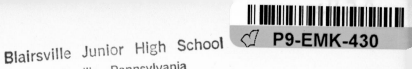

PLOTS AGAINST PRESIDENTS

Plots

Against

Presidents

By JOHN MASON POTTER

AN OBOLENSKY BOOK
ASTOR-HONOR, INC.
New York

Dedication

To the memory

of

ABRAHAM LINCOLN

JAMES A. GARFIELD

WILLIAM McKINLEY

JOHN FITZGERALD KENNEDY

TABLE OF CONTENTS

PLOTS AGAINST PRESIDENTS

I

Presidents Are Prime Targets

When the funeral services were over in the rotunda of the Capitol, the President, accompanied by members of his cabinet, Congressmen, Senators and officers of the government, walked out onto the portico. Waiting, beside a column, was Lawrence. The President was only a few feet away when Lawrence suddenly whipped a pistol from his right hand coat pocket, aimed it and fired point blank. . . .

The former President stood up in the open automobile and acknowledged the cheers of the throng that had been waiting Schrank moved near the car and was only a few feet away when he pulled a pistol from his pocket. He had to hold it between the heads of two cheering men. He fired and the former President staggered from the bullet which had hit him in the chest. . . .

No one noticed him when he aimed his revolver at the President-elect. Everyone in the vast auditorium was looking at the man who had been chosen to be the next President. The applause was like thunder. He fired six shots in rapid succession. . . .

The car was moving slowly along a curve on its way into the city. Only a moment before the Governor's wife had commented: "Mr. President, they can't make you believe now there are not some in Dallas who love you and appreciate you, can they?" Three shots rang out in rapid succession. . . .

A man—any man—who is elected President of the United States is a prime target for assassins and would-be assassins. He may be shot at—or at least conspired against—by someone or by several persons who wish to kill him. He is in danger from the moment he is elected, and even before. In 1860 men were betting that Abraham Lincoln, then the Republican candidate for President, would not live to see the White House. He received many letters warning him of his peril both before his victory at the polls in November and after. Nor is a man who has stepped down from the Presidency safe; former Presidents are assigned guards to protect them against anyone who would do them harm. One former President barely escaped death at the hands of an assailant.

A President of the United States is a prime target because he is a public figure—one of the foremost public figures in the world. He must appear before the public on many occasions, for he is the living symbol of the nation. He is also

3

head of the political party that helped put him in the White House. He must appear where he may be readily seen by the public—and by potential assassins.

At times he may need to enlist the support of the public in order to strengthen his position as head of state and as head of his party. He may seek to shore up a falling popularity by going before multitudes and addressing them; he may wish to enlist popular support for issues he is advocating; he may find it expedient to demonstrate his popularity in order to maintain leadership of his party. The late President Harding was taking an issue to the public, during a speaking tour of the West Coast, when he was stricken. The late President Kennedy was on a political excursion when he was assassinated. His popularity had declined in the months before his tragic death. He was mending political fences and demonstrating his leadership.

Many Presidents have found themselves in a similar situation and have "taken to the road".

Presidents must appear before the public and when they take precautions against the attacks, which are obvious, they feel, somehow, that the ties between them and the citizens are not as close as they desire. Yet these precautions are important, for all four assassinated U.S. Presidents were shot while in public, and those Presidents who escaped such attempts on their lives, were also in public. Only once has an attempt been made to invade the Presidential residence and that was when two Puerto Rican nationalists sought to force their way into Blair House, then a temporary White House, to attack President Truman.

The President, who is the center of attraction at a public gathering, may also be the center in the sights of a gun in the hands of an enemy who wishes to kill him. On the other hand if the President takes substantial precautions he is apt to be criticized, as a coward, or as a person so unpopular that he must fear the public. Lincoln was roundly criticized for avoiding the peril that was waiting for him in Baltimore while he was enroute to Washington in 1861 for his first inauguration.

A President is a prime target because he is a President. In more than one instance a man who sought to kill a President declared he had nothing personal against his intended victim, and one expressed some admiration for the object of his lethal plans. Another who wanted to kill a President revealed afterwards that he just wanted to kill a President and was undecided at first whether to try to assassinate the incumbent President or the one about to succeed him.

Four Presidents have fallen victim to assassin's bullets and several others have escaped attempts on their lives. If a political leader becomes unpopular with the majority, the normal thing is to vote him out of office—as Lincoln reminded voters while he was on his way to assume the Presidency.

In the United States, its citizens take pride in removing a President by means of the ballot box. It would seem, therefore, that the ballot, not the bullet, is persuasive. The facts seem to prove that all four Presidents who fell to an assassin's bullet were not the objects of a political coup d'etat. All the assassinations were the accomplishments of deranged minds.

However, alien to the American concept of democracy, it still remains strange that all the assassination attempts, both successful and unsuccessful, took place after 1860, except for the attempt on President Andrew Jackson's life. During the period of instability in the new nation, the U.S. President's safety was more secure. It is almost hard to believe that the frequency of the assassination attempt has increased with time as the American political system has matured.

In comparison, the chief of a foreign state, may become victim to the coup d'etat, which is political in nature and in many cases fatal to a government's leader. It is this contrast, in the nature of an assassination, that seems to differentiate the U.S. from the non-U.S. variety of this species of murder.

The record is not that clean or commendable for the attempts on Andrew Jackson, and Lincoln, on the way to his first inauguration, tends to indicate some political feeling. However, no organized power group seemed to have appeared on the scene and no political upheaval ensued.

Twenty men have occupied the Presidency during the past 102 years. Four were assassinated, and attempts were made to kill four others. Every President in modern times has received threats against his life. Of the twenty Presidents, from Lincoln to Johnson, one out of every three has been the object of an attempted assassination.

The above ignores, as apparently it should, the rumors of assassination that followed the death of Warren G. Harding in 1923—rumors similar to those which followed the deaths of Presidents Harrison and Taylor in the previous century.

The murder or attempted murder of a President is, as a matter of politics, senseless. It changes nothing. There has been no reversal, no significant change in direction, following the death of a President. If there has been any noticeable effect it has been simply this: the successor has sought to carry out his predecessor's policies as his own, and with vigor, and these policies appear to have greater acceptance with the people. When Lincoln died, he was succeeded by Andrew Johnson, whose ideas of how to deal with the defeated South were quite different. Yet Johnson made Lincoln's policies his own and attempted valiantly to carry them out. Prior to the death of President Kennedy many persons believed that the views of the Vice President on various issues lagged behind those of the late Chief Executive. As Kennedy's successor Johnson led the fight for legislation originaly proposed by Kennedy, and successfully completed what was undertaken and begun by his predecessor.

While Americans like to think of assassination as being contrary to our history and tradition the fact is that few countries can equal the record of the United States in this regard. Nor can we claim that the assassins and would-be assassins are from other countries or that they imported alien concepts and practices. The four killers were all Americans, and only two of the would-be assassins were not American-born. One man was born in Italy, and other in England. The two men who sought to kill President Truman were Puerto Ricans and as such were also United States citizens. It has never been established that any foreign power was involved in any way in the killings. There are some people who think Lee Harvey Oswald was an agent for a Communist nation but the most thorough investigation has never established a semblance of proof.

The assassins and the would-be assassins obviously have been acting without the prior knowledge of other countries. Even though there had been an international crisis with

PLOTS AGAINST PRESIDENTS

Russia and Cuba during the Kennedy administration, there was no sudden action, no sudden move, by either of these countries when John F. Kennedy was slain and the nation had a new and is yet untried leader. And when Booth killed Lincoln there was no effort on the part of the South to take advantage of the situation, even though Booth himself claimed to be acting as a Confederate.

The assassins and would-be assassins have been the agents of no one but themselves. They were lonely, frustrated, confused and troubled men.

It was a misfit who made the first attempt to kill a President of the United States. . . .

II

Two Tries In Seconds

It was a damp raw day, with rain threatening momentarily to pour down from the black clouds hovering over the roof tops of the nation's capital city. Men and women arriving at the Capitol to attend memorial services for a deceased Congressman looked anxiously at the lowering skies as they mounted the broad stairs and disappeared into the interior of the structure.

Coaches which had brought them to the capitol this murky forenoon—Friday, January 30, 1835—waited along the un-paved and muddy streets of the Capitol Plaza and coachmen found shelter inside their vehicles, except for those few who preferred to chat with each other while they enjoyed a smoke. These latter kept a weather eye alert for the first sign of rain as they puffed mediatively on their pipes.

Inside the Capitol, in the chamber of the House of Representatives—now Statuary Hall—funeral services for the late Congressman Warren B. Davis of South Carolina, were scheduled to begin at noon. Colleagues in the House, members of the Senate, government officials and leading members of the Washington community planned to pay their last respects to the deceased Congressman. The rain held off but continued to threaten as they arrived at the Capitol and mounted the stairs.

Shortly before noon Andrew Jackson, seventh president of the infant republic—it was still less than fifty years old—arrived, mounted the steps and entered the rotunda. As he crossed the circular hall to the chamber of the House of Representatives, a small slender man, standing to one side, watched him steadily. The man, warmly clothed against the chill dampness of the day, had a thin face with a moustache. Above it dark eyes glistened. He was about thirty-five years old, a good-looking man. In the pockets of his coat were two loaded pistols; he had come to kill the President.

The thin man made no attempt to kill Jackson as he passed through the rotunda because, as he explained later, he did not wish to interfere with the funeral services. But he did not give up the idea of killing the President.

The President, with members of his Cabinet, took his seat in the chamber of the House of Representatives, while the thin man watched through a window in a door. The services began.

After a while the thin man left the window, crossed the

11

rotunda and went out onto the east portico and found a vantage point behind a thirty-foot high Corinthian column near the door leading from the rotunda. He waited. He could look across the park-like grounds of the Capitol to what was known as the Old Capitol, a boarding house preferred by members of the two houses of Congress, but which had served as the Capitol for a while following the burning of Washington by the British in 1814. (Since then the building has been torn down and the Supreme Court Building erected on the site.) Beyond he could see the roof tops of many other buildings.

The services inside lasted nearly an hour. The gray-faced President listened to a discourse on the uncertainity of life and how death hovers over all mankind. The President knew about the nearness of death; he had faced it often in wars against the Indians, and in the war against the British that had assured the continuation of the Republic. He had faced it, too, in the duels he had fought in defense of his honor, in the bitter border brawls he had been in, and in his struggle against sickness and disease. No one knew better than Andrew Jackson that death could be near at all times, but it is certain that he had no knowledge that dismal morning that a short distance away an armed man waited to kill him.

The sermon came to an end and President Jackson took his place in the funeral procession, some distance behind the coffin. Next to him was the Secretary of the Treasury, Levi Woodbury, and the President took hold of Woodbury's right arm. The procession moved to the rotunda and on to the door leading out onto the east portico. There was a delay. Some of the people had hurried down the steps to the street below where their carriages waited, anxious to avoid the rain that threatened momentarily to begin, and had caused a temporary traffic tie-up.

The procession resumed and the thin man drew his two pistols from the pockets of his coat, cocked them and held them ready, concealed beneath his overcoat. Few, if anyone noticed him; they were too anxious to avoid the rain and get under cover.

The President and Secretary Woodbury emerged onto the portico, walking slowly. The thin man, waiting to the left of them, tossed his overcoat aside and sprang in front of the two men. Standing about thirteen feet away he raised his right arm, leveled the pistol at the President's heart and pulled the trigger.

The percussion cap exploded, but it did not ignite the powder in the barrel of the pistol. The sound of the exploding percussion cap on the portico broke the silence of the moment.

The procession suddenly came almost to a complete stop, then quickly disintegrated. Cabinet members and Congressmen rushed at the thin man.

He dropped the useless pistol, and with his right hand snatched the other pistol from his left and aimed it, too, at the President, ignoring the men who were rushing at him. He fired point-blank at the enraged and onrushing President, who was attempting to strike him down with his cane.

The percussion cap exploded, but again there was no discharge from the weapon in the thin man's hand.

A Naval lieutenant named Gedney was the first to reach the would-be assassin. He grabbed him by the shoulder and threw him down. Secretary Woodbury, joined in the scuffle, grabbing the thin man by the collar. Representative Ransom H. Gillet of New York, a powerful man, threw himself upon the thin man and those wrestling him to the ground.

Friends of the President who had rushed to his side now tried to calm him, but with difficulty. Jackson who was trying to cane the thin man, shouted: "Let me alone! Let me alone! I know where this comes from!"

As a matter of fact he did not, but it was reasonable for him to think that he did. He had many enemies in addition to the man who now struggled with the Naval officer, the Cabinet member and the Congressman.

The scuffle quickly ended, and the thin man was escorted down the steps into a hack by a United States marshal. Some of those who watched him may have remembered seeing him before for he was a familiar sight in Washington, especially at the Capitol, where he frequently attended sessions of Congress, sitting in the spectators gallery.

The hack started for the jail, and the marshal asked the thin man why had he tried to kill the President. The thin man said that Jackson had killed his father. The President, he said, had influenced many people to persecute his father, who as a result had died poor. This simply was not true, for the father had died of natural causes before Jackson had become president.

But the thin man thought it was so. He thought a great many things were true that were not.

The thin man was Richard Lawrence, about thirty-five years old, house painter by profession, a man who fancied many things, who lived in a world of unreality. He was a man who craved distinction and he gave it to himself generously even though it was unearned and unreal. The only real distinction he ever achieved came to him that damp January noon—he became the first man ever to attempt to kill a President of the United States.

Only the afternoon before, he had stood outside the White House for a while looking at the mansion, his two pistols in his pockets. But he made no attempt to enter and after a while he turned and walked back to his room in a boarding house. About a week before the attempted assassination he had gone to the White House and asked the President for money. The President put him off, saying that he was busy, asking Lawrence to come back another day. That was the second time that Lawrence had made this request; he had made it earlier in January and apparently Jackson took him to be a harmless lunatic. Lunatic he was, but not a harmless one. The first time he had had his two loaded pistols in his pockets, and was prepared, even then, to shoot Jackson.

Lawrence had inherited a brace of pistols from his father a number of years previously. However, they were not a matched pair, and so in 1831—four years before the attempted assassination—he kept the better pistol and exchanged the other for a weapon nearly identical to the one he had retained. Lawrence was said to be a good marksman with a pistol. No one knows why the two pistols did not discharge. Authorities checked the two and found that they had been loaded correctly, and there appeared to be no reason for their failure to go off. The two pistols were muzzle-loaded as were firearms of that period. When the trigger was pulled the hammer struck a precussion cap on a nipple. The explosion of the percussion cup was intended to set off the charge inside the barrel of the pistol, and invariably this happened.

But on that damp January morning, neither one did. While some people said that the weather had dampened the powder, others said simply that it was a miracle. Authorities who tested the two pistols found that they were easily capable of killing the President. Lawrence said he thought it was due to the dampness in the air. He was held for trial.

Naturally the question came up: Was Lawrence the agent for some one else, for some of Jackson's other foes? The President thought so, and it soon became known that he believed Lawrence to be the agent of Senator George Poindexter of Mississippi, a former friend who had become his bitter enemy as a result of a quarrel over patronage.

The Senator was enraged. He insisted that the Senate appoint a committee to investigate, which it did. Within a few days the committee exonerated him. Newspapers revealed that Lawrence had visited the Senator a few days before the crime but only to solicit work.

Many of Jackson's friends believed that Lawrence was the agent of the Whigs, who wished to see Jackson removed. This was a period in our history when feelings ran high in national affairs, when the duel was an accepted thing, and when differences of opinion—especially if that opinion were strongly held—were settled on the dueling field, or in fist fights, brawls and other physical encounters.

In prison awaiting trial, Lawrence was well treated. Authorities investigating the crime apparently became convinced fairly soon that he was not an agent for some one else, but for himself only, and that he was obviously a madman.

The trial began on April 11, 1835 in the United States

Circuit Court in Washington. Lawrence was indicted on two charges of assault with intent to kill. This was a misdemeanor in those days and the penalty, if convicted, was either a fine or imprisonment or both. Even though the attempt to kill was made against the life of the President of the United States there was no indictment possible that might carry the death penalty.

Lawrence's defense was simple and the obvious one— insanity. It was not as much of a defense then as it would be now, for then if a man were insane he could be held responsible for his acts if he had periods of lucidity, if he could distinguish between right and wrong, and if he committed his crime during a lucid period.

The prosecutor was Francis Scott Keyes, author of "The Star Spangled Banner," and District Attorney for the District of Columbia. Keyes, a distinguished man of his day, had been lawyer, patriot, poet and Episcopal churchman. It quickly became clear that Keyes had resisted all pressures for a prosecution based on hatred. He appeared anxious that Lawrence be treated as the madman he so obviously was.

At the trial it came out that Lawrence's father, before migrating to the United States from England, had been confined briefly in an institution for insanity, that his aunt had died insane in Washington. An examining physician testified that he had been laboring under mania and general derangement, and was obsessed with the idea that the President had injured him and his father. Another doctor said that Lawrence had a "morbid delusion."

One of those delusions was that he was the King of England, and also of the United States; once he interrupted the trial to assert that he was a sovereign and not subject to the court's jurisdiction.

"I desire to know if I, who claim the crown of the United States, likewise the crown of Great Britain, and who am superior to this court, am to be treated thus?" he once asked the court. Another time he told the jury: "It is for me, gentlemen, to pass judgment on you and not you upon me."

The trial did not take long. Late in the afternoon of the first day the case went to the jury, which deliberated five minutes, and then reported: "We find him not guilty, he having been under the influence of insanity at the time he committed the act." Lawrence was committed to jail for the rest of his life, serving in jails and mental hospitals. He died in the Government Hospital for the Insane, now St. Elizabeth's Hospital, in Washington, on June 13, 1861.

Richard Lawrence was born in England, and came to the United States with his parents when he was about twelve years old. As a boy he was quiet and reserved and rarely played with other boys and girls of his own age. He was well behaved, neat in appearance, industrious, and all in all appeared to be a very fine lad. His parents were Protestants, but as he grew up he professed allegiance to no church even though he sometimes read the Bible, and occasionally attended religious services.

When he was old enough, he was apprenticed to a house painter and eventually became a competent worker. In his youth he was steady in his habits. He worked on such well known Washington buildings as the National Hotel at the corner of Pennsylvania Avenue and Sixth Street.

He appeared to like painting and took up landscape painting as a hobby. He did not gamble and was only a moderate drinker. He seemed to be almost a model young man. There is no record of his showing any interest in the company of young women.

Sometime around 1832 he began to change. His family noted that while he was once a mild man, he now became violent at times, and threatened violence at other times, that he became suspicious of others, and that he was becoming subject to moods of extreme feeling, sometimes suddenly laughing for no apparent reason, or giving in to spells of cursing. He talked to himself frequently. He imagined many fantastic things.

The most fantastic thing was the belief that he was the king of both the United States and of England. This idea became fixed in his mind and he went about calling himself King Richard III. The boys in the neighborhood quickly dubbed him "King Dick."

Occasionally he changed this story, that he was about to become King, that he was the rightful heir to the throne. The United States, in his mind, was still a British possession and therefore subject to his rule.

At times "King Dick" believed that his realm included not only the United States and Great Britain, but also Holland and Rome. He imagined that he owned two great estates in England, Tregear and Canelly, which were connected with the throne.

He began to dislike Jackson, a feeling that eventually grew into hatred. Compared to him, the King of the United States and England, Jackson was only his clerk. He felt that it was an outrage that he, a sovereign, had been apprenticed to a painter.

In November of 1832 he left Washington for New York,

19

with the intention of going to England but returned home the next month convinced that he had been prevented from sailing because the steamship owners had gotten together in a conspiracy in which they hoped to gain possession of a large fortune awaiting him in Europe. They had wanted to keep him in America where he would be unable to get control of it, he declared.

The following spring he tried again, going to Philadelphia, but returning with the story that the government was against his going to England, and that he would have to wait until he acquired a ship and capain of his own.

He moved in with a married sister, a Mrs. Redfern, and informed her that while it was proper for her husband, a storekeeper, to work, he did not need to because he held claims for large sums of money which he said the government owed him.

The idea of money owed him by the government became an obsession. He began frequenting sessions of Congress. He rode to the Capitol on a hired horse, but the saddle was his own. He felt that the livery stable's saddle was not good enough for a man of his importance.

He recalled that once he had stopped Martin Van Buren, the Vice-President, in the rotunda, and told him he needed money. He said he told Van Buren that if he did not get the money, Van Buren and Jackson would fall. There is no record that he ever got any money or that Van Buren paid any attention to this request.

As time went on Lawrence worked less and less as a painter. He felt that he should receive more pay for his work because of his imagined royalty, and so when he did accept a job he usually quit in a short time because he received the same wages as other painters. The other painters were happy to see him go; one of them said he was fearful of working with him.

The obsession about Jackson and about large sums of money became greater. Sometimes he was heard going about muttering to himself: "Damn General Jackson! Who is General Jackson?"

He began to have trouble with his sister and her household. He became suspicious of other people, imagined all kinds of wrongs being done to him, and reacted violently. He went into a rage one day and threatened to kill the Redfern's colored maid because he thought she was making fun of him. Things reached the breaking point when he had a quarrel with his sister. He attempted to kill her with a four pound weight. The brother-in-law interceded, disarmed Lawrence and had him put in jail.

However, he was not there very long. A grand jury refused to indict him, finding him not responsible for his actions. A doctor who treated him for a physical ailment about this time found him insane, in his opinion. This was about a year before his assault on Jackson.

Out of jail, Lawrence found quarters in a boarding house and in time ran up a considerable bill. He refused to pay it, however, until he had received from Congress several millions of dollars due him. He clung to the fixation about a fortune awaiting him. The landlady protested and he flew into a rage and he told her that he would blow out her brains or cut her throat. The landlady's husband told him that he would go to court and obtain a judgment against him. Lawrence was reported as having said: "If you do I will put a ball through your heart!"

Nevertheless the husband secured the judgment, and Lawrence made no attempt to harm either the landlady or her husband.

Yet he got along very well, with other people, and appeared to them to be a quiet, reserved person of peaceful mien, who bothered no one. That was the view of a fellow boarder, told to the authorities after the attempt on Jackson's life. He was able to talk rationally on many subjects, for example, landscape painting, both before and after the assault.

But he appeared unable to talk about Jackson with rationality. He thought all his troubles and misfortunes traced back to the President. He was confused in his thinking, but he was certain that Jackson was an arch enemy of his. He told doctors examining him after his arrest that Jackson had been his enemy ever since he was a child, and that Jackson had even succeeded more recently in turning his sister and her husband against him. Jackson, he claimed, blocked his just claims to huge sums in the Bank of the United States. He believed that with Jackson out of the way and Martin Van Buren succeeding him in the White House there would be no difficulty in his getting that fortune. However, he added that if Van Buren blocked him as Jackson had, he, Lawrence, would assassinate him, too.

With Jackson dead, Lawrence expected that he and the leaders of the nation would be able to work together to bring prosperity to the United States. He was quite willing to assume a position of leadership. In fact he was sure that he could not assume this position of leadership in the nation's affairs until Jackson was dead.

Jackson was one of the most hated men ever to sit in the White House, despite the popular following that had given him the Presidency. Much of the nation's press was violently opposed to him. Orators of the political opposition railed against him. He was pictured as a tyrant, a despot and a backwoods ruffian. He was called a murderer because he had killed two men in duels; he was called an adulterer because he had married his wife on their assumption that her first husband who had deserted her was dead when in fact he was not. He was held up to scorn and ridicule as no other President, before his time or after, has been.

Lawrence was to say later that the public attitude did not affect his own views, but there were many who simply did not believe him. He himself made statements that indicated he had been so influenced even though he said he had not been. After the attempt on the life of Jackson he told the marshal taking him to jail that he had tried to kill Jackson because he was a tyrant. The marshal wanted to know how Lawrence knew this and was told that it was common knowledge, and that he had read this in newspapers.

As time went on, Lawrence's mental condition grew worse. The idea of his being the sovereign of Great Britain and of the United States, that Jackson was his personal enemy conspiring against him, that large sums of money were due him from the Bank of the United States, or awaited him in England, were main delusions, but he had others.

He became careful of his dress. He was always neat in appearance, but now he gave more thought to his attire. Sometimes he would change his clothes several times in a single day.

Children continued to call him "King Dick," but there is little evidence to show that he minded this. He followed the debates in Congress with increasing interest, but apparently he did not always understand them. But he liked them because most of them were against Jackson.

Gradually the idea came to him to kill Jackson, although just when is not known.

He had no confidants, and he discussed his plans with no one. However, he assumed that everyone knew that he planned to kill Jackson, he said later.

Sometime that winter of 1834-1835,—probably in January—he decided to go to see the President and ask him for some of the money he believed due him. He took his two pistols and went to the White House. When he asked to see the President, attendants said that it was impossible that day. He returned to his boarding house to brood. Later he said that if he had seen Jackson and had been refused the money he sought, he would have shot the President in the White House then.

About a week before he tried to kill Jackson, Lawrence made another visit to the White House. It was an easy thing for a visitor to see the President in those days, and a porter escorted him to Jackson's quarters. Jackson was talking with a Congressman from Pennsylvania, Joel Barlow, Lawrence recalled afterwards. Jackson turned to his visitor and Lawrence said that he needed a thousand dollars for a trip to England and that the President should give him a check for that amount, drawn upon the Bank of the United States.

Jackson said that he was busy right then, and that he had another caller waiting, and that Lawrence should come back another day. Lawrence left; he did not have his revolvers with him that day.

He had them with him on the afternoon of January 29th. He had them in his pockets as he arrived at the Executive mansion. He did not try to enter or to seek an appointment with the President. Instead he waited outside by one of the entrances on Pennsylvania. He stood there for a long time, silently, staring at the mansion. Whether he had planned to enter and shoot the President, or wait for him to appear outside before attacking him, or whether he decided simply that he would have an opportunity the next day, is not known. Certainly he knew from reading the newspapers that the President would attend the funeral for Congressman Warren Davis.

The next morning dawned damp and gloomy. Lawrence left his boarding house and went to his painter's shop, there to await any orders for work that might come in. He had no work and had not had any for some time. He picked up a book, sat down on a chest and began to read. From time to time he chuckled but whether it was from what he read or from thoughts flashing through his warped mind, no one knows. After a while he tossed the book down and exclaimed aloud to himself: "I'm damned if I don't do it!"

He thrust his two loaded pistols into his pockets, donned an overcoat and went to the capitol to make his unsuccessful attempt to assassinate the President.

After the arrest that followed, there was a public clamor. The authorities however were quick to decide that Lawrence was insane. After he was found insane and committed, the clamor continued. Many people thought that the very speed of the court action indicated there was something being withheld from the public that would not stand close investigation. There were even some who suggested that the whole incident was an attempt to win sympathy for Jackson, whose policies had made him so unpopular with many of the nation's leading citizens. There appears to be nothing, however, to indicate that Lawrence was involved in any conspiracy, or that he was directly influenced by any group.

Certainly many people thought that Lawrence had been influenced by the speeches attacking Jackson which he had heard in Congress. The New York Evening Post said that the would-be assassin had "inhaled the latent seed of his malady in the heated and poisonous atmosphere at the United States Senate Chamber," adding that he was probably "wrought up to a frenzy by the incendiary harangues of Clay, Webster and Calhoun and their besotted followers."

Others believed that Lawrence had been the tool of Jackson's enemies. John C. Calhoun, the fiery Southern leader, detained the Senate with a denial of any complicity in the attempted assassination. Calhoun had been elected vice president under Jackson, but had broken with him and had resigned, the only vice president in the nation's history ever to do so. Calhoun had sought and won election to the Senate, where he was a principal opponent of many of Jackson's policies.

John Quincy Adams, former president who had been defeated in his try for re-election by Jackson, stood up on the floor of the House of Representatives of which he was a member to assert his loyalty.

Nevertheless, the rumors and suspicious continued for a long time.

Lawrence had been agitated by Jackson's attitude toward the Bank of the United States, then a lively political issue. Jackson had in fact vetoed a bill to recharter it in 1832. The charter had not run out, and would not do so until 1836. Lawrence thought that Jackson's financial policies had ruined business—he had read this in the newspapers—and put many people like himself out of work. He himself was nearly destitute from his long unemployment but this was due more to his irrationality than any other cause. With Jackson dead and Van Buren the President—and himself a close and influential associate of the new chief executive, money from the Bank would circulate more freely, bringing prosperity to the common people, he reasoned.

Added to all these reasons for his hatred of Jackson was still another. He was convinced that Jackson was responsible for the separation then existing between the United States and Great Britain, and that he was conspiring with the Duke of Wellington to deny him his rights.

Lawrence, the first of the small group of men who were to attempt the assassination of a President, had a greater opportunity than did any of the men who followed in his ill-starred footsteps. No attempt was made in those days to protect the President from harm. Lawrence could have made his attempt in the White House or at any number of public events which Jackson attended.

Lawrence died in June, 1861. There is no record to indicate whether he read in the newspapers of February—four months before his death—of the plot to kill Abraham Lincoln while he was on his way to the White House. Lawrence had thought Jackson a tyrant, other men were to think Abraham Lincoln a tyrant, too.

III

"Like A Thief In The Night"

Joseph Lee of Salem, Massachusetts was worried, not about the outcome of the election still three weeks away, but about the personal safety of the man he expected to win it. So on October 13, 1860, he sat down and wrote a letter. It was not an easy letter for him to write, because he was not accustomed to writing letters. The one he wrote that day reveals his lack of knowledge about grammar, spelling and so on. It also revealed his deep anxiety about the safety of Abraham Lincoln.

He wrote:

"Mr. Lincoln Sir i rite to you to tell you to be on your gard du not eeat every Thing you have orded to be brought

28

be Carful not to be Posined by those rufings Mr. Lincoln Sir i hope that the Lord Will Spair Your Life to mak the Country in A beter condison sir i like the Republican Movent and i hope sir we shall put everthing Rite may the lord keep you from the Snars That lies before der sir the day this not Fair disent sir Whe hope that your life Will Be Long and plesent the four years and We Will put you theor a gain so no more At Present From Your Frind."

It was only four days later that B. S. Bassett of Lawrence, Kansas was similarly worried about the safety of Abraham Lincoln. He also sat down and wrote to Lincoln a letter which read in part:

"I want to warn you of one thing—that you be Exceeding Careful What you Eat or Drink as you May be Poisoned by your Enemys as was President Harrison and President Taylor."

On the same day as Mr. Bassett wrote his letter, F. R. Shoemaker of Chester, Pennsylvania wrote one, too. It read:

"Mr. President I now endever to do all I can to put you on your gard. When you cross Masons & Dix. line keep you eye's OPEN and look out for your enimeys or they will poison you or do something to take your life. Same as they tried to serve Old Buc. Look, Sharp."

These were not the first letters that Lincoln received warning him of the dangers of assassination or making allusions to Presidents Harrison, Taylor and Buchanan (Old Buc). There were many Americans who believed that the first two had been poisoned in the White House because of their strong anti-slavery attitudes, and that President Buchanan had faced the same danger. While there appears to have been very little foundation for the stories of secret assassinations of Presidents Harrison and Taylor they were widely believed.

Harrison was a northerner, a Whig opposed to the extension of slavery. He had died a month after being inaugurated, and had been succeeded by Democrat John Tyler, a Virginian, slave owner and pro-slavery in his attitudes.

Zachary Taylor, hero of the Mexican War, was southern in birth and not opposed to slavery, but he had taken a forthright stand against the extension of slavery. About eighteen months after his inaugural he died in office and was succeeded by Millard Fillmore, who also had been opposed to slavery. After Fillmore stepped into the Presidency many people thought that his attitudes were less forthright than they had been, that he was more willing to make concessions to the South.

James Buchanan was widely critized by many people for his failure to act energetically against secession, and by others for not giving in to Southern demands for the surrender of Fort Sumter.

There was a story—apparently without foundation—that a pro-slavery group of politicians had called upon Buchanan and threatened him with the fate of Harrison and Taylor if he persisted in defying the South. Many Americans believed this accounted for his weakness in dealing with the issue of secession.

There was a story to the effect that U. S. Senator Lewis Wigfall of Texas had organized a group of southern men who planned to kidnap "Old Buc" and take him South and keep him prisoner. Vice President John C. Breckinridge, Southern and pro-slavery, would become the acting head of the Federal government which would then become pro-South and unopposed to the secession of the slave states.

Letters of warning continued to be received by Lincoln, both before and after his election. One well-wisher urged him to discharge all the servants in the White House, who presumably were agents of the pro-slavery elements. Another urged him to trust no doctor except his own, who should be brought to Washington.

Gradually the letters began to sound a new note. They spoke of organized groups determined to kill him before he could become President. Some of these letters came from individuals of importance and prominence. On October 20th, Captain David Hunter sat down in his quarters in Fort Leavenworth, Kansas, and wrote to Lincoln about a group of "young men in Virginia" who had "bound themselves by oaths to cause your assassination, should you be elected."

The captain was later selected to accompany Lincoln on his journey from Springfield to Washington, as one of a group who were to serve as escorts.

It was not surprising that Lincoln received these and other warnings, or that the rumored assassinations of two Presidents and the intimidation of a third be accepted by many Americans. It was a period when violence was often resorted to in the settlement of arguments.

It was a time when an editor with strong views might have to defend them at the risk of his life. Political leaders, clergymen and others in similar situations also faced the same peril. Duels were commonplace even though almost every state had laws against them. In large parts of the country, men habitually carried firearms or knives on their persons.

Women, too, frequently carried pistols to defend themselves from molestations or even slights upon their honor.

It was a time of great bitterness. The arguments over slavery had reached a point where many Americans took irrational attitudes and violent measures. There had been riots in the North concerning the return of runaway slaves, and there had been angry demonstrations. A great deal of blood had been shed in Kansas, Missouri, and in other border areas over the issue of slavery, and it was not surprising that the atmosphere surrounding the election of Lincoln should be charged with the threat of violence. It was a time when too often men took the law into their own hands.

The frontier, often lawless, frequently violent, dominated large areas of the country, and even after the frontier had departed from an area, its attitudes and codes of conduct usually remained.

Across America men were wagering that Lincoln would never reach the White House, they said he would be killed before he reached Washington, that before that happened the South would have seized the city for its own capital, that southern sympathizers in the nation's capitol would block Lincoln on inaugural day. He continued to receive warning letters in his mail, more and more the writers mentioned the cities of Washington and Baltimore as places of especial peril.

Lincoln received other letters, of course, in which writers discussed political issues facing the nation, the growing secession movement in the South, the need for strong, prompt action—even before he took the oath of office. Some of them sought special favors.

Lincoln had much to think about, with state after state in

the South voting secession, during those late fall days. He paid more attention to those letters dealing with political matters and concentrated on the problems facing the nation —also the formation of a cabinet and adoption of a wise policy. However he did not ignore the warnings. Late in January he asked a close personal friend, Leonard Swett, to go to Washington and talk with General Winfield Scott, commander of the Army. It was significant that he did not ask Swett to see Secretary of War, John Buchanan Floyd, an avowed pro-slavery man who later became a Confederate general. According to at least one letter received by Lincoln about this time, the Secretary of War was moving troops— and munitions and arms—so that, in the event of war, the Federal forces would be widely dispersed, and the munitions and arms would be in places easy for the Confederates to seize.

Perhaps, too, he was taking into account the story about Senator Wigfall and his group of would-be-kidnappers.

Swett went to Washington and General Scott told him to tell Lincoln he did not need to worry about his inauguration being blocked. The general said that if it were necessary, he would plant artillery at both ends of Pennsylvania on Inauguration Day. As it happened later, he did just that. Swett went back to Springfield and reported to Lincoln.

If Swett and Lincoln were satisfied with this answer, General Scott was not. He assigned a trusted subordinate who had just returned to service in this time of crisis, to investigate the loyalty—or lack of it—among a number of newly formed military companies in Washington. The officer was Colonel Charles Stone. He was to find out, if possible, if the companies were the means by which the inauguration was to be blocked, and the city seized.

Meanwhile the warning letters continued to be received in Springfield. Increasingly they mentioned Baltimore as a place of special danger. About the time that Swett was in the nation's capital, Lincoln received a letter from Captain George W. Hazzard, who mentioned the danger awaiting the President-elect in the Maryland metropolis and urged that he either take a different route by which to reach Washington, or go through the city secretly accompanied by only one or two men as body guards.

The captain had been assigned to be a member of the party escorting Lincoln on the latter's journey to Washington.

Lincoln paid some heed to these letters of warning, but his real concern was with the problems of state, and with the division that was occurring in the country. He received a flood of mail from all parts of the country, South as well as North, concerning the split that was occurring between the two major sections of the country. They suggested courses of action that might be taken to prevent the split from progressing, and to heal the breach. Some of the letter writers felt that the South was only bluffing and all that was needed was a strong stand be taken by the Federal government. Others felt that the South was not serious about seceding and if they were left alone they would return or remain within the Union. He was urged to take strong stands, and no stands, to act quickly and to delay action.

As he toiled to organize his administration and to plan its policies and course, he had little time to give to the warnings that continued to come in.

Others told him that the South was determined and war inevitable, and that he must not only take a strong stand and move vigorously, but that he should not wait until he became President to make his views known and bring pressure on the Buchanan administration to take immediate measures to halt the secession. Other men said that the South should be allowed to secede, that peace between the two sections should be preserved.

Lincoln was faced with the need to evaluate all these views, decide which was right and plan accordingly. He had little time to give to consideration of personal safety. He had not only to organize his cabinet, but also to chart a course that would, hopefully, preserve the Union.

There were other rumors of violence about the land, besides those aimed at the President-elect. A man who became very much alarmed was Samuel M. Fenton, president of the Philadelphia, Wilmington and Delaware Railroad. His line was the only one connecting directly the city of Washington and the North, and he had heard rumors that Southern sympathizers might destroy bridges and other railroad property of the P. W. and D. to deny its use to the Federal government, and especially to the movement of Northern troops and supplies along it.

Fenton did not know how seriously he should take these rumors. In January, 1861, he asked Allan Pinkerton for help. Pinkerton was the most famous detective in America, at that time, and most of his fame was based on work which he had done for railroad lines. He headed the nation's first large scale detective agency.

There were two places where the railroad was especially vulnerable, Fenton told the detective; Havre de Grace,

Maryland, where ferry boats carried the trains across the broad Susquehanna, and Gunpowder River, where a long high bridge spanned the stream. Fenton had heard that gangs of men—toughs and Southern sympathizers—planned to destroy the ferry boats at Havre de Grace, thus severing that connection, and that other such gangs planned to burn bridges across the Gunpowder and other rivers. On the first day of February, Pinkerton and a group of his men began investigating these rumors. He assigned agents at various points along the railroad, and established a secret headquarters in Baltimore.

At the end of ten days he reported to Fenton that he and his men had been unable to uncover any definite conspiracy to harm the railroad or its property, but conceded that possibly he might have failed to uncover one that really did exist. He suggested that extra men be hired as railroad workers whose real job would be to guard the property, as a precaution against this possibility, or spontaneous acts of violence and destruction.

His job completed, Pinkerton ordered his own agents back to his headquarters in Chicago, and prepared to leave himself. But on Sunday, February 10th, 1861, he received a letter which made him change his plans again, and quickly recall the agents of his organization. He had received a letter from an official of the P. W. and B. in which it was stated:

> "I am informed that a son of a distinguished citizen of Maryland has taken an oath with others to assassinate Mr. Lincoln before he gets to Washington, and they may attempt to do this while he is passing over our road . . . . . This information is perfectly reliable."

Without waiting for authorization from Fenton, Pinkerton began seeking the identity of the "son of a distinguished citizen of Maryland," and the others who planned to kill the President-elect. He ordered additional agents to join him in the task.

He assigned one man—one of his best—to Perrymansville (now Perryman), and others at strategic points. He continued his secret headquarters in Baltimore, and had several agents working in that city.

He had little time in which to uncover the plot if he were to prevent the assassination. Lincoln was saying his goodbyes in Springfield when Pinkerton received the letter, and in thirteen more days Lincoln was scheduled to pass through Baltimore.

He did not wish to alarm Lincoln until he had to, so instead of getting in touch with him personally, he sent an agent to deliver a message to Norman Judd, an old friend of his who had been instrumental in securing the Republican nomination for Lincoln and who was to be a member of the official party accompanying Lincoln to Washington.

The Pinkerton agents frequented the hotels and bars and other places popular with the Southern sympathizers in the city, and soon one of the agents, using the alias of Joseph Howard, was able to convince the Southern element of the city of his pro-Southern sympathies. He became the close associate of a young Baltimore aristocrat, who soon revealed that he was a member of a conspiracy to kill Lincoln on the day he was to travel through the city. The agent was equally successful at Perrymansville and was admitted to an informal Pro-Southern cavalry troop at Bel Air, a town that later was to be better known as the home of John Wilkes Booth. The troop, he learned, was awaiting arms; it was also to work in concert with an assassination group in Baltimore.

Howard's efforts brought him into contact with a "captain" Cypriano Ferrandini, a barber at Barnum's Hotel, who was the ringleader of the Baltimore plotters.

It was a dismal Monday, February 11, 1861, when Lincoln went to the railroad depot at Springfield, to board the train that was to carry him on the first lap of his journey to Washington. It was raining, but nevertheless several hundred friends and well-wishers had gathered to bid him goodbye. Lincoln was visably moved, as he spoke to the throng. He told them, according to one account: "I now leave, not knowing when or whether ever I may return."

Accompanying Lincoln were four Army men assigned by General Scott. They were Hunter, now a major; Captain Hazzard who had warned Lincoln in letters of the dangers of possible assassination; Colonel Edwin Vose Sumner, a veteran Indian fighter, and Captain John Pope, who had been the center of a storm the year previously for attacking the fortification policy of President Buchanan as being favorable to the Southern secessionist. There was a fifth man, "Colonel" Elmer Ellsworth, who headed a military company of zouaves, and who, officially, was responsible for the personal safety of the President-elect. Also a member of the party was Ward Lamon, close friend of the President-elect who was destined to become the marshal of the District of Columbia during the Lincoln administration.

The train moved eastward across the prairie, and despite the rain, crowds gathered at every hamlet and crossing to cheer Lincoln. On the surface it was a gala, happy journey that first day, but behind that facade of good feeling and enthusiasm was the danger of assassination. Apparently the members of the party tried to keep the latter from the public, and in general succeeded very well. One historian, writing a biography of Lincoln shortly after the President's death, said there was an attempt on Lincoln's life during that first day's journey, but he did not elaborate, and how, where and in what fashion that attempt was made—and failed—is not known.

That evening, however, while Lincoln was receiving the plaudits of his admirers in Indianapolis, a group of political leaders from Illinois talked with Lamon, and impressed upon him the necessity of protecting Lincoln. This strange meeting is easier to understand if the story of the attempted assassination mentioned by the historian is accepted.

It was in Indianapolis that evening that Norman Judd, received a telegram from Pinkerton saying that he had an important message for him and asking where he could be reached on the journey.

* * * *

The next day, Lincoln's birthday, saw the party move eastward across Indiana toward Cincinnati, and as on the first day, the journey was a triumphant one. And again, beneath the surface there were dark overtones of danger. Shortly before the train was due to arrive at State Line, the engineer of another train found an obstruction on the track. The engineer had taken his train down a stretch of track where the Lincoln train was due in a few minutes, and rounding a turn had discovered a device for putting cars on tracks so placed that it would derail any train running onto it. It was at a spot where it could not have been seen at any distance and where usually trains ran on full speed. In such circumstances it could not only derail a train, it could wreck it and probably cause injury and possible death to many of the passengers.

The device was quickly removed before the arrival of the Lincoln train.

Was it an attempt on the life of Abraham Lincoln? It is impossible to say, but apparently some people at the time were not willing to dismiss it lightly. The news of this incident was kept from the press at the time, as were other incidents of this sort. The next day, however, when the train left Cincinnati, it was preceeded by another locomotive that would make sure that the tracks were safe for the Lincoln train.

A Pinkerton agent reached Judd on February 12th, just before the departure from Cincinnati and delivered a note from Pinkerton which had been written three days previously. It told of the existence of a plot to kill the President-elect as he passed through Baltimore on February 23rd. Pinkerton also wrote that he did not know the details even though he was convinced that the plot did exist. He promised to keep Judd informed and suggested that Lincoln not be told—yet.

Pinkerton was engaged in a race against time. He had learned of the plot only thirteen days before it was scheduled to be carried out, and by the time he had got word to Judd, three of those days were gone. He and his operatives, including two women, worked feverishly to learn more about the plot—who was to be the assassin, how the act was to be

carried out, the identity of other members of the conspiracy, how widespread it was, its connection with other
groups, and so on. The time left for them to find these
answers narrowed day by day.

Even while directing the operation of a group of agents,
Pinkerton, himself, managed to find an opportunity to make
friends with one of the Southern sympathizers of prominence
in the city, and through him he was able to meet and con-
verse with Ferrandini. Pinkerton posed as a broker from
the South and as a man loyal to the South. Ferrandini, captain of one of four pro-Southern troops newly organized in
the city, talked of them and of a group determined to block
Lincoln from reaching Washington, by assassination. He
swore to Pinkerton that Lincoln would die in the city if he
had to do the deed alone.

Day by day the detectives learned more about the conspiracy. Meanwhile two New York police officers working
for General Scott, became convinced of the existence of a
plot to kill Lincoln although they had not managed to secure
much specific information.

* * * *

On Tuesday, four days before Lincoln was due to arrive
in Baltimore, Howard, a Pinkerton agent, attended a meeting
of the group of which he had become a member. It was this
meeting that decided who should assassinate the President-
elect. It was agreed to draw lots from a box containing a
single ballot of red and other ballots of white. The man who
drew the red ballot was to be the assassin of Lincoln. He was
not to reveal he had drawn the red ballot to the other
members so that his identity would be unknown even to the

41

other members of the group. But Farrandini and some of the other leaders in the conspiracy had doubts about the courage and determination of some of the members, so they had secretly put several red ballots in the box.

When Lincoln emerged from his railroad car in response to cheers, there would be several persons, not simply one, in the throng who would move in on him and attack him with knives.

Firearms were ruled out because the shots would tell the crowd at once that something was amiss, while a knife could be used silently, and it was just possible that the assailant or assailants could escape from the area before anyone learned of the attack.

Members of the pro-Southern troops would be at hand to help the assassins escape to a waiting ship that would take them south to safety.

Other members of the conspiracy would telegraph news of the attack to the cavalry at Bel Air and at other points. This would be the signal to cut telegraph lines, burn railroad bridges, tear up railroad tracks and take other such actions, so that Maryland would be cut off completely from communication with the North.

By the time that Pinkerton had all this information he came to the conclusion that possibly he did not know the full details of the plot, and that only by changing his itinerary would Lincoln escape the danger awaiting him in Baltimore.

Pinkerton had been in touch with Judd, telling him of progress being made in the investigation. However Lincoln and the other members of the party had not been told.

Pinkerton had not gone to the Baltimore police about the plot, because Police Marshal Kane was pro-Southern and might be a party to the plot. He had said that he would be unable to assign additional police to maintain order when Lincoln arrived. There was no Federal agency—nor anyone else to whom he could turn.

Pinkerton continued to keep Judd informed. On Thursday, two days before Lincoln was scheduled to arrive in Baltimore, he talked with Judd in Philadelphia and they agreed that the time had come to tell Lincoln and to plan evasive action. It was their idea that late that night Lincoln should change his plans and leave for Washington, traveling over the Philadelphia, Wilmington and Baltimore railroad and when in Baltimore take the Baltimore and Ohio line which ran from Baltimore to Washington. Lincoln would make the trip accompanied by only a body guard, and without telling anyone of his change in plans. The plotters in Baltimore who had planned so well probably would not anticipate this change in Lincoln's plans and he should be able to slip through the city and into Washington without being detected and attacked. Pinkerton and Judd planned to see Lincoln at the end of the day, tell him of the plot, their plans to defeat it and secure his cooperation in carrying out their plan to spirit him past the conspirators and into Washington safely during the dark hours of that night.

The big questions in Pinkerton's mind were: were the conspirators watching Lincoln all the time as he made his way toward their city? Would they be alert to any change in his schedule and travel arrangements? Would the change defeat the plotters or merely change the time of their

43

attack on Lincoln. If the President-elect should change his plans and suddenly start for Washington would it be the signal for the plotters to mobilize and act?

* * * *

The train left Cincinnati, preceeded by a pilot locomotive as a precaution against any further obstructions on the track, such as that of the previous day.

The train was not far out of Cincinnati when a grenade was found on the train. Again this news was not revealed at once and it was some time later before a newspaper learned of it and printed the story. Years later a close associate of Abraham Lincoln spoke of an attempt to assassinate the President-elect on this date and presumably the grenade was involved. But at the time the whole episode was kept as secret as possible.

The next day the train bearing Lincoln continued its way eastward, across Ohio and into a section of Virginia that separated Ohio and Pennsylvania. That long north-pointing finger of land is now part of West Virginia, but then it was part of the South, slave territory. There was tension on the train until the Pennsylvania border was reached, and it eased when the train was safely across the line. Some of Lincoln's fellow passengers began to sing.

The train began to lose momentum and soon came to a stop. Up ahead a freight train had been derailed, only a short time before the Lincoln train was to pass there. Had the rails been loosened by the heavy rains that had pelted the area for several days? Or had they been loosened by some group wishing to do harm to Lincoln? It was two hours before the Presidential train was able to continue its journey.

* * * *

In Baltimore and the surrounding Maryland area the Pinkerton agents were working hard. They overheard many conversations pertaining to the planned attempt on Lincoln, but more important, they were gaining the confidence of men who appeared to be engaged in the conspiracy. The agent at Bel Air had joined the cavalry troop which was ready to act for the South as soon as it obtained the arms it lacked. Another agent within Baltimore was making progress in his friendship with a society scion who boasted of his links with the conspirators.

Meanwhile General Scott, unaware of the work Pinkerton was doing, but much concerned with the rumors he continued to hear about the conspiracy in Baltimore, decided to find out, if possible, just what the situation was there. He needed the services of experienced capable detectives. He had no Federal Bureau of Investigation to turn to, no Secret Service or Central Intelligence Agency. He did not even have an army Intelligence organization to help him. He had no one to whom he could turn. So he asked the Superintendant of Police of New York City, John Kennedy, for assistance. Kennedy assigned two of his detectives to help the General. They went to Baltimore to investigate the situation.

The General took two men into his confidence: Senator William Seward of New York, who had been designated by Lincoln to be his Secretary of State, and Elihu Washburne, a new Congressman from Illinois, who was an old friend and associate of the President-elect.

On Sunday, February 17th, Lincoln rested in Buffalo, New York spending some time with ex-President Millard Fillmore. Did Lincoln ask him about the purported assassination of President Taylor? No one knows, but possibly not. There is no indication that Lincoln ever took that story seriously.

It was known that they discussed the political situation, the secession of several of the Southern States, the organization of the Confederate States of America and the pro-secession sentiment in some of the other slave states.

While they talked, workmen were examining the rails over which the Lincoln train was due to pass the next day. Not a single rail was ignored, and by the end of that quiet Sunday in Buffalo, the railroad people had made certain there were no obstructions or loose rails along the route that might cause a wreck.

The next morning the train carrying the Presidential party left Buffalo, and reached the State capitol at Albany late in the afternoon. There was a great crowd of people waiting to greet Mr. Lincoln and cheer him as he left the train and was taken then to adddress the legislature. In the throng, but certainly not cheering, was the young actor, John Wilkes Booth, who had been warned only a few days before by the manager of the theatre where he was playing, that he had to stop making hostile remarks about the Federal government and its leaders.

The next day Lincoln entered New York City, where the cheers were not as strong or as cordial as they had been. Police Superintendant John Kennedy of New York City was in personal charge of the detail guarding the President-elect. Lincoln thanked him, but Kennedy said nothing about the investigation his two men were engaged in, in Baltimore. It was in New York that Norman Judd received additional information about the situation in Baltimore from a letter delivered by a woman agent of Pinkerton's. Judd was urged again to tell no one.

* * * *

Abraham Lincoln was exhausted. He had been making speeches, shaking hands with well-wishers, suffering the buffeting of enthusiastic crowds and conferring with political leaders ever since he had left Springfield ten days before. This day, February 21st, 1861, had been one of the hardest, and he needed rest badly. The next day would be a hard one, too. He was now in Philadelphia.

He made his way through the corridors of the Continental Hotel arriving at his room a few moments after ten o'clock. He told Elmer Ellsworth, the dashing young Zouave officer who was charged with his personal safety during the journey to Washington, that he did not wish to be disturbed, and retired.

It was only about fifteen minutes later that there was a knock on the door. Colonel Ellsworth opened it and before him stood a short, stocky bearded man who said that he had a letter that was to be given to the President-elect at once. Colonel Ellsworth demurred, offering to give it to Lincoln the first thing in the morning. The stranger insisted that it had to be given to the President-elect immediately. They argued, and finally the stranger said that the letter was from

Norman Judd. The Colonel knew that Judd was an old friend of Lincoln's, that he had played a key role in Lincoln's political rise and that he was accompanying Lincoln, as he himself was, on his journey to assume the duties of President. The Zouave officer finally consented to go to Judd's room.

Judd said that the President-elect should be awakened and given the letter. He told the officer that the stranger was Allan Pinkerton, the famous detective. Judd and Pinkerton would wait for Lincoln's arrival.

In about ten minutes both Lincoln and Ellsworth were in Judd's room. Then the Zouave left the room and stationed himself outside the door of the room in order to block the entrance of some of Lincoln's admirers who had followed him and also wished to enter.

Judd introduced Pinkerton to the President-elect and the detective recalled that they had met before. The three men seated themselves, and Judd explained to Lincoln why they had asked him to see them at this time of night.

He said that there was a plot to kill him before he would have an opportunity to assume the office to which he had been elected. The conspiracy was centered in Baltimore, through which he was scheduled to pass in about thirty-six hours.

Lincoln was to be attacked at the very moment that he was being acclaimed by his admirers in the Maryland city. The plan appeared to be well organized, the plotters determined to carry out their attempt to assassinate him and it was necessary that changes in his route to Washington be made by the three of them, said Judd, that would insure Mr. Lincoln's safety.

Judd talked, while Pinkerton watched Lincoln for his

reaction. Lincoln showed no emotion as he listened quietly while Judd unfolded details of the plot in Baltimore. He said that the plan had been uncovered by Pinkerton and his men, and that the detective had been in touch with him, Judd, during most of the ten days journey from Springfield. Lincoln had not been told of the plot until now, because they had been anxious to spare him; he had enough things to think about. But now the time had come when it was necessary to tell him, so that steps could be taken to avoid the danger that awaited him at Baltimore.

Lincoln continued to listen while Judd talked. Occasionally Pinkerton joined in the discussion, as a story of the plot and proposed counterplot was revealed. It was explained that even though the existence of the plot was known, it was not possible to plan counter measures until it was learned how the attack was to be made. Pinkerton said that he and his operatives had infiltrated several pro-Southern groups in and about Baltimore, and that one of them, who used the alias of Joseph Howard, had gained admittance to the inner circle of the Baltimore group headed by Cyriano Farrandini, an Italian barber at Barnum's Hotel, a favorite gathering place for the Southern element of the city. Farrandini appeared to be the leader of the conspiracy.

The conspirators were well aware of Lincoln's plans to arrive at Baltimore around noon on Saturday, go to a hotel for lunch and a conference with local Republican leaders, and then continue to Washington. At that time railroads did not run through Baltimore. Trains arriving at the station on one side of the city were dismembered, and the individual cars pulled by teams of horses to another station on the other side of the city, where the trains were reassembled and the journey resumed.

While no official reception had been planned for Lincoln —the only major city on his route that had not made such plans—it was expected that a huge crowd, most of it hostile, would be on hand to watch him as he rode in an open carriage from the first railroad station to the hotel, and later on to the other station. Baltimore was a Southern city and most of its citizens favored the South, even though there were still many of its inhabitants loyal to the Federal government.

When Lincoln stepped from his railroad car in answer to cheers and to shake hands, several conspirators would move in, attack him with knives, and then attempt their escape during the excitement. They would make their escape South by sea.

Semi-military troops, made up of Southern sympathizers, would be on hand to assist in the conspiracy, if they were needed.

It was explained to Lincoln that while several men had been selected to kill him, each thought he was the only one assigned to the task. They had drawn lots, and did not know that Farrandini had arranged it so that the success of the plot would not depend upon a single person.

Lincoln was told that they could not turn to the Baltimore police for protection. The head of the police, an avowed Southern sympathizer—he later was to serve in the Confederate army,—had said that he did not have enough men to spare to protect Lincoln from the crowds. There was no one to whom they could turn for protection. Besides, Pinkerton said, he did not know the identity of all the conspirators, nor could he say if there were other plots in addition to this one. They now had to make plans to outwit the known plotters, and also the unknown.

Judd and Pinkerton urged Lincoln to leave for Washington that night slipping through Baltimore when he was not expected.

Lincoln refused. He explained that he was scheduled to raise the American flag over Independence Hall the next morning—on Washington's birthday and to give a short address. Then he was to go to Harrisburg and address the State legislature. Once he had completed these official appointments, he would accede to their wishes and do whatever they deemed best.

Lincoln then said good-night and left the room. A small crowd had gathered outside, attracted by the news that the President-elect was there. He shook hands with many of his well wishers as he made his way back to his own room. There, a stranger was waiting for him.

It was Frederick Seward, son of Senator William Seward, who had been designated as Secretary of State in Lincoln's cabinet. The young man gave Lincoln a letter from the Senator. In it the Senator told of a plot to kill Lincoln in Baltimore, uncovered by New York detectives working for General Scott, then Secretary of War, who was very much concerned about the safety of the President-elect. He urged that Lincoln change his travel plans and leave for Washington, accompanied by a portion of his entourage on a night train to avoid the danger that awaited him in Baltimore.

Lincoln questioned young Seward, and found that while the Senator's son knew about the Baltimore plot, he did not know how his father had learned about it. Actually the investigation, independent of the one undertaken by the Pinkertons, and conducted by police officers from New York working for the General, had uncovered it. The latter had turned over the information to Senator Seward, who now wanted Lincoln to do substantially what Pinkerton had urged.

Lincoln said he did not have to decide what to do then and bade good-night to the disappointed young man, and retired once again.

The next morning Lincoln raised the flag as planned over Independence Hall, spoke of the principle of equality espoused by the Founding Fathers and told the cheering throng, "If this country cannot be saved without giving up that principle, I was about to say, I would rather be assassinated on this spot than surrender it."

Men were to recall that statement later.

Lincoln went back to the hotel for a short time before leaving for Harrisburg. Just before his departure he and Judd told young Seward that his father's suggestion would be followed, and the published schedule for Mr. Lincoln would not be followed. Then Lincoln left for Harrisburg just before Seward departed for Washington with the message for his father.

Four and a half hours later Lincoln and his party arrived at Harrisburg, to be greeted by a tremendous outpouring of men, women, and children intent on seeing the man who had been chosen as the sixteenth President of the United States. He made his way through cheering throngs to address the Legislature. Afterwards he attended a reception given by the Governor, Andrew G. Curtin.

Meanwhile Pinkerton had been working steadily, not even

taking time for sleep, as he made arrangements that he hoped would get Lincoln safely to the nation's capitol.

Lincoln, joined by the Governor, gathered members of his entourage about him at the Jones House and told them of his decision to follow the advice given him by both Pinkerton and Senator Seward, Judd having informed them of the existence of the plot. One of the members of the group was Major Hunter who several months before had written Lincoln, telling him of his belief that a plot against him existed in Baltimore, and suggesting that he slip through the city unannounced, accompanied by a few trustworthy companions.

Lincoln said that he would be escorted by his friend, Ward Lamon, a large burly man of undaunted courage, who later was to become U. S. Marshal of the District of Columbia. They planned to leave the city in about two hours, after attending a dinner given in the hotel by the Governor.

A few minutes before six o'clock, Lincoln and his group were enjoying their dinner, when one of his secretaries arrived with a message. Mr. Lincoln stood up, left the room and went to his chamber where he stuffed a soft hat in his pocket, put a shawl over his arm and then left after rejoining the Governor. In the corridors people assumed they were on their way to an evening reception at the Governor's home. Lamon met them at the hotel entrance where they all entered a waiting carriage and drove off.

They rode to the outskirts of the city, where they found a train, consisting of locomotive, baggage car and passenger coach, waiting on a siding. The baggage car, located between the locomotive and the passenger coach, made it impossible for the engineer and fireman to see the passengers.

Lincoln and Lamon said good-by to the Governor and entered the passenger car where they were greeted by two railroad officials whose cooperation had been enlisted by Pinkerton. It was exactly six o'clock.

At that moment Harrisburg was cut off from communication with the rest of the world. All telegraph wires had been cut with the exception of one used by the railroad itself. No trains were to leave there until morning. When Lincoln did not appear at a reception in the city attended by other members of his official party, word was given out that he was sick.

Pinkerton had been very much concerned lest word reach the Baltimore conspirators regarding the secret departure of Lincoln. He thought that the plotters might have agents in various communities watching Lincoln's movements, ready to send word of any change in arrangements. He also feared that such news might be circulated by newspapermen, talkative telegraphers and others. So he had arranged for the temporary isolation of Harrisburg and the additional precaution of railroad workers seeing and recognizing Lincoln as he rode in the train.

The train moved swiftly across the state. It was due to arrive in West Philadelphia at 10:30 P.M., where Pinkerton and another railroad official he had enlisted in the counterplot were to meet them. But the train arrived twenty-seven minutes early, nevertheless Pinkerton and his friend were waiting. Lincoln put on the soft hat, drew the shawl around his shoulders in order to change his usual appearance. Lincoln, Lamon and the two railroad men who had travelled with them from Harrisburg left the train and walked to the carriage that Pinkerton had waiting for them. Lincoln said good-by to the two railroad men and then got into the carriage. He was seated between Pinkerton and Lamon. The railroad official, Henry F. Kenney, rode up beside the driver and following instructions previously given him by the detective, told the driver to go to a certain street where they hoped to locate the home of a friend.

Actually there was no friend, the whole idea was to keep Lincoln under cover and guarded for more than an hour before going to the Philadelphia railroad station a mile away. So the carriage went from house to house along a street, looking for an imaginary resident, and keeping the attention of the driver from the three passengers behind them. Finally, after enough time had elapsed, the search was ended and the driver told to take them to the station.

Meanwhile Pinkerton's own group of operatives had taken posts assigned to them, ready to carry out instructions. Added to this group were a small number of other people, who did now know the details of the plan in which they were engaged.

Lincoln arrived at the station, in company with Pinkerton and Lamon. He walked stooped, hiding his height which might attract attention. Kenny waited for them just inside the station.

Lincoln and his two companions walked to the last car of a waiting train—a sleeper—where a female Pinkerton operative had reserved four berths, one of which was for her "sick brother." The moment that Lincoln, Pinkerton and Lamon entered the sleeping car, Kenney ran across the station waiting room, attracting attention to himself, and gave a parcel of "dispatches" to the conductor, who had been ordered by wire to hold the train until he received the parcel. This ruse having been arranged by Pinkerton and the railroad official so that the train would be held up until Mr. Lincoln was safely aboard.

The so called "dispatches" were merely a parcel of newspapers addressed to E. J. Allen, Esquire, Willard's Hotel, Washington." This name was an alias Pinkerton often used in his work.

The train started immediately and Lincoln retired at once to his berth which was too short for him, forcing him to lay on it diagonally. Despite the fact that he had delivered two speeches, shaken hands with thousands of people, spent eight hour in travel, and had had many conferences with political leaders since he had awakened that morning—or actually, on the previous morning—he remained wide awake. It had been at least nineteen hours since he had been in bed. Now however he could not sleep nor could the other members of his party—Pinkrton, Lamon and Mrs. Kate Warne, the female operative.

The train moved through the night—toward Baltimore. There was little talk among the four, and the tension mounted.

Pinkerton studied reports which his female operative had given to him regarding the arrangements for his secret journey to Washington. Everyone had been given his or her assignment and everything appeared to be in order, but Pinkerton did not relax, nor would he until the trip was completed.

The train stopped at Wilmington, Delaware. A telegrapher waited ready to send any message Pinkerton might want transmitted, but he, Pinkerton, remained in the train as he did not need to send any message at the time. As the train resumed its journey, the telegrapher flashed word of its departure to another person waiting for it ahead on the route. At Havre de Grace, the train was dismantled and ferried across the broad Susquehanna to the Southern side. This was a potential danger point, but nothing happened. Pinkerton stepped outside, to the rear platform of the car, and saw a light, operated by one of his men, flash, "All's well."

The train continued south, Pinkerton had men stationed at every depot, every bridge or other point where danger might lurk. As the train passed they signalled their message that "all's well," to the master sleuth waiting on the rear platform of the last car.

Despite the reassurance of these many messages signalled in the darkness, the tension mounted momentarily. The crucial place was ahead of them—Baltimore.

The train arrived at the Calvert Street Station about 3:30 A.M. Here it was to be dismantled, and the individual cars pulled by teams of horses along tracks to the Washington Branch station on the southern side of the city. When the train stopped Pinkerton got out, looked around but saw nothing amiss. The female agent after saying good-by to the President-elect, left the train and Pinkerton hired a carriage to take her to a hotel, her role of sister to a "sick brother" was over. The detective then rejoined Lincoln and Lamon and told them that everything appeared to be going well.

The sleeping car was slowly pulled through the darkened streets. Pinkerton remained alert, ready to spring to the defense of Lincoln at any moment; as so did Lamon. Lincoln appeared to be more relaxed than his two companions and he told several amusing stories to pass the time.

They arrived at the Washington Branch Station without

incident, only to find that further progress on their journey was being delayed. A connecting train from the West had not arrived.

The three men remained inside the car. They could hear a drunk singing outside as well as orders being given, shouts and bits of conversation. Lincoln continued to be calm and made joking remarks about some of the sounds that reached them. Nevertheless, Pinkerton was extremely alert and tensed for anything that might happen. While they were still in Baltimore he was fearful of their being discovered. Despite all his efforts to shield Mr. Lincoln some of the conspirators might be watching them even then.

Finally the Western train arrived, there was a transfer of passengers and baggage. Then Lincoln and his two bodyguards felt their own train begin to move—they were on the final phase of their journey.

Every mile reduced the danger and the chances of Lincoln being discovered and attacked, but Pinkerton remained vigilant. Nearly two hours later the train rolled into Washington. It was now daylight, and presumably Lincoln had arrived safely.

Still wearing the soft cap, but carrying the shawl over his arm, Lincoln left the train and entered the station, accompanied by Pinkerton and Lamon. Pinkerton scanned the crowd looking for anyone who might recognize Lincoln and who might be a party to the conspiracy in Baltimore. He saw one man looking intently at Lincoln and then walk toward him. Pinkerton moved fast, trying to protect the President-elect, but he was too late. The man grabbed Lincoln by the elbow, and said: "Abe, you can't play that on me."

Pinkerton struck the man who staggered back; Lamon reached for one of his pistols and Pinkerton was about to strike another blow, when Lincoln exclaimed: "Don't strike him, Allan, don't strike him! This is my friend Washburne. Don't strike him!"

It was Congressman Elihu Washburne of Illinois, an old friend of Lincoln's. Senator Seward had informed him of the Baltimore plot, and of Lincoln's message that he would arrive secretly in Washington. The Congressman had come to greet Lincoln in the event that he was on the morning train. Senator Seward and he had been meeting every train from the North, waiting for Lincoln but not knowing just when he would arrive. The Congressman was alone that morning as the Senator had overslept.

The Congressman wanted to chat, but Pinkerton was still nervous. "No talking here," he snapped.

The Congressman silently led them outside where they boarded a hack and started for Willard's Hotel. Pinkerton was cautious to the very end. He ordered the cab halted a block from their destination. Lamon went on alone, while Lincoln, Washburne and Pinkerton proceeded on foot, entering the hotel through the Ladies Entrance. The journey was over.

Pinkerton left to wire the news, in code, to members of his organization and to the key railroad men who had helped him, that Lincoln had reached Washington safely.

He then went back to Willard's Hotel. He had not slept since Thursday and it was now close to noon on Saturday. He went to see Lincoln who had managed to get a short nap—the only sleep he had had since Thursday. Mr. Lincoln shook hands with Pinkerton and thanked him for bringing him safely to Washington. It was a moment that Pinkerton remembered the rest of his life.

At noon that day—at the time that Lincoln had been scheduled to arrive in Baltimore—a huge throng waited at the railroad station. Word had reached the city of Lincoln's passage through there during the night, but many people either had not heard it or did not believe it. There was little police protection, the railroad cars were invaded by members of the mob looking for Lincoln, even before the train was dismantled. Mrs. Lincoln was insulted and a man resembled Lincoln was chased by members of the throng.

When the news was flashed across the country that Lincoln had slipped through the city—"like a thief in the night," one paper stated—he was critized widely and bitterly. Others later said there had been no plot except the one Pinkerton had invented to gain publicity for himself. However publicity about Pinkerton did not appear until many years later but the records of Pinkerton and his agents clearly indicated the existence of a definite plot.

Only two months after Lincoln had made his midnight passage through the city of Baltimore another mob, which probably contained many of the members of the first mob, attacked the Seventh Massachusetts Regiment as it marched from one railroad station to the other killing several soldiers.

Furthermore, during this period, the bridge across Gunpowder River was burned, other damage was done to the railroad, and troops en route to Washington were forced to go part of the way by sea.

IV

A Shot In The Dark

Abraham Lincoln was scheduled to be sworn in as the sixteenth President of the United States nine days after his arrival in Washington. During those nine days Lincoln conferred with many political leaders in Washington, as he made final preparations for his administration. During those nine days, other men were busy making plans to safeguard him from possible assassination on Inaugural Day.

There were good reasons why these precautions should be made. No one knew for sure if the Baltimore conspirators had given up, or if they planned to attempt an assassination sometime on Inaugural Day. While some of the members of the group had disappeared, there was no way of knowing if they fled from the area or were simply waiting in hiding for an opportunity to strike. Neither did anyone know if there were other conspiracies against which precautions should be taken. Nor was the possibility overlooked of a single person making an attempt unassisted.

The actions of General Scott to protect the President-elect on that Monday March 4, 1861, indicate eloquently his concern about the safety of the incoming President. Stories persisted of groups of men determined to keep him from reaching the inaugural stand at the Capitol where he was due to be sworn in. There was a story, for instance, of a group of horsemen in Virginia who were prepared to rush into the city and seize Lincoln while he attended the Inaugural Ball that evening—if he lived to be sworn in.

General Scott had managed to get some regular army troops into the city—only 653 men, brought from as far away as Leavenworth, Kansas, to serve as protection for Lincoln. He had some 900 local militia who were considered loyal to the Federal government, also the garrison of the Marine Barracks—a force of small size but of unquestioned loyalty and ability. Added to these, of course, was the police force of Washington itself. All in all, this was not a very large force, considering the length of the route that Lincoln would follow from the Willard to the Capitol, and the need to guard against a foray from outside the city, a sudden attack from the spectators, and so on. Furthermore they had to maintain order among the onlookers who had no hostile intent.

On Sunday, March 3, thousands of strangers had reached the city in anticipation of the events of the following Monday. Many of these visitors were obviously of good intent, but sprinkled among them were members of the criminal class, some described by one observer as "Baltimore thugs," and others.

A report reached Scott that an attempt would be made to blow up the temporary platform at the east portico of the Capitol which had been erected for the swearing-in ceremony. A guard was quickly placed underneath the stand, and at daybreak on Monday, March 4, a battalion of District militia marched to the site, and formed a semi-circle around it.

The sun was out, but it was a cold, windswept day. Tension hung over the city—a Southern city with many ties to the states which had seceded or were planning to do so. Few houses were decorated with bunting, as had been the custom at previous Inaugural Days, and some of the houses along the route Lincoln and Buchanan would ride had closed their shutters, as though to shut out the sight of the procession.

A battery of artillery was stationed near the Treasury Building, close to the White House, and not far from the Hotel Willard where Lincoln was staying. Two other batteries were placed at the Capitol grounds. All three batteries were ready for any action demanded of them.

A few minutes after 12:00 o'clock noon, President Buchanan and President-elect Lincoln emerged from the Willard, arm in arm. A cavalry troop on Fourteenth Street and an infantry detachment in front of the hotel presented arms. The two men entered an open carriage and started the ride down Pennsylvania Street toward the Capitol. Beside them rode a troop of District Militia. Colonel Stone, in charge of protecting the president-elect, spurred his horse repeatedly, making him rear up or to move suddenly, so as to keep the horses of the nearby militia troop nervous, too. He hoped that any individual attempting a shot at the occupants of the carriage would be unable to aim accurately.

There were few cheers among the spectators. Had they come to witness an assassination rather than an inaugural? Occasionally some one would cheer for the new Southern Confederacy, sometimes insults were shouted.

It was difficult for the throngs to see the President-elect, because of the cavalrymen riding beside the carriage. Behind the carriage came infantry.

Parallel to the procession regular army troops marched along F Street, ready for action, under the personal direction of the aged, and valiant General Scott.

Troops at the Capitol grounds had kept everyone out of the grounds except authorized persons with passes. With the arrival of the procession, Lincoln and Buchanan went into the Capitol by the north door, using a passageway guarded by marines and enclosed by a high wooden fence. In the Senate chamber the new Vice-President, Hannibal Hamlin of Maine, was sworn in.

The President-elect then moved outside to the platform where he was to deliver his Inaugural speech. He did not know it, but beneath the floor of the platform were fifty men concealed from view and ready to spring to his defense if necessary. Also ready was a group of riflemen stationed two to a window, in the wings of the Capitol, where they could watch the proceedings. Nearby were the troops which had escorted Lincoln and Buchanan to the ceremony.

His speech finished, Lincoln placed his left hand on a Bible and took his oath of office as President. The two batteries fired a roaring salute. The sound echoed off into the distance, being heard in much of the city.

Watching the ceremony was Senator Lewis Wigfall of Texas, leaning against a column, a contemptuous look on his fierce face.

* * * *

While Senator Wigfall had not attempted the kidnapping of "Old Buc," as he planned, he had not given up the idea of kidnapping Lincoln, in the opinion of some of the men close to Lincoln. Ward Hill Lamon, a former law partner of Lincoln's who had been brought to Washington to serve as marshal of the District of Columbia during the war years, wrote later:

> "When Mr. Lincoln was inaugurated in March, 1861, the the organization of plotters was still intact; but no plan of assassination had as yet received the sanction of the con-spirators as a body. It was their purpose to kidnap Mr. Lincoln and hold him in captivity, without injury to his person, until such concessions were made to the southern leaders as their plan of compromise rendered necessary."

In the days and months following his inaugural, Lincoln was constantly threatened, sometimes in person by individ-uals who managed to get in to see him at the White House. Apparently, however, no organized attempt was made on his life during this period, although the people near him had to be constantly alert.

John Hay, one of his personal secretaries, recalled years later:

"From the very beginning of his presidency, Mr. Lincoln had been constantly subject to the threats of his enemies. His mail was infested with brutal and vulgar menace, and warnings of all sorts came to him from zealous or nervous friends. Most of these communications received no notice. In cases where there seemed a ground for inquiry, it was made, as carefully as possible by the President's private secretary or by the War Department, but always without substantial result. Warnings that appeared most definite, when examined proved too vague and confused for further attention. The President was too intelligent not to know that he was in some danger. Madmen frequently made their way to the very door of the executive office and sometimes into Mr. Lincoln's presence. But he himself had so sane a mind, and a heart so kindly, even to his enemies, that it was hard for him to believe in political hatred so deadly as to lead to murder."

Even though he knew that "incitements to murder him were not uncommon in the South "he thought such danger remote" noted his wartime secretary.

In August of 1862, however, there occurred an incident that should have told him that such danger was not remote.

Despite the Baltimore plot, and the ceaseless flow of threats and warnings, he refused to take even ordinary precautions. He often went about the city—which still contained many persons of southern allegiance, many zealots and fanatics— unaccompanied by either a body guard or even a companion.

His friends, worried bout his safety, finally persuaded him to have a troop of calvalry stationed at the White House, and they also convinced him of the need for a military escort when he rode through the city. These precautions were long overdue; General Ben Butler, arriving at Washington in the middle of the night, in 1861, to report a victory, found the White House entirely without guards, and remarked that he could have captured the city with a corporal's guard.

During the heat of the summer Lincoln liked to ride out to the Soldiers' home, on the outskirts of the city, sometimes to spend the night, sometimes for only a few hours. The heat was less oppressive there and he liked to talk to the soldiers. Also the rides gave him periods of privacy for contemplation.

One night in August, 1862, while going to the soldiers' Home, an attempt was made on his life. He was riding a horse, which had been given to him and which bore the name "Old Abe." According to the account he gave to Ward Lamon the next day, the horse was responsible in part for his escaping injury. He said to Lamon, according to the latter's book some years later:

> "Last night, about 11:00 o'clock, I went out to the Soldiers' Home alone, riding Old Abe as you call him and when I arrived at the foot of the hill on the road leading to the entrance of the Home grounds, I was jogging along at a slow gait, immersed in deep thought, contemplating what was next to happen in the unsettled state of affairs, when suddenly I was aroused—I may say the arousement lifted me out of my saddle as well as out of my wits—by the report of a rifle, and seemingly the gunner was not fifty yards from where my contemplation ended and my accelerated transit began."
>
> "My erratic namesake, with little warning, gave proof of decided dissatisfaction at the racket and with one reckless bound he unceremoniously separated me from my eight

dollar plug hat with which I parted company without any assent, expressed or implied, upon my part."

"At a breakneck speed we soon arrived in a haven of safety. Meanwhile I was left in doubt whether death was more desirable from being thrown from a runaway federal horse, or as the tragic result of a rifle-ball fired by a disloyal bush-wacker in the middle of the night."

He recounted the story of the attack with a sense of amusement that was not shared by Lamon. The latter was unable to persuade Lincoln to be more careful, and in fact, Lincoln continued to elude his guards on many occasions.

Meanwhile the mail continued to contain threats from those who wished him harmed, and warnings of danger sent by those who wished him well. Many of the threats came from persons who were obviously crackpots. The idea of killing Abraham Lincoln persisted.

One man to whom the idea appealed was William C. Quantrill, a "colonel" of guerillas who led a raid on the Kansas community of Lawrence in August, 1963. It was one of the most brutal incidents of the war, for the guerillas had massacred more than 150 men and boys and had left the town in flames. The next year he got the idea of going east, to assassinate Lincoln. He moved his force toward Washington, but before he could reach it, he was mortally wounded in Kentucky in a clash with Federal cavalry.

By this time the idea of removing Lincoln from the White House—by kidnapping, or if that should fail, by assassination—became a topic of discussion for many individuals in the South, who hoped by a single stroke to achieve a great triumph for the Confederacy.

V

A Plan To Kidnap Lincoln

Early in November, 1864, a Colonel Margrave is supposed to have submitted to the Confederate government in Richmond, a plan to kidnap Lincoln and bring him inside the Rebel lines, according to a story which appeared in the New York Tribune the following March. A correspondent for the Tribune entered Confederate territory and spent several months in Richmond and in other parts of the South before returning to Washington to write his stories. On March 15th he wrote an account, which appeared on page one of the Tribune on the 19th, under a heading that read "Plan to Assassinate or Kidnap President Lincoln."

Colonel Margrave, who went under the "nom de guerre"

of Margrave, although his real name was Rhett, had served under the filibuster, William Walker in his Central American expedition. He had resumed his use of the name at the outbreak of the Civil War, and at one time he was a member of the staff of General Beauregard. He was wounded in the battle of Shiloh but later recovered, and was sent on secret missions to the North.

According to the Tribune story, Colonel Margrave submitted a plan to the Secretary of War. Under the proposed plan, a group of 150 carefully picked men would secretly make their way through Union lines and take up lodgings in Washington, Georgetown, Alexandria and Baltimore, where they could be in daily communication with each other. On command of their leader, they would spring into action.

The scheme was for the group either to force itself into the White House at a quiet hour and seize the President, or it might be found more convenient to take the President as he left for church or as he returned. He was to be thrown into a carriage and driven rapidly away.

Outside the city the carriage was to be joined by 25 to 30 armed men on horseback. The group would then drive on to Indian Point (Indian Head) about 25 miles south of Washington and on the Potomac. They would use two or three relays of fleet horses which were to be stationed along the route they would follow.

Pursuit by Federal troops would be made difficult. Every bridge between Washington and Indian Point was to be mined, and blown up as soon as Lincoln and his captors had passed. In addition, other men were to be stationed along the road, and cut down huge trees after the party had passed. These latter men were to escape through the woods as best they could.

At Indian Point the prisoner and his captors were to be ferried across the Potomac to a point a few miles south of Occoquan. They would hide in the woods, and travel by night, until they reached Confederate lines.

If it were found impossible to reach the safety of the Rebel lines, the conspirators would kill Lincoln.

The Tribune story did not say what they proposed to do with Lincoln if he were brought safely within Confederate lines.

The Tribune correspondent reported that the Confederate Secretary of War thought that the plan would succeed, but he had some reservations about it. He questioned if it were of a military nature, and if it was justified by the rules of war. He promised, however, to submit the plan to President Jefferson Davis and to Judah Benjamin, Secretary of State.

About a week later, Colonel Margrave left Richmond for the North. The Tribune man asked a Mr. Wellford, "who is familiar with all the secrets of the War Department if the plan had been adopted," and he answered: "You will see Old Abe in the Spring as sure as God."

Curiously, another man had conceived the idea of kidnapping Lincoln and spiriting him South. In September 1864, two months before Colonel Margrave is supposed to have submitted his plan, a well known actor had confided such an idea to friends. He was John Wilkes Booth, a member of the most famous theatrical family in America. His brother, Edwin, was generally considered to be the most accomplished actor in America, just as his father, Junius

Brutus Booth, had been the most famous Shakespearean actor of his day.

Wilkes Booth, as he liked to be known, was a handsome young man with gracious manners and a magnetic personality. He was liked by both men and women, and apparently he was able to influence many persons easily. The family estate was located at Bel Air, Maryland, where his father had settled a generation before with a common law wife. Edwin and the other members of the family were pro-Northern, but Wilkes had been partisan to the South from the start of the Civil War and before. He frequently spoke out against the Federal government and against Lincoln to relatives and friends and sometimes, to others. Because he was so likeable, he was usually forgiven these utterances, although on a few occasions he found himself in difficulty because of them.

He continued to play before Northern audiences, and sometimes in Southern cities in Union hands. He was a good actor, but he lacked the greatness of his brother and father. Nevertheless he was a strong box office attraction. Reviewers were not always kind, but those in the South appeared to like him more than did the Northern critics.

Between engagements he sometimes smuggled medical supplies into the Confederacy, and presumably also carried information as well.

As a boy he was given to dreams of great exploits, and as an adult the dreams took on a dangerous character. Years later, Edwin said that while the family knew that Wilkes was mad, they had not realized that he was dangerous. There was a history of mental instability in the family which revealed itself in Wilkes.

Whether Booth embraced the kidnapping idea after hearing of Senator Wigfall's scheme, or of other schemes is not known. Nor is it known if he transmitted the idea to Colonel Margrave, or if the Colonel discussed it with Booth before he worked out the details and submitted the plan to the Confederate War Department. It is not known if the Colonel and the actor knew each other, or even if they ever had any contact. But the Colonel's plan and the one Booth had before he gave it up for assassination, were remarkably similar. And under the Colonel's plan, if they were unable to get Lincoln within the safety of the Confederate lines, they were to kill him.

Shortly before Lincoln had passed through Albany on his way to Washington in 1860, the manager of a theatre there had been forced to warn Booth against his intemperate statements. Even though he was acting in Northern theatres, before northern audiences he was strongly pro-southern.

Acquaintances were to recall later that he had spoken in praise of assassins, had commented that a man could become famous by killing Lincoln, and that some day he might do some great deed that would enshrine himself in history forever. Apparently the idea of assassinating Lincoln was in his subconscious mind long before it emerged. Long before he spoke of becoming the assassin himself, he had started planning to kidnap Lincoln.

The idea of kidnapping Lincoln was pretty much the same as the one that Senator Wigfall had had. Kidnap Lincoln, spirit him to some spot beyond the reach of Federal arms, and then negotiate for concessions. It is not known if Booth was aware of the Wigfall plot. Certainly Wigfall had had some contact with at least one member of the Baltimore conspiracy, and the Senator was well known in Baltimore circles, as was Booth.

The idea was to kidnap Lincoln, with 70,000 Confederate soldiers then held in Northern prisons to be released as his ransom. That was a larger number of men than General Robert E. Lee had in his entire army during the fighting in the Wilderness campaign a few months before. The South was in desperate need of men, and 70,000 men, released for action, might tip the tide of the war.

The South needed the men desperately. General Grant, upon becoming the Federal commander-in-chief, had terminated the arrangement under which the North and the South exchanged prisoners. While the North was having difficulty in obtaining enough men for its armies, the plight of the South was even more acute. It needed soldiers more than anything else.

It is not known when the idea of kidnapping the President first entered Booth's mind. The fact was that many people in the South had that idea—of kidnapping Lincoln for transport to Rebel lines, or failing that, of killing him. The Tribune reporter who told of Colonel's Margrave's plan recalled that during the summer of 1863—the summer of Gettysburg and the Confederate high tide—"a club or society of wealthy citizens of Richmond was formed for the purpose of raising funds" to finance a plan for kidnapping Lincoln. "Circulars were sent to trustworthy citizens in every city and town in the Confederacy inviting cooperation in the grand undertaking and an immense sum of money was subscribed. The firm of Maury and Company, bankers in Richmond, subscribed $10,000 and Suram and Arenta, auctioneers, subscribed $5,000 and I have heard on good authority that there were several in the capital who subscribed even more liberally, than the parties named but who they were I did not learn. One man in Charleston, South Carolina whose name I have forgotten, subscribed $20,000. It was proposed when all was ready to obtain a furlough for Mosby and make him leader of the enterprise. Whether these schemes have been abandoned or whether the kidnappers are only awaiting a favorable opportunity to execute them remains to be seen."

It appeared that a great many people in the South were occupied with the idea of killing Lincoln. A man advertised in a newspaper in Selma, Alabama, offering to assassinate Lincoln for a large sum of money.

John Wilkes Booth, younger brother of Edwin Booth, the most famous actor of the day, had been obsessed with the hatred he felt for the North and especially for Lincoln. As the war progressed and the fortunes of the Confederacy waned, he became more intemperate in his anti-Federal sentiments, and at least once had to take an oath of allegiance to the Union, in order to get out of a scrape that might have sent him to prison.

In September, 1864 he was supposed to have first broached the idea of kidnapping Lincoln to Michael O'Laughlin, a stable worker in Baltimore who was also a deserter from the Confederate army. He also is said to have told Samuel Arnold, a farm hand at Hookstown, and a former Confederate soldier. Both had gone to school with Booth in their early youth.

Was this the start of Booth's scheming against the person of the President? Or was it the start of a new phase in his scheming?

A PLAN TO KIDNAP LINCOLN

On November 17, 1864 General Charles A. Dix, army commander in New York City, wrote a letter to Charles A. Dana, who served in the War Department, sometimes as the personal representative of Lincoln. In it General Dix told how a woman riding on a horse car in Third Avenue found a mysterious letter.

A day or so after the election in November, 1864, which saw Lincoln win re-election, a Mrs. Hudspeth was riding on a Third Avenue horse car with her daughter, when she noticed a man, a fellow passenger, who was wearing false whiskers. A sudden jolt of the car had tipped the man's hat forward. He was engaged in conversation with another man and apparently was unaware of the scrutiny that he was receiving from the curious woman, who wondered why he was wearing the false whiskers.

She noticed that his hand was small and graceful, that he was a young man, and she deduced an educated one from his speech. She also noticed that he carried a pistol in his belt.

She heard the man with the false whiskers tell his companion that he was leaving for Washington that day. He left the car before Mrs. Hudspeth did.

After he had left, the daughter of Mrs. Hudspeth picked up a letter from the floor of the car, and the mother stuffed it into her handbag. Later, when she got home, she discovered that it was not a letter he had dropped, as she thought, but an envelope containing two letters. One of them read as follows:

"Dear Louis: The time has at last come that we have all so wished for, and upon you everything depends. As it was decided before you left, we were to cast lots. Accordingly, we did so, and you are to be the Charlotte Corday of the nineteenth century. When you remember the fearful solemn vow that was taken by us, you will feel there is no drawback —Abe must die, and now. You can choose your weapons. The cup, the knife, the bullet. The cup failed us once, and might again. Johnson, who will give this, has been like an enraged demon since the meeting, because it has not fallen upon him to rid the world of the monster. He says the blood of his gray-haired father and his noble brother call upon him for revenge, and revenge he will have: if he cannot wreak it upon the foutain-head, he will upon some of the bloodthirsty generals. Butler would suit him. As our plans were all concocted and well arranged, we separated, and as I am writing—on my way to Detroit—I will only say that all rests upon you. You know where to find our friends. Your disguises are so perfect and complete that without one face no police telegraphic dispatch would catch you. The English gentlemen 'Harcourt' must not act hastily. Remember he has ten days. Strike for your home, strike for your country, bide your time, but strike sure. Get introduced, congratulate him, listen to his stories—not many more will the brute tell to earthly friends. Do anything but fail, and meet us at the appointed place within the fortnight. Inclose this note, together with one of poor Leenea. I will give the reason for this when we meet. Return by Johnson. I wish I could go to you, but duty calls me to the West; you will probably hear from me at Washington. Sanders is doing us no good in Canada. Believe me, your brother in love,

Charles Selby

The other letter was in a woman's handwriting, and read as follows:

St. Louis, October 21, 1864

Dear Husband:

Why do you not come home? You left me for ten days

only, and you now have been from home more than two weeks. In that long time only sent me one short note—a few cold words—and a check for money, which I did not require. What has come over you? Have you forgotten your wife and child? Baby calls for papa until my heart aches. We are so lonely without you. I have written to you again and again, and as a last resource, yesterday wrote to Charlie, begging him to see you and tell you to come home. I am so ill, not able to leave my room; if I was I would go to you, wherever you are, if in the world. Mama says I must not write any more, as I am too weak. Louis, darling, do not stay away any longer from your heart-broken wife.

Leenea

After the tragic events at Ford's Theatre in Washington, Mrs. Hudspeth was shown a photograph of John Wilkes Booth and she said that was the man wearing the false whiskers.

Mrs. Hudspeth turned the two letters over to the military authorities in New York, who forwarded them to Dana in the War Department, who in turn rushed over to the White House and showed them to Lincoln. The latter made no special comment; but later they were found in an envelope which the President had marked "Assassinations."

In forwarding the letters to Dana, General Dix commented that while the whole thing sounded more like something written for one of the New York Sunday newspapers, the letter in the women's handwriting convinced him both were genuine. Dix also said that the man who had lost the letters was of medium size, and had black hair. The name "Charles Selby" was obviously "an manufacture" in his opinion.

PLOTS AGAINST PRESIDENTS

If the Selby letter is to be taken as genuine, as Dana obviously thought so for he wrote about it many years later, then it appears that Booth was party to a plot to kill someone at that time—at the time that he was telling his old boyhood friends about a plan to kidnap Lincoln.

There was a reference to "the cup" failing once. J. C. Holland, author of the first comprehensive biography of Lincoln after his death, wrote in 1865, after talking with many of Lincoln's associates and friends—and with Lincoln before the assassination—that both in Canada and in Europe, as well as in this country, it was well known that there were conspiracies to kill Lincoln. He also wrote: . . . . "and it is believed that on one occasion, the President actually took poison in the drugs which were prescribed for him by his physician, and prepared for him in one of the shops of the city."

Holland, who later became editor of *Scribner's Magazine,* was a careful, conscientious and responsible historian.

Was the incident that Holland referred to the same one that "Charles Selby" wrote of? This is not known. It is easy to conjecture, of course. It is known that David Herold, who was a member of the gang which had planned to kidnap Lincoln—and later to kill him, had clerked for a while in a drug store in Washington, and once had delivered some castor oil at the White House for Mr. Lincoln's use.

Was this the time that poison had passed the lips of Lincoln? Had Herold put poison in the castor oil? If he had it might explain why poison had passed his lips without his life being taken. For when a man takes poison usually doctors try to move the poison quickly through the body before it had time to do much harm. This is done by liberal doses of laxative, such as castor oil. Herold was not very bright. At the trial of the conspirators it was noted that he was mentally retarded, with the intelligence of a child of about eleven.

Was Booth the man with the false whiskers? And if so, was he the Louis who had received the letter? Or was he the Selby who sent it? It is known that Booth was in New York the day that the letter was found, and that he went to Washington that night.

There was no Louis among the gang of conspirators rounded up after the shooting of Lincoln, but there was a Lewis—Lewis Paine. And Paine was not his real name, but Powell. It was he who later nearly killed Secretary of State Seward while Booth was shooting Lincoln.

Two months before the incident on the Third Avenue horse car, Booth had started organizing the group that ultimately was to be involved in his plans for kidnapping, and in the assassination, according to two of the men involved. Was Booth organizing his own group, after being a member of another? Was he organizing a new group especially for kidnapping? Or was the man on the street car not Booth but some one else, and the plot referred to in the letter not a threat to Lincoln's life but to some one else? It is not difficult to add together a number of facts and what appear to be facts but possibly are not, and come up with a conclusion that you are seeking. But there are too many questions unanswered, too many inconsistencies, too many blanks, to flatly state any conclusion.

It was at Barnum's Hotel in Baltimore that Booth met Arnold and O'Laughlin for a few drinks and talk—talk that eventually led to a discussion of a plan to kidnap the President of the United States. The two guests had known Booth as a boy when all three went to the same school together. Booth had been their leader then and now they were flattered by this attention from the scion of the famous Booth family.

This first meeting, ironically, was in the same hotel where much of the plotting to kill Lincoln while he was travelling to Washington had taken place. As far as is known, Booth was not a party to that plot, nor were Arnold and O'Laughlin.

Neither O'Laughlin or Arnold had amounted to much, and now they both were working in small jobs for their brothers. Booth offered them money and a chance to attain glory if they assisted him. The two mild-mannered men agreed and Booth made plans for the carrying out of the plot he had embraced—if not conceived.

Booth raised some money by disposing of some property he owned, and doled out modest sums to Arnold and O'Laughlin, and later to the other conspirators. He went to Canada and set up arrangements for credit, in case he should have to flee the United States, and he talked with a fellow Marylander named Martin, who dealt in contraband. As far as is known he did not get in touch with the representatives of the Confederate government in Montreal. Martin gave him a letter of introduction which led him to Doctor Samuel A. Mudd, a well-to-do physician in southern Maryland, and to John H. Surratt, Jr., a Confederate courier and spy, who travelled regularly from Richmond to Washington and to Canada. He was employed by an express company whose president in 1861 had helped defeat the Baltimore plot against Lincoln, but gave up the job to devote himself fully to his spying, carrying of messages and the plotting to kidnap Lincoln.

Surratt was familiar with the area in southern Maryland through which Booth planned to spirit Lincoln after the capture in Washington. Booth visited the area to acquaint himself with the roads and general terrain. The plan was to take Lincoln down the eastern shore to Port Tobacco, about twenty-five miles south from the capital, and there take him across the Potomac into Confederate territory. Surratt helped Booth to recruit George A. Atzerodt, a German-American who did odd jobs, and picked up some extra money by taking blockade runners across Pope's Creek. Atzerodt lived in Port Tobacco with his common-law wife and their child. He was fierce in appearance, but he was essentially a coward—and frequently a drunk.

During the fall of 1864 Booth made several trips to the sparsely settled area south of the city, and once, at least, he spent the night with Doctor Mudd at his home near Bryantown.

Meanwhile the gang was growing slowly, but not as fast and to the size that Booth desired. Surratt enlisted David Herold, who liked to hunt partridges in the area through which Booth planned to take Lincoln. Surratt had known Herold since the latter had attended school in southern Maryland, and Booth had also known him for about two years. Herold stood in awe of Booth, and often trailed after him in Washington.

There were two others who eventually were to be involved in the events that transpired at Ford's Theatre on April 14th—Mrs. Mary E. Surratt, mother of John Surratt, and Edward Spangler.

When Booth went to see John Surratt at the rooming house in Washington run by his mother, he made a favorable impression upon the mother, and upon John's sister. Mrs. Surratt was strongly pro-Southern, and it was said that she sometimes harbored blockade runners in her home. In her home hung pictures of many leading Confederates—Jefferson Davis, Alexander Stephens, vice president of the Confederacy, and General Pierre Beauregard. She also had pictures of Union generals Grant, McClellan and Hooker.

Sprangler was a scene shifter at Ford's Theatre who had known Booth since he was a boy. Booth's father had hired him to do some work at the Booth farm at Bel Air. Spangler had not forgotten, and he sometimes did odd jobs for him at the theatre. He was staunchly pro-South, and a serious drinker.

This was the group that Booth had at his bidding—six persons. Later another member would be added to the group.

There have been many persons who believed that Mrs. Surratt was not a party to the conspiracy which was so often discussed in her home, and in which her son was involved. Certainly her boarding house became the meeting place of the conspirators. And there are those who think that Dr. Mudd was not a party to it, either; that he had helped Booth after the killing, not knowing the identity of the patient, nor of the deed he had committed. In any event, it was far from the fifty to one hundred men that Booth had expected to have. He had told a fellow actor he expected to have that many when he sought to recruit his fellow thespian.

It is interesting to note that Booth's plans were very similar to those of Colonel Margrave, who had envisioned a group of from one hundred to one hundred and fifty, while

Booth spoke of fifty to one hundred. Both men envisioned the capture of Lincoln and then rushing him southward by way of lower Maryland. Margrave's plan spoke of crossing the Potomac at Indian Point—he probably meant Indian Head—to Occoquan. Booth, after scouting the area, chose Port Tobacco as the place to cross. The two were separated by about a dozen miles.

It was a bad winter for the South. It had used up much of its resources in manpower, in supplies and material, while the North had increased the size of its armies, it had more and better equipment and supplies than ever before, and it was braced for a final, massive onslaught. General Sherman had marched across Georgia to the Atlantic Ocean and turned North toward a meeting with General Grant, who was maintaining a siege of Petersburg and Richmond.

More and more Southerners realized the Confederacy was doomed; the desertion rate was up and steadily increasing.

But Booth remained fierce in his allegiance, in his belief in an eventual triumph of Southern arms, and went ahead with his plans to kidnap Lincoln. It was for this purpose that he had organized the group, not for assassination, even though the idea of killing Lincoln should the opportunity present itself, persisted in his mind. Paine knew this, but whether the others did is not known.

Booth continued to make plans for the kidnapping. During the second week in January, 1865, Herold went into southern Maryland to see about obtaining relays of horses. In Port Tobacco, Atzerodt was trying to find a floatboard that he could hire, capable of carrying a carriage and ten or twelve men.

Meanwhile Booth had gone back to the family farm at

Bel Air to visit his sister, Asia, and to sign a statement he had written some time before, which was intended for a fellow actor which he could use as he saw fit. It was a statement in which he sought to justify what he intended to do. In it he wrote, in part, "My love (as things stand today) is for the South alone. Nor do I deem it a dishonor in attempting to make for her a prisoner of this man, to whom she owes so much misery. If success attend me, I go penniless to her side. They say she had found that 'last ditch' which the North have so long derided and been endeavoring to force her in, forgetting they are our brothers, and that it is impolitic to goad an enemy to madness. Should I reach her in safety, and find it true, I will proudly beg permission to triumph or die in the same 'ditch' by her side."

It is generally believed that Booth and his group first planned to kidnap Lincoln on Wednesday, January 18, 1865. It had been announced that the President would attend the performance of the play, "Jack Cade," at Ford's Theatre. It is probable that the conspirators were ready to seize him at the theatre, but Lincoln did not appear as expected.

Booth continued to try to enlist fellow actors in his scheme, but failed. He was a personable, and at times quite likeable man, and very persuasive, but as far as is known, he was unable to win new recruits until February.

In February, while standing outside Barnum's Hotel in Baltimore, Booth met Lewis Paine, as he was known, even though his real name was Powell. Somewhere, possibly in Montreal, they had met before and they greeted each other. Paine had just been released from arrest for beating up a colored maid. He was down and out, penniless, and quickly joined the conspiracy when Booth told him about it and gave him funds with which to keep going.

Paine and his two brothers had been in the Confederate army, and the two brothers had been killed. He himself had been wounded and captured at Gettysburg.

He escaped, but did not return to the South. He took an oath of allegiance to the North about the time that he beat up the Negress. He was a man of low intelligence, and one of the doctors who later examined him said he might have been insane.

In Washington Booth urged Paine—who called the actor "Cap"—to step into the White House and shoot Lincoln. When Paine was reluctant to do this, Booth urged him to wait in ambush in the bushes near the White House and shoot Lincoln on the grounds.

Considering later events, one cannot but wonder why Paine hesitated.

VI

A Laugh And A Shot

On the morning of March 4, 1865, a fellow actor visited Booth at his room in the National Hotel, and found the latter examining a knife, a pistol, and a map. Booth turned and lunged at the visitor with the knife—he was not one of the actors Booth had sought to recruit.

"What in the name of sense is the matter with you," the startled actor exclaimed. Booth put down the knife and the two conversed. That afternoon Booth attended the second inauguration of Lincoln, using a pass obtained for him by the daughter of a United States Senator.

At the inauguration police guarded a passageway from the interior of the Capitol to the stand on the steps of the building. A man tried to break into the passageway, but was repulsed by a police officer. He tried repeatedly, and a few minutes before Lincoln was due, the policeman seized the man and took him to a guardroom in the basement and locked him up. The man was not searched. After the ceremony was over and Lincoln had left, the man was released from the guardroom.

Later, after the assassination at Ford's Theatere, the police officer was shown a picture of Booth, and identified him as the man he had confined in the guardroom. A grateful Congress rewarded the policeman with a promotion.

Time was running out, and Booth knew that he had to do something soon if he was to aid the South. He brought the conspirators together on March 17, 1865—Saint Patrick's Day—in Washington. This was the first time that Arnold and O'Laughlin, brought in from Baltimore, met the other members of the group.

Booth still expected to capture Lincoln in Ford's Theatre. He knew that Lincoln liked the theatre and had been at Ford's a number of times—once when he himself was starring in a play. He engaged the Presidential box and it was occupied by Paine and Surratt, so that the former could become more familiar with the interior of the theatre.

After the show was over, the full group met at a restaurant nearby. To Booth's anger and dismay, Surratt wanted to abandon the scheme as too dangerous. He believed that the government had wind of the plot and was preparing to defeat it. In this he was partly right, for a boarder at his mother's house had become suspicious of the meetings, the coming and going of strange persons, and the general tone of hostility to the North that he found there. He had tipped off the police, who were engaged in an investigation. The government might have known about the plot—or it might not have. Certainly it was suspicious, certainly it had been doing some investigating. History has never revealed just what the police knew, nor what it planned to do.

Surratt also said that he had heard rumors of a plot against the President. He did not know if the rumors were about their conspiracy, or some other one.

Arnold suggested that instead of trying to grab the President at the theatre they try to do it outdoors at some spot away from crowds. Arnold said that the whole enterprise was getting too dangerous and that if Lincoln was not taken within a week, he would withdraw from the plot.

Booth became angry and called Arnold a traitor and said he should be shot. The meeting continued through the night.

At one point Booth implied that they might kill Lincoln instead of kidnapping him, and one of the conspirators declared he would quit the group. Booth apologized and said they would stick to the idea of kidnapping the President, and that it would be done outdoors, as Arnold wanted.

It was early Saturday morning, March 18, when the group broke up. Booth had managed to persuade the conspirators to remain together with him as their leader. That night Booth appeared in a play at Ford's Theatre—the last time he was ever to act in a play. He was warmly, even enthusiastically applauded. In the audience were three of the conspirators, Surratt, Paine and Herold. After the performance he told them he had learned the President planned to attend a performance of "Still Waters Run Deep," at the Soldiers' home on Monday afternoon.

The group quickly met, and plans were made to kidnap Lincoln on his way to the performance—and in the open as Arnold wanted.

Herold was sent down to Surrattsville, which took its name from a tavern and post office that Mrs. Surratt's husband had run for a number of years, in Maryland south of Washington and on the way to Port Tobacco. He was to pick up two rifles, some tools, and some rope and there await the arrival of Booth and the others, with the President in their hands, as they sped toward Port Tobacco. Some of the conspirators were to string ropes across the road behind them to trip and delay any pursuit. Here again, the plan of Colonel Margrave was being followed, even though ropes instead of fallen trees were to be used to slow up the pursuit.

Back in Washington the other six conspirators, Booth, Surratt, Arnold, O'Laughlin, Paine and Atzerodt, made their plans carefully. They would wait in a clump of trees outside of the city and as the President passed on his way to the Soldiers' Home they would rush from cover, surround and capture him and strike southward for Herold and for Port Tobacco, en route to the Confederacy.

Lincoln would be overpowered by Paine and others and kept prisoner in the carriage. The coachman would be forced from his seat, the reins taken over. During the first few miles, until they had left the city, Lincoln would be kept in the carriage, but once in the open, the vehicle would be abandoned, and the entire party would ride at breakneck speed for lower Maryland and Port Tobacco.

The conspirators, with the exception of Herold, rode in pairs to a group of trees along the route they expected Lincoln to take on his way to the Soldiers' Home. The spot they chose was between Seventh Street and Florida Avenue—about two miles from the White House. After capturing Lincoln they would have to ride across the city, passing near the capitol, before reaching Maryland.

For some reason Booth did not remain with the conspirators after they had met at the appointed place. He went on to the Soldiers' Home—did he plan to kill Lincoln if the President escaped the ambush?

A carriage came along as was expected and the five mounted men dashed from cover and surrounded it. One of the group flung open the door of the vehicle—Lincoln was not inside. Another man was riding in the Presidential carriage. The conspirators turned and fled, leaving a puzzled and very angry passenger to continue his journey.

At the Soldiers' Home Booth learned that the President was not coming after all; he was at a military review instead.

The conspirators were alarmed; they thought their plan had been discovered by the authorities and that at any moment they might be arrested. Young Surratt reached his mother's boarding house first, stormed inside, pistol in hand, and exclaimed:

"I will shoot anyone that comes into this room! My prospects are gone, my hopes are blighted!"

A few minutes later Paine arrived, also pistol in hand. A short time then Booth came in, exasperated.

The plot was dead, although Booth continued his efforts to keep it alive and the group together. Time was running out; the Federal troops in the South were about to throw themselves upon the weakened but still valiant Southern army.

The gang broke up for a while. Surratt returned to his

job as courier for the Confederate government and left for Montreal. Arnold, got a job as a clerk in a store at Old Fort Comfort, in Virginia. Booth, while still clinging to his hope of abducting the President, went to New York. Still in Washington, however, were Paine, Atzerodt and Herold, living on the money provided them by the actor, waiting for orders from him.

The intended victim also left the city. Lincoln departed three days after their abortive attempt to kidnap him for City Point and a visit to the Army. He did not return until April 9th, 1865.

It was probably sometime after Booth's return from New York that he visited a fellow actor, Charles Warwick, then living in a rooming house run by William Peterson across the street from Ford's Theatre. Warwick, noting that Booth appeared to be tired, suggested he stretch out for a while on his bed. Booth did so and rested on the bed that a short time later was to serve as the death bed of Lincoln.

The war began to end. On April 3rd Richmond fell, and the government fled westward, trying to reach Danville, which had been designated the new, temporary Confederate capital. General Lee was cut off before he could reach that city, and surrendered at Appomattox Court House on April 9th.

Washington became delirious with joy. There were fireworks, band concerts, parades; church bells rang, cannon boomed, bonfires were lit; there was singing, laughter and drinking everywhere.

On Tuesday evening, two days after Lincoln's return to the city, hundreds of persons moved on the White House to cheer the President, and to express their exhilaration. In the throng was Booth, and possibly he was accompanied by Paine or Herold.

Lincoln addressed the throng, and told them of his plan for limited franchise for Nergoes in Louisiana. Booth became enraged and declared that Lincoln would not live to make another speech.

He was now determined to assassinate the President, even though some of his gang of conspirators balked at this. He had talked about it for some time, and now there seemed to be no choice for him. Even if he succeeded in capturing Lincoln, it would be hardly possible for him to reach the Confederate lines, if any were left. Richmond was gone, Lee's army was gone. True there was Johnson's army, not yet surrendered, and other isolated groups of Confederate forces, but the President of the Confederacy, Jefferson Davis was in flight with his cabinet and a handful of troops. There was no longer a place to which Lincoln could be taken, and from which negotiations could be conducted for concessions from the North.

So Booth thought of murder, and the more he thought of it, the larger grew the plan in his mind. If the Federal government were to be rendered leaderless, then the South could rise up again and perhaps wrest a victory at the very moment of defeat. If he were to kill the head of the Federal government, he might yet make a Southern victory possible.

He thought of this, and decided that he needed to make sure there was no leader to take over should Lincoln die. He decided that the Vice President, Andrew Johnson, should die, as well as the secretary of State, William Seward. With the three top men dead, there would be the question of who held the commanding position in the Federal government.

The line of secession was not clear; very likely Congress would squabbe over this, ambitious generals might try to seize power, there might be an internal disorder and strife that would render the government powerless for a long time.

Thursday, April 13, 1865, Booth went to Grover's Theatre and after chatting for a while with the manager, asked if the theatre planned to take part in the general celebration of the raising of the American flag over Fort Sumter, to be held the next night. The manager said it would, and then Booth wanted to know if he was going to invite the President. The manager said he would send an invitation right away. Later Booth sent a friend to rent the box next to the one the theatre had reserved for Lincoln's use.

At noon the next day, Good Friday, April 14th, Booth entered Ford's Theatre to pick up any mail there might be for him, and learned from the acting manager, Henry Clay Ford, that Lincoln had accepted an invitation to attend the performance that evening of "Our American Cousin." He had seen the show before, but this time he was making an event of it. He would be accompanied not only by Mrs. Lincoln, but also by General and Mrs. Ulysses S. Grant.

Booth went outside and sat on the steps, looking over his mail. But his mind was not on the letters he held in his hands; it was on the opportunity he now saw before him of achieving his dream of killing Lincoln. He would do it here in the theatre he knew so well.

He went back into the darkened theatre and walked about; studying it, making mental notes about this and that, planning the assassination.

The President and his party would be in the Presidential Box, on the right of the stage, as seen from the audience. It was really two boxes, seven and eight, with a thin partition in between. When the President attended the theatre the partition was removed, so there was plenty of room for four persons. Entrance to the box was gained from a passageway in its rear.

Booth went to Box Seven, and sitting about where Lincoln was to sit, listened to the rehearsal by the cast. He knew the play, but he listened and watched. There was a moment when there was only one person on the stage.

That would be the moment that the assassination would be done he decided. Killing the President at that moment, he could leap to the stage below—he had made longer leaps than that in some of the plays in which he had appeared. He would have only one man to contend with on the stage— even if that man recovered in time from his surprise. He could escape from the stage and the theatre at that moment, he told himself.

A few minutes after leaving the theatre Booth encountered James Ford, brother of the theatre's owner, who was seated in a carriage laden down with flags. He pulled over to the curb and talked with the actor for a few minutes. He said it was a dull day—Good Friday was traditionally the poorest day of the year for the theatre,—but he expected that this day would have a full house. The flags were for decorating the box Mr. and Mrs. Lincoln were to occupy with their guests, General and Mrs. Grant, the manager said. There was some idle chatter, and the two men parted. The time was just before noon—and Booth had just decided that Grant should be killed, too.

He went around the corner to a livery stable and arranged for a good horse to be available for his use at four o'clock in the afternoon, and at another stable ordered his horse be taken to the stable in the rear of Ford's Theatre.

It was about this time that he also went to the Kirkwood House where the Vice President, Andrew Johnson, had a two room suite. He left a card which read, "Don't wish to disturb you. Are you at home? J. Wilkes Booth." and then left.

Why did he make that visit, and why did he leave the card? Historians have never been able to find a satisfactory explanation.

There was another resident of the Kirkwood House known to Booth—George Atzerodt. The conspirator had been living at a small third rate hotel, but Booth arranged for him to move to the fashionable Kirkwood House where he was a fish out of water, but handy to the Vice President. He had been sent there the night before by Booth to spy on Johnson. The Vice President's suite was on the street floor and Atzerodt's room was on the second floor. The bar was on the street floor and Atzerodt spent most of his time in it and in the lobby. In his room were clothes and weapons delivered by Herold.

Booth went to the National Hotel where he lived and changed his clothes. He put on a black coat and tight black trousers suitable for riding. He donned a black hat, put on calf riding boots with new spurs, slipped a small compass into his pocket together with a gimlet for boring holes in wood, a small derringer and a long sheathed knife.

*   *   *   *

George Atzerodt had been absent from the Kirkwood House for a while, and when he returned he carried a bundle.

97

He asked the clerk in the lobby where Johnson's suite was and the clerk pointed it out. It was almost directly under Atzerodt's. The clerk added that the Vice President had just come in. Atzerodt appeared surprised.

The conspirator went to his room and opened the bundle. He hid two large pistols under the pillow on his bed, and concealed a knife beneath a sheet.

A short time later Atzerodt went downstairs, and paid a visit to the bar, as was his wont and frequent pleasure. Then he left the hotel.

Shortly after, Johnson left and walked to the White House to see Lincoln. The President was holding a cabinet meeting and Johnson waited. In those days the Vice President was not considered of political importance, except when running for office. He was not customarily invited to cabinet meetings, and his only function was to preside when the Senate was in session.

Booth went to the hotel where Paine was living, and discussed his plans with the Confederate deserter. He told Paine to check out and that there would be a horse waiting for him in the little stable behind Ford's Theatre.

At the boarding house on H Street, Mrs. Surratt had told a roomer that she had to drive out into the counry again— she had made several such trips in recent days. It was the same roomer who had become suspicious a few days before about the people he had seen going in and out of the house, and the secret meetings that had been occurring there, and had notified the police.

When Booth arrived the boarder was leaving to hire a horse and carriage at a nearby livery stable. When he returned a few minutes later Booth had gone, but Mrs. Surratt told him that she had a package to deliver to the Surratt Tavern for Booth. She did not say what was in the package although she displayed it to him. Inside however was a field glass that Booth expected to pick up during his flight south. On an earlier trip—April 11—she had left word for the tavern keeper to have the "things" that had been left several days previously, ready for Booth to pick up that night. The "things" were two carbines, some rope and a monkey wrench, left by her son John, Atzerodt and Herold.

It is not clear how Booth and the conspirators spent all the day. Booth went back to his hotel—the National—sat down and wrote a letter in which he explained and attempted to defend what he planned to do that evening. It was written for the newspaper, The National Intelligencier, to be printed the next day, after the assassination. Leaving the hotel, he encountered an actor friend, John Matthews, who had refused to join the conspiracy to kidnap Lincoln. Without telling Matthews the contents, he asked him to deliver the letter to the newspaper offices the next day, before noon.

Sometime that afternoon Booth learned that General Grant and his wife were not going to accompany the President and Mrs. Lincoln to the theatre after all. They had arranged to leave town that evening to visit a daughter and had given that as an excuse to Lincoln. Mrs. Grant had no desire to spend the evening in the company of Mrs. Lincoln. Earlier that month, Mrs. Lincoln had harranged Mrs. Grant severely, and she hoped to avoid any possibility of that happening again.

Sometime around four o'clock or shortly after, Herold went to a livery stable where he had arranged for a horse. He obtained a mare, with an English saddle and rode off.

He had missed Booth at Ford's and at another appointed spot for a rendezvous.

Booth, who had expected to see Atzerodt when he visited the Kirkwood House, noticed him on a side street. He dismounted and they had a short talk. Booth told Atzerodt that he was to kill the Vice President at 10:15 PM that night—at the same moment that he planned to shoot Lincoln. Atzerodt, his courage running out fast, said that he had agreed to help in the kidnapping but not in the killing. Booth sneered at him, called him a coward and said that it was too late for him to back out now. He was persuaded to stay in the plot, and try to kill Johnson. He had been drinking heavily all day, trying to find the courage he needed. He went to a livery stable and rented a mount, which he took to another livery stable and left, in the hope of confusing his trail, should anyone ever seek to follow it. He did not go directly to the other livery stable, however, but rode about aimlessly for a while, stopping at saloons to have drinks. He passed Ford's Theatre which he looked at carefully as he rode by. Not far from the theatre he threw away a bowie knife which he had been carrying.

That afternoon Lincoln and Mrs. Lincoln went for a carriage ride and they talked about what they would do after he finished his term as President. He still had most of the four years of his second term to serve. He was in a happy mood, and Mrs. Lincoln was to recall that he had apparently lost the melancholy that was almost habitual with him.

Shortly after six o'clock Booth returned to Ford's Theatre. He rode down the alley to the rear of the theatre, and rapped at the rear entrance. Spangler and another stage hand came out and Booth asked them stable his horse and to use a strong halter because his mount was skittish. He did not want her to break the halter and run away. After this had been taken care of, Booth invited the pair to have a drink with him in the tavern next door. They accepted his offer and left the empty theatre. They did not have to return to it so he bought a bottle of whiskey for them and urged them to drink before leaving. He then went back to Ford's.

The theatre was empty and dark, except for a couple of gas lights on the stage. Booth could see the flag draped box which had been prepared for Lincoln and his guests. Ironically Spangler had been asked by the manager if he thought the decorations on the box were all right, and Spangler had said they were.

Booth picked up a piece of pine board, one and one half inches by three inches, normally used to prop up sheet music for the musicians. He went down into the orchestra to the rear and then up the stairs to the dress circle and then continued on toward the decorated box. He came to the door of the corridor leading to the box and before it was a cane chair. He entered the corridor and then looked around the box, and then went back to the door. There he found that he could brace the door with the piece of wood, although he had to gouge out some plaster from the wall near the door to do so. He was careful of the plaster he had worked loose, catching it in a hankerchief, and leaving no trace of it on the floor to attract attention and rouse suspicions.

With the piece of wood in place, the door was braced from the inside so that it could not be opened from the outside.

He put the piece of wood in a dark corner near the door. The board was important. If he had to stab the guard at the door, he would be able to quickly brace the door from the inside and be free to carry out the assassination.

Now he turned his attention to the interior of the box. The partition had been removed so that Boxes seven and eight were now one box. A rocking chair had been placed inside for Lincoln, and there was another chair for Mrs. Lincoln. Inside, too, was a sofa for the use for the President's guests.

There were two inner doors, leading from the corridor to the boxes. He tried them and found that they opened easily. As he knew, the locks were broken. He paid special attention to the door of Box Seven.

Closing this door, he took the gimlet from his pocket and made a small hole in one of the door's panels, so that he could peer in and see the chair that Lincoln would occupy. He enlarged the hole with his knife, and then removed the shavings and bits of wood before leaving the theatre. He then returned to the National Hotel, ate his dinner and rested.

* * * *

It had been a happy day for Lincoln. He had been in good spirits during his ride with Mrs. Lincoln, and he had talked with laughing nostalgia with old friends. But there had been one time during the day when his spirits were not high. He had told William H. Crook, one of the guards on duty at the White House that day, "Crook, do you know I believe there are men who want to take my life?—And I have no doubt they will do it."

"Other men have been assassinated," he had added.

Crook told Mr. Lincoln he hoped this would never happen.

"I have perfect confidence in those who are around me—in every one of you men," Lincoln had declared, "but if it is to be done, it is impossible to prevent it."

As he left the White House for home that night, Crook said, "Good night, Mr. President," as was his custom. And customarily Lincoln had always replied, "Good night, Crook." But this night, Lincoln said it differently.

He said, "Good by, Crook."

On his way home Crook thought about that.

That afternoon Lincoln had asked that Major Thomas T. Eckert, chief of the War Department's Telegraph Office, be assigned to guard him at the theatre. Eckert was a strong and brave man, and Lincoln had confidence in him. But the Secretary of War, Stanton, had refused to let him go. He said he was needed at the Telegraph Office, which he was, for there was news to be received concerning the Confederate units still holding out. So another guard was assigned, John F. Parker.

Parker was as bad a choice as Eckert had been a good one. He had a long record of being up on charges as a police officer; they included drunkenness, shirking his duty, being in a house of prostitution, and insulting a woman. But it was hard to get policemen in Washington, and he was kept on the force. The records show, strangely, that he had been assigned to White House duty eleven days earlier at the request of Mrs. Lincoln. On this night, he was three hours late in reporting for duty. He was told that he was to guard the President at Ford's Theatre, and was to leave for there fifteen minutes before the President and his wife drove away in their carriage.

* * * *

There was a final meeting of the group of men who were pledged to carry out the assassination conspiracy. Just where it was held is not known, nor the exact time, but it was shortly before they were to ride off on their various assignments. Present were Booth, Herold, Paine and Aszerodt. Several were absent. Mrs. Surratt presumably was back at the rooming house. Spangler was at Ford's Theatre. O'Laughlin and Arnold were back in Baltimore as they had pulled out when the assassination had been substituted for kidnapping. John Surratt was in upper New York State doing a final mission for the dying Confederacy. Doctor Mudd, who had been involved slightly in the recruitment of the would-be kidnappers, was at his farm in southern Maryland.

The four conspirators went over the plan of action. Booth was to go to Ford's Theatre, gain entrance to the Presidential box and shoot Lincoln. Paine was to go to the home of Secretary of State Seward, across Lafayette Park from the White House, gain entrance to his bedroom and stab him to death. Atzerodt was to go back to the Kirkwood House, knock on the Vice President's door, and when the official opened it, shoot him.

The killings were scheduled to be done at about 10:15 P.M. At that moment the stage at Ford's would have only a single actor on it. Paine was not familiar with Washington, and Herold was to ride with him to Seward's home, and after the assassination there, guide him to the bridge at the Navy Yard. The conspirators would all go to the bridge, and expected to reach there about the same time.

Booth had arrived at the meeting carrying a small but lethal derringer, a knife, a false mustache and a wig, as well as a makeup pencil. He also brought two large revolvers. Paine had a knife and received a revolver from Booth.

The plan was simple as far as flight was concerned. They would rendezvous at the Navy Yard bridge after they had carried out their assignments. From there they would dash southward stopping long enough at Surratt's Tavern to pick up the other guns, rope and compass, and then continue on to Port Tobacco. From there they would cross the Potomac into Virginia, then secretly make their way to safety. They had not determined just where that safety was, but presumably they hoped to find some Confederates still holding out. If so they could join them in the expected resurgence of Southern power during the time of chaos in the North.

The plan was remarkably similar to the one of Major Margrave's which had been described in the New York Tribune more than a year before.

* * * *

It was around 8:15 P.M. when the President and Mrs. Lincoln left the White House. They drove in a carriage to the home of Senator Ira Harris on H Street—not far from the Surratt boarding house. When General and Mrs. Grant declined the invitation to attend the theatre with them, Mrs. Lincoln had invited the Senator's daughter, Clara and her fiance, Major Henry R. Rathbone to go with them. Except for two cavalrymen behind the carriage, Lincoln had no protection as he rode to H Street, and then on to Ford's Theatre.

The first act was in progress when they arrived. The actors in the comedy stopped, while the Lincoln party made its way to the box, to the music of the orchestra which was playing, "Hail to the Chief." Parker the guard, sat in a chair outside the door leading to the corridor, off which was the Presidential box. About twenty minutes later he left his post, walked along the rear of the theatre and down a staircase to the orchestra floor. Outside he found Lincoln's coachman and his valet, and at his suggestion, the three of them went next door to a tavern for some drinks. Lincoln was unguarded.

About this time Edwin McMasters Stanton, Secretary of War, visited Secretary of State Seward. The latter had broken his jaw and his arm in a carriage accident few days before and was confined to his bed. Doctors had placed an iron frame about the jaw and neck to protect them—it was to save Seward's life. Members of the family had arranged a schedule by which they took turns in caring for the Secretary. In addition, two convalescent soldiers had been assgined to help them.

Seward was in pain, efforts of Stanton to cheer him up were in vain. After a short while, Stanton left.

A little later, about 9:30 P.M. Booth arrived at Ford's Theatre. He rode his horse down the alley to the rear of the theatre, and called for Spangler again to hold his horse at the rear door. Spangler was to keep the horse ready for Booth when he came out of the theatre. It was the exit Booth had chosen for his escape after the shooting.

Booth used a passageway under the orchestra floor to reach the main entrance to the theatre. Instead of going in, he went next door to the tavern and had a drink of bourbon. He chatted with some friends about the theatre and one of his friends told him he would never be the actor his father was.

"When I leave the stage for good I will be the most famous man in America," he replied.

He returned to the entrance of the theatre. While he was chatting there with some stagehands, the chief of the Washington Cavalry Patrol came along and invited Booth to have a drink with him. Booth declined the invitation as he said he wanted to watch Laura Keene, the star, in a passage of the play. He entered the theatre, borrowed a bite of chewing tobacco from the doorkeeper—who admitted the actor without a ticket. He hummed a tune, quietly, as he went up the staircase to the Dress Circle, enroute to the Presidential box.

Meanwhile Paine, accompanied by Herold, was on his way to the Seward home. He rode a one-eyed mare which Booth had purchased from Doctor Mudd several months previously. Herold had suggested that Paine carry a small bottle and tell them at Seward's that he was bringing some medicine ordered by the doctor, for the bedridden Secretary.

Herold was not to go inside with Paine. He was to remain in the street, unless Paine needed assistance, and then, after the assassination, he was to guide Paine to the Navy Yard bridge.

Atzerodt, who had been drinking heavily, went to the livery stable where he had arranged for a horse. It was the same stable from which Herold had hired his mount. Herold was overdue in returning his horse, and the stable owner, who had seen Herold and Atzerodt together, decided to follow Atzerodt on foot, hoping that he might lead him to Herold—and his horse. He followed Atzerodt to the Kirkwood House, where Atzerodt hitched his horse and went inside. In a little while he came out, wiping his lips. Apparently he had had more drinks. The stableman by this time had concluded that Atzerodt was drunk.

Atzerodt appeared to be wandering about aimlessly and the stableman decided to return to his livery stable and look for Herold later.

It was not quite aimless though. Atzerodt was killing time until he was supposed to go to the Kirkwood House and kill the Vice President of the United States. It was a simple assignment; all he had to do was to go to the first floor of the hotel, rap on Johnson's door and shoot Johnson when he opened the door. In the event that it was not Johnson who opened the door, Atzerodt, armed with a huge revolver, was to fight his way inside and kill Johnson. He was then to run out of the hotel, mount his horse and race for the Navy Yard bridge where he was to meet Booth, Herold and Paine.

Atzerodt rode up Tenth Street, past Ford's Theatre. Outside was the President's carriage, and a few soldiers lounged about.

Perhaps Atzerodt, who had no stomach for murder but could not defy Booth, hoped to see the actor there, hoped that Booth would tell him he did not have to carry out his assignment.

Atzerodt did not know it, but Booth was probably still

in the bar next to the theatre. Soon he would leave the bar, and enter the theatre.

It was now a few minutes after ten o'clock on Good Friday, April 14, 1865. The theatre, because of the President's presence, was crowded, but the other theatres in the city were half empty. But the solemnity of the day had not dampened the spirits of the city. The theatres and the public buildings, and many private ones, too, were "illuminated." Lights were placed in windows, to provide a gala effect. There were celebrations in many homes, and the bars were doing a good business. Victory and peace were at hand after four long years of bitter struggle.

Booth had chosen 10:15 P.M. as the moment to strike because he knew that about that time only one person would be on stage. It would be the best time for him to strike. The attention of the audience would be on the play, and when he leaped from the box to the stage, there would be only the single actor who might attempt to stop him. He was confident that in the confusion he would be able to escape; probably the actor would be so surprised that he would not react in time to do anything to stop him.

In the box the President and his wife sat near the rail of the box, he in the rocking chair, and Miss Harris and her major, who was in civilian clothes—not in uniform as many artists were to envision him—sat on the sofa on the opposite side of the box.

Lincoln had seen the comedy once before and had liked it. Now he sat back in his chair, relaxed and again enjoying the humor of the play. He reached over and took the hand of his wife. She demurred.

"What will Miss Harris think of my hanging onto you so?"

Lincoln did not take his eyes from the stage, but he answered, "Why she will think nothing about it." These were probably the last words that Lincoln ever said; no one in the box recalled his saying anything again.

Booth reached the door of the corridor leading to the Presidential box. He had expected to find a guard sitting in a chair, and was ready to attack him with the dagger he carried, and quickly fight his way into the box. The chair was empty, Parker was still next door drinking at the bar.

On stage an actress, playing the part of a pompous English matron, had just said, "I am sure, Mr. Trenchard, that you are not used to the manners of good society, and that alone will excuse the impertinence of which you have been guilty." Then she stalked off the stage.

Henry Hawk, playing the role of Trenchard, had the stage to himself.

Booth had slipped quietly into the dark corridor, taken the piece of wood from the corner where he had it, and braced the door behind him. He had then peered through the small hole he had made in the door to Box Seven, and saw the head of Lincoln. He silently stepped into the box, unobserved. The audience could not see him because of the wall of the box; the occupants of the box were engrossed with what was happening on stage.

Booth had the derringer in his right hand. He took a few steps and was then immediately behind the President, and a little to the President's left. He aimed the weapon at Lincoln, at a point just behind his left ear.

Hawk, on stage, chuckled in triumph as he answered the

English dowager. "Don't know manners of good society, eh? I guess I know enough to turn you inside out, old gal— you sockdologizing old man trap."

There was a roar of laughter. Almost no one heard the shot, even in Box Seven it was nearly drowned out.

Lincoln sagged and his head fell forward. He ceased to rock the chair.

Mrs. Lincoln was still laughing when she turned and saw the stranger next to her husband. Major Rathbone and Miss Harris, on the sofa, looked to see what was going on. There was a haze of gunpowder in the box.

The major reacted quickly, even before he knew that Lincoln had been shot. He lunged at Booth. The assassin dropped the derringer and pulled out his dagger. The major tried to grab Booth, who slashed at him viciously, while the major attempted to fend off the blows but the knife cut into his left arm to the bone.

Booth cried out, "Sic, Semper Tyrannis (Thus ever to tyrants)" and moved to the rail. The bleeding major grabbed Booth's coat but could not retain his hold. The actor leaped over the rail to the stage, eleven feet below. It was not a difficult leap for him, he had made bigger ones in some of the plays in which he had appeared. But the spur on his left shoe caught on the folds of a flag decorating the front of the box, and he landed unevenly, breaking the shinbone of his left leg. He still had the dagger in his hand as he scrambled to his feet and started to run off stage. He fell down once, but got to his feet and ran limping to the wings. The startled Harry Hawk, bewildered by what was going on, was motionless.

Most of the audience was not aware of what he had done

when Booth reached the wings. There was a loud piercing scream from Box Seven. Mrs. Lincoln had realized that her husband had been shot.

The dagger still in his hand, Booth ran out through the stage door where his horse was being held by the boy assigned by Spangler. According to some accounts, Booth kicked the boy who was stretched out on a stone waiting, the reins in his hands. Other accounts say that Booth struck the boy, using the butt of his dagger.

A man came running out of the theatre, shouting, "Stop that man," and attempted to seize the reins of the horse. But Booth was already in the saddle, and he spurred the mare and dashed out of the alley.

Inside the theatre there was pandemonium. The audience knew something had happened, but did not yet know what. The appearance of the man at the rim of the box, and his subsequent leap to the stage and flight had happened so quickly that they were not aware at first who it was.

Miss Harris had gone to the rail of the box and called for water. There was another scream from Mrs. Lincoln when she found that the President was unconscious. Someone in the audience called: "For God's sake, what is it: what has happened?"

A man's voice from the box answered, "He has shot the President!"

*   *   *   *

Paine went to the door of the Seward home and rapped. Nearby, in the street, Herold waited, holding his horse and Paine's. A servant answered the knock and Paine told him he had come from the pharmacy with medicine that the doctor had told him to deliver personally to the bed-ridden Secretary. He had a package in his hand.

The servant, a Negro, hesitated but Paine pushed inside and started up the stairs. Frederick Seward, who had been resting in bed, came out on the top floor landing and wanted to know what the commotion was about. Paine, standing at the top of the stairs, said that the doctor had sent some medicine which he had to deliver personally to the Secretary.

Young Seward said he did not wish to disturb his father. He went into the darkened room where his father was resting and came back and said his father was asleep. Paine now knew which bedroom held the ailing Secretary. Young Seward said to leave the medicine with him but Paine refused. He started down the stairs, but after two steps he whirled around, revolver in hand and fired at the young man. The revolver did not discharge. With a leap, Paine was on the landing and he struck young Seward with his revolver, smashing his head and sending him unconscious to the floor. He leaned over young Seward and struck him several times with the revolver. The Negro servant, who had seen the attack, ran down the two flights of stairs and out into the street shouting, "Murder! Murder!"

In the street Herold watched the servant, and then quickly dismounted. He tied the reins of Paine's horse to a tree and then remounting galloped off to meet Booth at the Navy Yard bridge.

Inside the house Paine stopped hitting the unconscious man, looked at his revolver and saw that he had broken it. He threw it at the figure on the floor and drawing a knife, pushed into the sick room, dark except for the light now streaming in from the hallway.

He saw the shadowy figure of a man and stabbed him; a male nurse with a wound in the forehead fell to the floor. Paine turned to the Secretary lying helpless but awake, and sprang upon the bed. He sought the Secretary's throat with his left hand as he stabbed time and again. But the iron brace holding the jaw covered most of his neck. Paine was able to severely cut the Secretary, but he did not wound him fatally as he could not reach his wind pipe.

Two persons suddenly grabbed him and tried to subdue him. He struggled, slashing away with the knife, striking with his left fist. The Secretary rolled off the bed, falling on his broken arm, and to a corner of the room. The three men continued to fight desperately; tables and chairs were knocked over. The male nurse, despite his wound, had gotten up from the floor and was helping Major Augustus Seward, another son, protect the elder Seward.

Despite their efforts to prevent him, he again attacked the Secretary. In the melee, Fanny Seward, a daughter, was hit and knocked to the floor unconscious.

Paine fought like a wild man. He hit the major repeatedly with the knife and knocked the wounded male nurse down again. Finally Paine managed to free himself momentarily and ran from the room, waving the bloody dagger and shouting, "I'm mad! I'm mad."

In the hallway Paine saw a man walking toward him, unaware of the danger he faced. Paine waited and when the man was near enough, he plunged his dagger deep into the man's chest. The man, a messenger from the State Department, dropped without making a sound.

Paine ran downstairs and out of the house. He looked for Herold, who had fled when the servant had come running out. He saw his horse hitched to a tree. Untying her and mounting he started off. The Negro servant, still outside, followed him on foot for a while shouting, "Murder." A group of soldiers were attracted by his cries, but instead of stopping Paine, they ran to the Seward house.

Paine continued to ride down darkened, unfamiliar streets. Without Herold, he did not know his way, but for a half hour he kept riding on. There was no pursuit.

He saw some soldiers coming toward him in the moonlight. He hid in a field. He did not know where he was but actually he was not very far from the Capitol in what is now known as the East Capitol section; only about a half mile from the Navy Yard bridge where he was supposed to rendezvous with Booth, Herold and Atzerodt.

* * * *

At 10:15, when Atzerodt was supposed to kill him, Vice President Johnson was asleep in his bed at the Kirkwood House. His secretary had gone home. There was no one to stop Atzerodt in his attempt to murder Johnson.

But Atzerodt made no attempt to kill Johnson. He was walking from saloon to saloon, aimlessly—seeking the courage to do so. He never did. He was still wandering around the city mounted on his horse now, when the word swept through the city that Lincoln had been shot. He became frightened, galloped back to the stable where he had hired his horse and turned it in. He did not want to go back to the Kirkwood House, so he boarded a horse drawn street car enroute to the Navy Yard. Near there he had a friend who ran a shop and he hoped to gain permission to sleep there that night on the floor.

The storekeeper refused. Atzerodt was only a short distance from the Navy Yard bridge and the escape route that had been agreed on. But he wanted nothing more to do with Booth or the other conspirators. He went back toward the center of the city, and finally found a place to sleep in the Pennsylvania Hotel. He went to bed sometime between two and three o'clock in the morning.

* * * *

Ford's Theatre was in an uproar. There were cries, shouts, pushing and shoving. A twenty-three year old physician in the audience responded to the call for a doctor. Lincoln was unconscious, the major was bleeding badly. Mrs. Lincoln and Miss Harris were hysterical.

People in the audience tried to leave and some succeeded, but others were prevented by people trying to get into the theatre. Many people still were unaware of what actually had happened—some thought that the whole thing was a hoax, perpetrated by pickpockets who wanted the audience to mill about while they plied their profession.

Lincoln was carried out of the theatre and across the street, to a boarding house run by a man named Peterson. He was still bleeding, and some people in the street sopped up blood with their handkerchiefs, as a memento of the tragic event.

Throughout the night doctors tried in vain to save Lincoln's life. Members of the cabinet and of his family rushed to the bedside. Among them was the Vice President, unaware that he had been marked for death in the same plot. They learned of the attack on Seward.

Outside, in the city, rumors mingled with facts as citizens told of the night's events. At first there was some question about the identity of the man who had shot Lincoln, but shortly the authorities had his name. Many of those who identified him were members of the cast of "Our American Cousin."

Some citizens wondered just who it was who had been attacked—Lincoln or Seward. The White House physician heard about the shooting of Lincoln and prepared to go to him, when he learned about the attack on Seward. He thought that the first information had been wrong, and hurried over to help the Secretary and the others who had been wounded by Paine. He was there when he received word to come to Tenth Street to aid the stricken President.

Booth found no one waiting at the Navy Yard bridge and he did not linger for any of the others. He told the guard at the bridge that he had spent the evening in the city and was on his way to his home in Maryland. The guard let him cross. A few minutes later Herold arrived and was also permitted to leave the city.

They met, a few minutes later and continued on together. Booth's leg bothered him, he was in constant pain. He did not know if it was a break or a sprain.

By the time they arrived at Surrattsville, Booth was having difficulty with the pain. Herold got the compass, but Booth decided not to take the two carbines. He got a quart of whiskey from the tavern operator, and then after a deep drink went in search of medical attention. He could not stick to his original plan of going to Port Tobacco and crossing the Potomac into Virginia. They had hoped to be on the other side of the river during that night.

The two of them rode through the dark night to the farm of Doctor Mudd. Booth did not trust the doctor, who had helped him recruit men to aid in the plan to kidnap Lincoln. He donned the false whiskers he had brought along, and wrapped a thick muffler about his neck, so that little of his face showed, except his eyes and nose.

They told the doctor that Booth had fallen from his horse and broken his leg—Booth used an alias—and that they were on their way home to Washington. No one knows if Mudd saw through the disguise or not, but when he put a splint about Booth's leg he did not know that Lincoln had been assassinated, according to testimony he later gave at their trial.

* * * *

Lincoln died at twenty-two minutes after seven o'clock the next morning, April 15, 1965, and Andrew Johnson became President. Martial law existed in Washington, the saloons were closed, and almost everyone who knew or had anything to do with Booth was questioned, and in many cases, arrested. Seward had been badly wounded, as had been his two sons, the male nurse and the State Department messenger. All of them were to recover. Paine found temporary sanctuary in a swampy area near the Potomac.

During the next twelve days Booth and Herold were like hunted animals, living in thickets and swamps. Booth was in no condition to travel, but he had to get away. After four days of hiding in some bushes on a farm run by a former slave owner and former Confederate army captain, they tried to cross the Potomac, but the current was too swift for them. Two days laters they succeeded and got into Virginia.

Things were no better for them there. Eventually a troop of Federal cavalrymen caught up with them while they were sleeping in a barn. Herold quickly surrendered, but Booth refused, and despite the pain in his leg, attempted to shoot it out with the troops. The barn caught on fire, and a soldier named Boston Corbett shot Booth as he was silhouetted against the flames. The bullet struck him behind the right ear. He died about fifteen minutes after seven on Wednesday, April 26th, 1865.

* * * *

In Washington the boarding house on H Street had been searched by the authorities, who arrested Mrs. Surratt, and Paine as well. The latter had hidden in a swamp near the Potomac for a day and then returned to the boarding house, in search of companionship, just in time to be taken into custody.

More and more conspirators were arrested as the details of the plot became apparent to the authorities. Not only was Atzerodt arrested, but so were Spangler, the stage hand at Ford's Theatre who arranged to have Booth's horse at the stage door; O'Laughlin and Arnold, who had broken with Booth when he proposed assassination and Doctor Mudd, too, was taken into custody. A search was made for John

Surratt, but he was supposedly out of the country at the time of the assassination.

After a military trial at which they were found guilty of participating in the plot to kill Lincoln, four of the conspirators were hanged. They were Paine, Herold, Atzerodt and Mrs. Surratt. Also found guilty but given life sentences were Arnold, O'Laughlin, and Doctor Mudd. Spangler was sentenced to six years in prison.

O'Laughlin died of yellow fever while imprisoned at Fort Jefferson, in the Dry Tortugas. Doctor Mudd distinguished himself in fighting the yellow fever epidemic that went through the prison, and President Johnson pardoned him, as well as the other conspirators in prison.

John Surratt escaped to Europe and served in the Papal Guards for a while. Discovered, he attempted to flee again, but was taken prisoner in Egypt. Brought back to this country, he was tried for complicity in the assassination, but there was a hung jury. He had claimed that he was in Elmira, New York, at the time of the killing, and had brought forth witnesses to prove his statements.

* * * *

The body of Abraham Lincoln was taken back to Springfield, after rites were held in the nation's capitol. The train, draped in black, which bore his body, followed the same route that had been taken when he had journeyed to take his oath as President. In the cities where he had stopped, the homeward journey halted temporarily, for special memorial services. Cities and towns along the route, and elsewhere, draped public buildings in black. Thousands of persons watched the movement of the train, took part in the solemn rites along the way, and wept for the dead President and for his grief stricken family and friends.

Never before had there been such an expression of grief by the American people, never before had so many persons seen or participated in the general mourning for a dead President.

It was not until nearly a century had passed that there was to be another outpouring of grief such as that which marked the funeral journey back to Springfield. Then on a weekend in November 1963, the body of John F. Kennedy was taken from the White House where Lincoln had lived, to the Rotunda of the Capitol—near where Lawrence had tried to kill Jackson, and where Booth probably planned to kill Lincoln—for rites. Millions of Americans in 1963 watched on television, the services for an assassinated President, and experienced grief such as that which swept across the United States following the death of Abraham Lincoln.

VII

An Uneasy Grave In Springfield

The body of Abraham Lincoln was brought back to Springfield from Washington, and placed in a tomb at the base of a small hill in Oak Ridge Cemetery. There had been some dispute regarding the burial site of the martyred President, and at the insistence of Mrs. Lincoln, the body was placed in the cemetery's receiving tomb, awaiting a decision regarding its final resting place in Oak Ridge.

A week after the body was deposited there, a group of prominent Springfield men, all friends of Lincoln, formed an association—the National Lincoln Memorial Association —to erect a shaft or monument in the cemetery. The base of the shaft would contain vaults where Lincoln and members of the family would also find their final resting places.

The eventual design of the monument consisted of a tall shaft rising from a broad base which in turn rested on a structure housing catacombs, a small hall, and some of the structure supporting the shaft and its base. At the foot of and in front of the shaft a statue of Abraham Lincoln was to be placed, and there would be groupings of statuary of soldiers and sailors of the War Period. The top of the bottom structure served as a terrace, reached by flights of stairs.

Meanwhile, pending the construction of the monument, the body of Lincoln was taken from the receiving tomb and placed in another, temporary resting place nearby.

It was a quiet cemetery, even though there was a steady trickle of people wishing to see where Lincoln's body was kept. In general Oak Ridge Cemetery fulfilled the wish that Lincoln had made a few days before his assassination, that he be buried in a quiet place. It was a desire that he had expressed to his wife while they were out driving, and after his death she resisted a movement to have her husband buried elsewhere.

But there were men who threatened to violate the serenity of the cemetery, to disturb the quiet rest of the murdered President. For years there were plots made to steal his body from the tomb, to hold it for ransom. The macabre chronicle of these plots was told in 1887 by John Carroll Power, in a book entitled *History of an Attempt to Steal the Body of Abraham Lincoln*. Mr. Power was custodian of the monument that was eventually erected in Lincoln's honor, and which had entombed in its base the remains of the late President, as well as the bodies of his three sons, and eventually, his widow. It is not a well written book, nor well organized, but it provides a story that is without parallel in our country, and one that is little remembered today. For there was an attempt to steal Lincoln's body, as well as a number of plots to do so which were never carried out.

Long before the monument was completed, and in fact only two years after Lincoln's body was brought back to Springfield, a lawyer in that city conceived the idea of secretly taking the body from its temporary resting place and taking it south, perhaps even out of the country, and then waiting for an offer of ransom, which presumably would come from private organizations, such as the National Lincoln Memorial Association.

No one knows who the lawyer was; Powers in his book admitted he did not know his identity. What Powers did not mention was the fact that the lawyer, unless he had come to Springfield within the seven years prior to his plot, undoubtedly had known Lincoln, and even might have been thought of as one of his friends. Springfield was a small community, and there can be no question about all its lawyers being acquainted with each other.

The lawyer told a telegraph operator about his scheme, seeking to enlist him as an accomplice, but the telegraph operator refused. The lawyer then told a mechanic, who also refused. Thereupon the lawyer, feeling, no doubt, that too many people now knew of his scheme, gave it up. The two young men left Springfield shortly after, and the lawyer is said to have died a few years later.

But the idea persisted, and one man who embraced it was James B. Kineally, alias Kinnelly, who had earned some notoriety as a passer of counterfeit money. He had served a five year term in the state prison at Joliet, Illinois for passing counterfeit fifty dollar bills in Peoria. On his release he went to St. Louis, not with the intention of mending his ways, but of going big time in his old ways. He got in contact with counterfeit engravers and arranged for delivery of bogus money, organized a gang to distribute it and also arranged for some criminals who made a specialty of doing so, to pass the counterfeit money for him. He set up a distribution system in which money was dropped in clumps of bushes, hollow logs, and other such places, for the gangs to pick up. He would watch the drop and the pick up from a distance, to make sure that all went well. The Secret Service had learned of his organization, and his system of distribution, but had been unable to catch him at a drop because he was always far enough away to make it difficult to establish any connection of the passing of the money with him.

He conceived the idea of stealing Lincoln's body and holding it for ransom, using one of the gangs with whom he worked.

In June of 1876 the Chief of Police in Springfield met Powers, the custodian of the Lincoln monument then nearing completion, while walking along a street. The Chief told him that he had learned of a plot to steal Lincoln's body from the catacomb in the base of the monument. The plotters would hide the body somewhere, and when enough ransom was offered an accomplice—who would not be present at the theft of the body and so able to prove he was somewhere else a long distance away—would find it seemingly by accident, collecting the reward which later would be divided among members of the gang, including the accomplice.

The Chief suggested that other members of the National Lincoln Memorial Association be told. After hearing the story, however, they simply did not believe it, and paid no attention to it.

Powers, in his book, describes the gang and what they intended to do, based on information he acquired years later. There were sixteen men, thieves and counterfeiters, in the plot. They had their headquarters in the town of Lincoln. Ironically the town had been surveyed by "the railsplitter" as a young man and had been named after him. It was the county seat of Logan County and was located some thirty miles north of Springfield.

Five members of the gang went to Springfield in March, and rented a store on the north side of Jefferson Street. They opened a saloon, which was to serve as their base of operations there. One of the five worked as the bartender. On the second floor they opened a dance hall.

Other members of the gang in Lincoln came to Springfield, arriving in twos and threes, and making contact with the original group. All members of the gang went to Oak Ridge at one time or another to familiarize themselves with the cemetery, the exterior of the monument and those parts of the interior open to the public. They talked with the people there, asking questions carefully while among legitimate visitors so as not to excite suspicion. They were particularly interested in the location of the bodies—but then, most of the visitors were.

The gang planned to steal the body on the night of July 3rd—on the eve of the nation's first centennial when attention would be on the celebration of the event. They would take the body, carry it away and bury it, coffin and all, in a sandy bar of the Sagamon River, under a bridge. The spot was about two miles from the cemetery.

The conspirators would then wait for a reward to be offered for its return and collect it through their accomplice.

The idea seemed like a good one to members of the gang, who felt there was every chance of success. One of the original five men who came first to Springfield, however, thought too much about the ransom and his share of it before the plan was carried out. He got drunk one night and while in that state visited a local brothel. He could not keep his secret. He told the madame that he was in a conspiracy to steal "old Lincoln's bones," and that he was going to receive a large sum of money for his part in the deed, and he expected her and her girls to help him spend it.

The plotter left town while still intoxicated, and on his return found that the secret was out. The madame had told the editor of a local paper who in turn had told the Chief of Police. There were rumors all over Springfield about the plot.

The plotters decided they should leave the town as soon as possible. That night they loaded the contents of the saloon into a wagon and left, leaving behind not only fresh fuel for the rumors but also an unpaid rent bill.

Kineally, who was behind the scheme, was furious and would have nothing more to do with the men in Logan County—at least, not in connection with stealing Lincoln's body. But he did not give up the idea, he simply looked for another group of men to carry out the theft.

Sometime later another gang prepared to carry out the scheme, presumably at Kineally's bidding. About eight men in the town of Mount Pulaski prepared a cavern in which to hide the body after it had been stolen. It was located in a wild and lawless area known as the Salt Creek Hills eight or nine, miles outside of Mount Pulaski. It was an area in which several murders had been committed.

The stolen body was to be rushed northward to a point where a relay of men and horses were to be met. After delivering the body to their confederates, the first group would rush back to Springfield and make a point of being seen in their usual haunts. The second group would rush to a second meeting place, and after delivering the body to a third set of conspirators, would return to Springfield also. The third set of men would take the body to the cavern.

The "cavern" might have been a pit or cellar dug under a small frame house in the area; or it might have been located in a clump of paw paw bushes. And there may have been two gangs and two plots at the same time, with similar methods of operation and identical aims. Powers is not clear about this, and there are many loose ends to his accounts of plots. Indeed, he speaks even of another hiding place, behind a brick wall, which could be sealed up after the body was inserted.

The best explanation of the confused account of the plots during the summer of 1876 is that Powers himself was confused. He sought out people—respectable people who had somehow learned details of the plots—and asked them for information. He did this some years later; some of the men had moved from Springfield, and some, certainly, had moved in fear, as many of the conspirators apparently had never been identified and would possibly kill to protect themselves.

Powers does not make it clear why the men did not carry

out the plot—or plots. In one case, however, a member of the gang tried to get a reward for turning in his companions. Accidently he divulged the fact that he had been involved in such a plot to a professional man in Mount Pulaski. Thereupon he suggested that he turn State's evidence, identify the others, and assist the law. He did not tell the professional man the details of the plot or the names of its members, but suggested that the professional man contact an acquaintance of his, and arrange for this second man to see the authorities and convey the offer. The conspirators would expect a large reward, enough not only for him, but also to share with the professional man and his friend.

The second man, who knew none of the details of the plot, only that such a plot existed and that there was a gang of men ready to carry it out, went to see the Governor of Illinois. The latter listened to the story and then suggested that he tell his story to officers of the National Lincoln Memorial Association. This he did, only to be told that respectable and loyal citizens did not expect to be rewarded for doing their duty.

It was then suggested that the man go to see Robert Lincoln, son of the slain President, who had his office in Chicago. The man did so, and talked with Lincoln, Leonard Swett, who had been a close friend of the elder Lincoln and Elmer Washburn, who had recently stepped down as Chief of the United States Secret Service.

Robert Lincoln, after listening to the story, said he was opposed to giving a reward; that the situation could be handled without one. Swett was sarcastic in talking with the man, who now regretted that he had become involved in the matter.

When the man returned to Springfield, however, he was conscious of being followed. The shadow remained in Springfield for about a week, watching and following him, apparently hoping to be led to the gang.

The rumors of plots to steal the body persisted during the summer of 1876, and it may be that at least one of them was foiled when the Secret Service arrested two members of a gang on counterfeiting charges. These two men, it was said, were "one-fourth" of a gang that planned to steal the body and their arrest ment that the plot had to be abandoned—or postponed. Word of these plots kept coming to the attention of Robert Lincoln in Chicago, and apparently their persistence led him eventually to take them seriously.

The Secret Service was anxious to break up the extensive counterfeiting operation set up by Kineally, and had managed to get an informer within a group in Chicago. Among the interesting bits of information that the informer, Louis C. Swegles, turned over to Captain P. D. Tyrrell was that the gang planned to steal Lincoln's body and hold it for ransom. The amount they would ask for would be two hundred thousand dollars, and the release from jail of a skillful counterfeiter whose services they needed. The counterfeiter had been sent to jail the year previously; his work was so good that it was almost impossible to detect it from genuine currency.

This information was learned on November 4th and a meeting had been held the previous night in Swegles's hotel room. One of the conspirators, Terrence Mullins, said that in addition to the other rewards they would win the respect of the American people. This puzzled the authorities when it was passed on to them.

The plot was being planned at short notice, for the gang had set November 7th as the date of the robbery. The effort would be made by a very small group—four men. The information was passed on to Robert Lincoln, Swett and Washburn.

While it would be easy to prevent the theft, Lincoln and his friends felt that it was necessary to break up the gang, and take its members into custody; otherwise, they reasoned, the gang would simply try again, and might eventually succeed in their plan. They were probably right in this, for the similarity of the various plots suggests one mastermind behind them.

The four men who were to carry out the plan included Mullins and a fellow criminal John Hughes, proprietor of "The Hub," a saloon in Chicago, another man who was not identified, and Swegles, the police informer.

They planned to steal the body November 7th because on that day the attention of the American people would be on the outcome of the national election. Rutherford B. Hays was running against Samuel Tilden. It was a hotly contested election—in fact an electoral commission appointed by Congress had to make the final decision regarding the winner.

Tyrrell learned on Monday morning, November 6th, that the gang was going to Springfield that night. At three o'clack that afternoon a meeting was held in Lincoln's Chicago office, at which plans for thwarting the execution of the plot and the arrest of the plotters were discussed. By nightfall they had obtained the assistance of two Pinkerton agents and a detective employed by the Illinois Humane Society. Lincoln sent a telegram to Stuart, head of the Association in Springfield, telling the custodian to call at the St. Nicholas Hotel and ask for C. A. Demorest.

At nine o'clock that evening, the four members of the gang boarded the first passenger car in the train going to Springfield, and Tyrrell and the two Pinkerton agents boarded the last sleeping coach on the same train.

The train arrived in Springfield at six o'clock in the morning and the gang went to the St. Charles Hotel, and the other three men went to the St. Nicholas.

At half past eight Swegles managed to get away from the others long enough to tell Tyrrell where they were and that Hughes and Mullins were asleep with orders to be called at ten o'clock in the morning.

At nine o'clock Stuart asked to see C. A. Demorest at the St. Nicholas and was directed to a room occupied by Tyrrell. The two men went to the Lincoln monument while the Secret Service officer explained the situation. They told Powers, the custodian, about the plot, and told him to continue as he always did, and if members of the gang came to the monument seeking information to treat them like other visitors, and to tell them the truth. He was given a description of the men. They also looked over the grounds and the tomb, to ascertain where to place their own men that night.

Around three o'clock that afternoon, two men answering the descriptions given Powers arrived at the monument and registered under false names, before being shown about the place. They asked a number of questions. One of the men was Hughes, the other was Swegles, who listened carefully to make sure that Powers did not reveal inadvertently that the plot was known.

While the two were at the monument, Mullins secured an old axe at a German saloon for use in breaking open the sarcophagus and removing the coffin containing Lincoln's body. At that time, in addition to the martyred President's body, the tomb also contained the remains of three of his sons.

Meanwhile Washburn, his former secretary, and the detective from the Humane Society arrived in Springfield at five o'clock. There was a meeting shortly after in Tyrrell's room of all the people involved in the effort to capture the gang as it tried to steal the body. Plans were out-lined so everyone would know his role. Washburn was suspicious of Swegles, the informer, at first, but later decided to trust him.

One of the Pinkerton men went to the monument with a note to Powers, telling the custodian that everything was all right and that Tyrrell and his men would be along in a little while. It was getting dark at that time. The day had been overcast, thick clouds were overhead. Powers said later that it was so dark at six o'clock that night that a man could hardly see his hand before him.

Powers took the Pinkerton man inside where they remained waiting in darkness behind the locked door of the monument, until the arrival of Tyrrell and his men about forty minutes later. They were admitted by Powers who carefully relocked the door behind them and then, lighting a lamp, led them to a point in the interior where no light could be seen from outside. Then Tyrrell took charge. They were in a labyrinth at the base of the shaft. He moved forward until he came to the tomb, which had a door leading to the interior, and one leading outside. Here, in the tomb, the bodies of Lincoln and his sons were encased in a sar-cophagus.

Washburn's former secretary was stationed by a wall ten feet thick, near the tomb, so that he could hear when the gang tried to open the sarcophagus. The other members of the law group were brought back to a room nearby, and told to take off their boots and wait, in total darkness. Nearby were lamps and matches, ready for use.

Swegles was not with this group. At six o'clock, before starting for the monument, Tyrrell had sent him to meet Hughes and Mullins. He was supposed to have arranged for a team and teamster to be at the cemetery at a certain time. As far as is known, he was supposed to have hired a legitimate, honest teamster. What explanation they planned to give him, and how they proposed to protect themselves from his talking later is not known.

A strong light streaming in through the bars in the locked door of the monument told the group inside that the conspirators were at hand. They were simply looking around, making sure that they were alone, and they checked the door that was on the opposite side of the base from the one leading to the vault. The men making the check were Mullins and Swegles. After they had gone, Tyrrell had Powers unlock the door, but had it still closed. A few minutes later Swegles came back, alone, gave a password, and the door was opened for him. He told Tyrrell that the others, Hughes and Mullins, were at work in the tomb. The other man, unidentified, had been posted at the entrance to the cemetery so that he could give the alarm if anyone approached.

About this time the secretary came back to report that he could hear the conspirators working inside the tomb.

Swegles told Tyrrell that he had not been able to come back as soon as the other two began working on the sarcophagus, as he was supposed to, because they had told him to hold their lantern while they worked at freeing Lincoln's coffin. He wondered if they were suspicious of him but he had no choice so he complied. He was sure Hughes and Mullins would kill him if he tried to leave then.

Now he was supposed to be on his way to the waiting teamster, to tell him to come up to the door of the tomb. He had made no such arrangements. He asked Tyrrell what he was to do. Tyrrell said to remain there. Tyrrell had been out of the monument once, in his stocking feet so as not to make any noise. He now made his plans to capture Mullins and Hughes.

The latter were supposed to be waiting inside the tomb, by the coffin which had been freed from the sarcophagus. But after Swegles left they moved to the shade of an oak tree about one hundred and ten feet away and waited.

Tyrrell, revolver in hand, burst into the catacomb where the two men had been working, but found them gone. He immediately sent his force of men outside looking for Hughes and Mullins. The latter saw what appeared to be two men walking toward the door of the tomb and went forward, assuming that they were Swegles and the teamster, but when they were about thirty feet apart, they saw there were several men. They remained quiet, and then silently fled. Meanwhile Tyrrell continued his search. Two of the detectives had gone up on the terrace of the monument searching for signs of the men, and to see if they were hiding there.

Tyrrell went up another flight of stairs to the terrace. In the darkness he saw two men and opened fire with his revolver. There was a return fire, as the two misty figures moved about, trying to hit the Secret Service officer. Tyrrell was not hit, and it was obvious that he had not hit either of his opponents. He called down for other members of his group to come to his aid, when one of the two men on the terrace called out, "Tyrrell, is that you?"

In the darkness Tyrrell had mistaken two of his own men for the conspirators; they in turn had assumed that the man firing at them was one of the gang. Fortunately, no one was hit.

The conspirators had fled, and there was little that the group under Tyrrell could do. They returned to the city. The next day newspapers across the country carried the story. In time, however, some people came to the conclusion that there was no attempt to steal the body, and that the whole story was a sham.

Some of the group that had been with Tyrrell, left the next day for Chicago and they looked through the train to see if Mullins and Hughes were on it. Their search was fruitless.

Mullins and Hughes had acquired a team of horses and a wagon to flee from the area and the next morning bought their breakfast from a farmer several miles outside of town. Then they disappeared for ten days.

When they returned to Chicago to Hughes' saloon, Swegles was there waiting for them. He told them of his imaginary escape and they did not suspect him. Swegles then tipped off Tyrrell regarding their arrival. He secured warrants and arrested them on the evening of November 19th. They were handcuffed and brought back to Springfield and placed in the county jail. There a number of persons identified them as the men who had broken into the tomb and pried Lincoln's coffin from the sarcophagus.

However, the prosecutors found, to their embarrassment, that there was no law in Illinois at that time against stealing bodies of dead persons. In fact, few if any states at that time had such laws.

So Hughes and Mullins were convicted of attempting to steal a wooden casket, valued at seventy-five dollars, and were sentenced to spend a year at hard labor in the state penitentiary.

It was learned later that Hughes had a partner in his Chicago saloon. The partner was Kineally. During the period in which Mullins and Hughes were making their plans, a visit was made by one of them to St. Louis, where Kineally was living.

There were no more attempts to steal the body. The casket was put back into the sarcophagus. Years later, when the body was to be moved to a new spot inside the monument, the casket was opened to make sure that there had been no mix-up, and that it contained Lincoln's body. It did.

The Assocsiation organized a group of men who volunteered their services as guards, and who kept a constant, vigilant watch from then on.

Lincoln, at last, had the quiet sleep that he desired.

VIII

Postponed Assassination

Fifteen years after the assassination of Abraham Lincoln, his son, Robert was Secretary of War in the cabinet of President James A. Garfield. As may be presumed, the murder of his father had been a shocking and tragic experience for the young man of 1865, and a decade and a half later the son, now middle aged, had vivid memories of that horrible night when his father was dying in a rooming house across the street from Ford's Theatre.

Garfield had been President for less than four months when he asked Robert to tell him about the assassination of his father. Robert complied, and Garfield listened intently. He had no idea that another man had been stalking him for days, waiting for a suitable occasion to shoot him. Several times the would-be killer had postponed committing the deed, which later, would be compared to Lincoln's assassination.

Unmindful of the danger that dogged his steps during the last few days of June and the first two days of July, Garfield went about the city unguarded and sometimes, even unaccompanied. There were no precautions taken against his suffering a fate such as Lincoln's.

That evening, July 1, 1881, after the talk with his Secretary of War, the President walked out of the White House about seven o'clock, strolled across Lafayette Park which faces the Executive Mansion, and entered the home of James G. Blaine. It was the same house occupied by Secretary of State Seward in Lincoln's time and again was the residence of a Secretary of State. If he had turned around he might have seen the man following him but it is doubtful that he would have realized that the man was trying to get near enough to shoot him.

The man who wanted to shoot Garfield was Charles Guiteau, who thought of himself as an agent of God, and the savior of his country. He first thought of killing Garfield on the evening of May 18—eleven weeks after Garfield had been inaugurated as President.

At first he resisted the idea, he said later, but it persisted, and on June 8th he entered a gun shop just around the corner from the White House and arranged to buy a British revolver with a white bone handle which, the shop owner said, "would kill a horse." Guiteau did not have the money to pay for it, but two days later, after borrowing fifteen dollars from a friend, he returned to get the revolver, a box of bullets and a ladies' pen knife, paying ten dollars total. He could have purchased a cheaper revolver, but he wanted a handsome weapon as he expected it to be displayed in a museum later, after he had used it to kill Garfield.

Guiteau, who had worked for the election of Garfield, but had not been given an important diplomatic post as a reward, was a man with grandiose ideas and of large scale delusions. He was thirty-eight years old—he was to have the dubious distinction of being the oldest man ever to attempt to kill a President of the United States.

He was only ten years younger than the man he sought to kill, and both Guiteau and Garfield wore mustaches and full beards, in the fashion of the times. Guiteau, a man with a twisted mind, had a dark complexion; blue-grey eyes which were wide set in contrast to the usual ideas that sinister characters have eyes placed close together. His hair, like his beard and mustache, was dark brown. He stood only five feet five inches tall, and weighed about one hundred twenty-five pounds. To the people who knew him, he appeared to have a nervous nature—and a light tread as he walked.

He had had an amazing career as a lawyer, author, publisher and lecturer, as well as cheat and montebank. During his career he had learned many things, but not how to handle a firearm. So he went to a wooded area not far from the White House and practiced shooting the next day, firing ten rounds.

At first he had thought of walking into the White House and shooting Garfield there, but decided that it was too risky. He did not know that the President's secretary had decided that Guiteau was a crank and that he would not have let him get in to see the President, should he attempt to. So he sat on a bench in Lafayette Park, for hours waiting for the President so he could shoot him. Sometimes he asked the White House guards when the President was coming out.

Garfield left the White House on Sunday, June 12th, in his carriage and went to a church on Vermont Avenue. Guiteau followed him and stood in the back of the church auditorium during the service. He thought that this would be an especially fine place in which to kill Garfield—while the President was at his devotions. He could see Garfield near a window. In his pocket Guiteau had the loaded revolver.

He decided against shooting the President there because he was afraid he might miss and hit some one else. After the service, Guiteau went outside and looked at the window near which Garfield had been seated, to see if it would have been possible for him to shoot through it and hit Garfield. He wanted to know, in the event that he might want to shoot him another Sunday at the church.

As the days went by, the idea of killing the President grew in magnitude in his mind. Guiteau thought of the acclaim he would receive for the deed. On Thursday, June 16th, he went to the Arlington Hotel, where he wrote out an explanation of why he had decided to kill the President. Garfield, he wrote, "had proved a traitor to the men that made him and thereby imperiled the life of the Republic."

"The expressed purpose of the President has been to crush General Grant and Senator Conkling and thereby open the way for his nomination in 1884," Guiteau wrote.

"In the President's madness he has wrecked the once grand old Republican party, and for this he dies."

After he had completed his writing Guiteau read in the newspapers that the President intended to go to Long Branch, New Jersey, with Mrs. Garfield who had been ill. The President, the newspaper said, would leave on Saturday.

Guiteau decided that here was his opportunity to carry out the assassination. He would shoot Garfield in the railroad station of the Baltimore and Potomac Railroad before he left the city. The station was located at the site of the present National Gallery of Art.

He got up at five o'clock, went to the woods along the Potomac and practiced briefly with the revolver, firing off several rounds and then went to the station.

When Garfield and his wife arrived, Guiteau moved to within a few feet of his intended victim, and then decided to delay the shooting because, as he explained later, "Mrs. Garfield looked so thin and she clung so tenderly to the President's arm that I did not have the heart to fire on him."

Twice he had changed his mind about the shooting at the last moment, first in the church, for fear of hitting someone else, and at the railroad station, lest he upset Mrs. Garfield. But he had not given up the idea; he continued to stalk the President.

Garfield returned to Washington two days later, and Guiteau was waiting for him at the station. Again he deferred the killing, this time because he did not feel like it. It was, he said later, "a terribly hot sultry day." Such days are not uncommon in Washington during the summer months.

Five days later Guiteau, who had given quite a bit of

thought to what was likely to occur after the assassination, went to the District of Columbia jail, hoping to see the accommodations there. It was visiting day but he could not gain much of a look at the interior. However he became convinced that it was "a very excellent jail."

He continued to spend long hours seated on benches in Lafayette Park, waiting for the President to come out. On Friday, July 1st, at about seven o'clock, his long hours of waiting were rewarded. The President came out, alone, and crossed Pennsylvania Avenue. Guiteau followed him. Garfield walked along Madison Street at the east side of Lafayette Street, to the house in which Paine had tried to stab Seward to death fifteen years before. It now housed James G. Blaine, the Secretary of State, and one of the most influential members of the Republican party—later Blaine was to be the Republican candidate for President but lost the election because of the ill chosen and bigoted statements of one of his supporters.

Guiteau, the revolver in his pocket, trailed the President from the other side of the street to Blaine's house, but was unable to get close enough to try a shot.

He waited outside the house, after going into an alley and taking the revolver from his pocket. If Garfield came out of the house alone, Guiteau intended to shoot him on the steps.

But when Garfield emerged, Blaine was with him and the two of them walked, arm in arm, back to the White House, and Guiteau again deferred his attempt to murder the President. He recalled later that the two men were chatting and laughing "in the most delightful and cozy fellowship possible, just as hilarious as two school girls." This

143

clearly indicated to Guiteau that Blaine was using Garfield as a tool against the Stalwarts, a faction of the Republican party.

He did not shoot Garfield that night, not only because Blaine was with his intended victim, but also because of the "hot, sultry night." Besides, he knew he would have another opportunity at the railroad station. He had read that on Saturday, July 2nd, the President was going on a two weeks vacation.

He spent that night in Room 222 in the Riggs House. Curiously, the President had been assigned a parlor car with that number, by the railroad. Guiteau got up around five o'clock, took a walk, and then went to Lafayette Park where he seated himself and read a newspaper. It was a fine morning and he enjoyed the weather.

About seven o'clock he returned to his hotel and had a leisurely breakfast. He then went to his room and wrote a couple of letters, explaining why he had to kill Garfield. In one he said "His removal is an act of God," and in the other, "I had no ill-will toward the President."

He put the two letters in a small package which contained, among other things, a note bequeathing his papers and revolver to the State Deparment Library.

He placed the revolver in his right hip pocket, took the package, and walked out of the hotel. He did not pay the hotel bill, even though he did not expect to return. He had a long record of not paying hotel bills.

He wandered back to Lafayette Square and spent some time there, watching the White House. A few minutes before nine o'clock he left the park and boarded a horse car that would take him to the railroad station.

He was convinced that by killing Garfield he would become a national hero, nevertheless he understood that he might be in danger immediately after the assassination from friends of the President or from mobs. He wanted to be sure that he survived these first few moments after the deed. His safety he thought rested with the police.

When he arrived at the railroad station he arranged for a hack to be waiting for him when he came out and then drive him to the Congressional Cemetery, near the District of Columbia jail. He planned to get out of the cab at the cemetery and run to the jail and give himself up. He promised the hackman two dollars—which he had no intention of paying.

He had made careful arrangements for the killing of the President. It was an event of supreme importance, and so he had his shoes shined so he would look his best. This left him with twenty cents in his pockets.

He still had his package. He took it to the newsstand in the station and asked the attendant to hold it for him. He was confident that it would be turned over to the police. He was correct in this.

Going into the mens' room, he took out the revolver, examined it and then put it back in his pocket. He then walked out and went to the ladies' waiting room.

He waited.

*　*　*　*

The fifty-year old President was in excellent spirits that Saturday morning. His first four months in the White House had been difficult; he had been engaged in struggles within the Party, and his wife had been ill part of the time. Now he was going away for a vacation. He would have a chance for some yachting on the Hudson, and he planned to deliver the Commencement address at Williams College, his Alma Mater.

There was some laughing and joking with his sons, and when one of them dared him to, he jumped over his bed.

It was about nine o'clock when Blaine came over from his residence and the two men then got into a State Department coupe and started for the railroad station. The Garfield boys followed in another carriage.

At twenty minutes after nine o'clock the coupe arrived at the station—ten minutes before the train was due to leave. Garfield and Blaine entered the station and started through the ladies' waiting room on their way to the train. There were only a few persons present at that time. One of them was a short, slight man dressed in a black suit and hat. It was Guiteau.

Blaine walked to the right of the President. They were talking and in no hurry. They were nearly through the parlor when Guiteau stepped from behind a bench, took a few steps, and then shot the President in the back.

"My God, what is this?" Garfield exclaimed. He flung up his arms and staggered.

Stepping closer, Guiteau fired again. The bullet missed, although it passed through the sleeve of Garfield's coat.

Garfield collapsed. Guiteau turned and raced away—into the arms of a policeman who had followed Garfield and Blaine into the station.

He did not resist the policeman, on the contrary, he was relieved to be safely in custody.

"Its all right. Keep quiet, my friend," Guiteau said. "I wish to go to jail."

He did indeed wish to go to jail, and was prepared for this. In his left hand he had a letter to General William T. Sherman, commander of the army, requesting that soldiers be sent to take over the jail, as a precaution against violence.

"Now Arthur is President of the United States," he told the policeman, and he referred to a factor of the Republican party to which he gave allegiance, "I am a Stalwart of the Stalwarts."

There were some shouts to "lynch him," in the station, but there were not enough people there to make a mob, and no one made a move against Guiteau, who was promptly taken off to the jail and placed in a cell recently vacated by a grave robber.

A horse drawn ambulance rushed the President back to the White House. The Cabinet was quickly summoned, and Secretary of War Lincoln, arriving exclaimed, "My God! how many hours of sorrow I have passed in this town."

Doctors found that the bullet had badly wounded the President. It was lodged behind the pancreas, after fracturing two ribs, going through the backbone and fracturing the first lumbar vertebra and cutting a large artery.

In the days that followed, Garfield fought for his life in the White House and Guiteau, apparently comfortable and contented, was engaged in writing his autobiography in his jail cell.

Mid-summer Washington is hot, and soon various devices for cooling the White House were installed and operated. Crude though they were, they succeeded in keeping the air in the President's bedroom comfortable and dry.

The severed artery continued to function, because of a temporary sac that formed. But his condition remained serious, he suffered loss of weight and great pain. Once he rallied enough so that he was able to sign an official paper.

The bullet could not be located precisely. This was before X-rays. The physicians attending the President thought it was near the pancreas, but they did not dare to try to get it out because of Garfield's weakened condition. Alexander Graham Bell, the inventor of the telephone, brought a device to the White House, somewhat similar in principle to a geiger counter, which located the bullet but unfortunately did not indicate how far beneath the skin it rested.

The physicians struggled on during the hot summer weeks. One of those attending the President was Joseph K. Barnes, Surgeon General of the United States. Barnes had been the White House physician when Lincoln was President and had attended him in the Peterson house after the shooting in Ford's Theatre.

By the middle of August Garfield was obviously losing strength alarmingly, by the end of the month his mind seemed cloudy.

Garfield wanted to be moved from the White House, and the doctors, in the hope that sea air might help him, agreed. He was taken to a house near Long Beach, New Jersey, in early September. But the change and the sea air apparently did little good. He steadily grew worse and died September 19th, 1881.

* * * *

Garfield had been killed by a man who wanted a job—a man who wanted to represent his country in a diplomatic post, a man who wanted to be important. He was shot by a man who thought he had been instrumental in winning victory for Garfield in the national election, and like Booth, Guiteau had expected to be praised and applauded.

"I come here in the capacity of an agent of the Diety in this matter," Giteau said when he was arraigned in court on November 14th, 1881. During the trial that stretched out over more than ten weeks, he recounted how the idea had come to him to kill the President and how he had become convinced that the idea had come to him from God.

Charles Guiteau was motivated by an overriding desire to be important, to be someone special. This was to lead to fanciful dreams, to grandiose plans and schemes, and eventually, it was to lead him to the hangman's noose. Completely amoral, he talked and wrote of morality, entirely without principles, he urged others to adhere to the highest principles. Denied an appointment to an important diplomatic post by President Garfield, he said that God instructed him to become a Presidential assassin.

He had an open, friendly manner, was a neat dresser, and of good personal habits—he neither drank or used tobacco. He appeared to be earnest as well as honest, and he was able to influence ministers, women, and lawyers. He was a complete scoundrel.

He was born in Freeport, Illinois, in 1841, the son of a minor city official who was a devotee of the Oneida religious colony in upstate New York, which practiced a kind of religious communism and preached that the second coming of Christ had already taken place, and therefore union with the savior was possible without further waiting. As a boy he had the usual schooling, plus one year of business school, and then decided to enroll in the University of Michigan. Arriving at Ann Arbor, he found he lacked credits for admission, and enrolled in a local high school. After a year he grew tired of this and went to Oneida and joined the religious colony. There he was active in some of the extra-curricula programs, such as debating, but he was not satisfied. He sometimes sulked, and he often day dreamed. Sometimes the day dreams became near to reality in his mind. He took to putting up signs in his room, such as one that read,

> Charles J. Guiteau
> Premier of England
> Will deliver a lecture
> In St. James Hall, London

He left the colony in April, 1865—the month of Lincoln's assassination, but told the colonists that he was going outside to carry on its work. He got a room in Hoboken, and spent some time writing out a prospectus for a newspaper, which he proposed to call The New York Theocrat. It was to be a publication with religious orientation, and was to be followed by the establishment of other newspapers of similar character in cities across the country. He was to be the editor of the first.

When he showed the prospectus to some professional newspaper men they laughed at the idea, and Guiteau gave it up. He rejoined the colony, but did not immediately return to the colony. He was assigned to work with the New York City office that merchandized many of the products of the colony. These products included lumber, animal traps, crockery and farm products. Later he returned to the colony itself as assistant shipping agent for the animal trap factory. After about a year, he grew tired of this, and left without telling anyone of his intention, returning to New York City.

He joined the Plymouth Church in Brooklyn because the Reverend Henry Ward Beecher was its pastor.

He spent his time writing a phamphlet in which he urged that criminal proceedings be instituted against the Oneida community. There, nightly, young innocent girls and women were "sacrified to an experiment easier imagined than described." He himself had had sexual relations with three women there, he declared, but declined to put his name on the pamphlet.

When his funds became low—he was living off a modest inheritance from his maternal grandmother—his mind turned once again to journalism, and he sought a position with New York papers, but in vain. So he decided to become a lawyer, instead.

For some unexplained reason he went to Chicago to achieve this. There he got work in a well known and highly respected law firm, studied, and a few months later was able to pass the examination and was admitted to the bar. It might be remembered that in those days the standards for admission to the bar were generally low, and that men prepared for careers as lawyers by working as clerks in the offices of already established attorneys.

He went into practice, but most of it consisted of debt-collection cases. It has been said that when he collected any money, he usually kept it for himself.

It was during this period that he met and married an

attractive and devout sixteen year old girl. Ultimately they had a child who died at birth.

It was not a happy marriage for her. They lived in hotels or boarding houses, but he never paid rent if he could help it. The usual procedure was to sneak out from a hotel at night with their belongings, after they had run up a bill. Sometimes the hotel or boarding house would act before they had a chance to leave, and would seize their luggage as collateral. Whenever she protested against this mode of living, he would lock her in a hall closest for a night. He took a certain pride in his ability to escape paying rent, and told her that the world owed him a living.

It was also during this period that he displayed the pretensions of grandeur that were to be more marked as time went on. Once he asked her if she did not think he looked like a good foreign minister.

Late in 1871 he and his wife left Chicago, going to New York again, where they continued to live in hotels and rooming houses without paying their bills. Shortly after his return to the eastern metropolis he rented a desk in a law firm's office and resumed the practice of law. He also joined the Calvary Baptist church and immediately persuaded his wife to borrow ninety-five dollars from the pastor of the church which he never repaid.

The following summer Horace Greeley, editor of the New York Tribune, sought the Presidency, running as the candidate of the Democratic party and as a Liberal Republican. His opponent was Ulysses S. Grant, the victor of Appomattox. Greeley had long been venerated by Guiteau, and so he was not only deeply interested in the campaign, but he also tried to help Greeley's election. He hung around the party headquarters a great deal, talking with the campaign workers, and occasionally delivering an address at open-air rallies. If Greeley had been elected, Guiteau had planned to ask him to appoint him United States Minister to Chile. Greeley was defeated, and twenty-four days after the election he died.

Guiteau's wife left him the following year, and in 1874 she divorced him. She charged him with adultery, and when the Calvary Baptist church questioned him, he admitted an inability to resist the lures of prostitutes. He was expelled.

His unsavory practice of collecting debts for clients and keeping the money for himself came to the attention of The New York Tribune—the paper that Greeley had edited— and it ran an exposé. He promptly initiated a suit against the paper, seeking one hundred thousand dollars in damages, but did not press the case, because he did not wish to have the paper as an enemy if he should ever run for President. He continued his law practice.

In December the hotel where he was staying apparently found out about his past record for skipping out without paying. He was arrested, found guilty of preparing to defraud the hotel, and sentenced to spend five weeks in jail. While in prison he decided that he had had enough of New York. When he was released he went back to Chicago and applied for work with a law firm, telling his prospective employers that he had recently resigned as United States Consul in Marseilles. There was no position available but the law firm allowed him to use a desk in their office.

He rewarded their kindness a few weeks later by taking his desk with him when he left the firm. He removed it when everyone else was at lunch. The law firm caught up with him, eventually, and forced him to pay for the stolen desk.

The idea of becoming a newspaper editor returned to him, and for a while he worked on a project to purchase the Chicago Inter-Ocean, a daily paper. He worked hard gaining information about the operation of a newspaper, and trying to obtain funds for its purchase. He planned to make it a strong Republican newspaper modelled after the New York Tribune, and to make himself another Greeley.

He offered to drop his suit against the Tribune if the editor would provide financial backing for his plans. He received no answer. He offered to support an Illinois Congressman if he should seek the Presidency in 1876, and in return for two hundred thousand dollars with which to purchase the paper. The Congressman did not accept the offer. He tried to secure backing from other political people, but failed. All he had for his efforts was a single twenty-five dollar subscription from a Chicago lawyer, who later was to defend him after the assassination.

Guiteau returned to the practice of law, but it was not long before he was involved in something else, this time religion.

At that time the revival movement started by Dwight L. Moody, retired business man and Ira D. Sankey, was going strong in Chicago, and Guiteau began attending the meetings, and soon was an usher. From that position he moved ahead, apparently impressing the two leaders of the movement, for he sometimes was permitted to deliver sermons. Ambitious, he decided to drop his career as a lawyer and to become a theologian and lecturer. He spent a month studying the Second Coming and by January, 1877 he had prepared a sermon. He hired a church, placed advertisements in the Chicago newspapers and distributed handbills. Anyone who could not afford the twenty-five cents admission fee could attend free, he announced. On the night of the lecture the weather was frigid, and only thirty persons were present; their contributions totalled one dollar and eighty cents. In May, his second attempt, in Evanston, was more successful; about three hundred attended, responding to an advertisement in the local newspaper to the effect that "Charles J. Guiteau, the lawyer and theologian from Chicago, will deliver his great lecture on 'Christ's Second Coming, 70 A. D.'"

During the next three years he went about the country giving lectures, publishing the lectures in pamphlet form, and selling the pamphlets. He hired church halls, lived in hotels, and patronized print shops, usually without paying his bills. He also did not buy tickets when he travelled on railroads, telling the conductors, "I am travelling for the Lord; I have no money." Usually he was permitted to ride to the next stop—where he would wait for the next train. A couple of times he had to get off a train while it was in motion.

He made little money, in fact he was sometimes destitute, and lived off the free lunch counters in saloons.

He appeared to enjoy the life he was living, even if his debtors did not. He sometimes described himself in his advertisements as "The Little Giant from the West," or "The Celebrated Orator." He did not hesitate to give himself the title of Reverend. He was said to have a premonition that someday he would become President of the United States.

Times grew hard for him, people failed to attend his

lectures—several times the halls were totally empty. Train conductors increasingly took a dim view of his riding without paying, and once he had to flee from a deputy sheriff who arrested him for non-payment of debts, and then fell asleep, giving Guiteau the opportunity to escape.

He kept moving about the country, sometimes having a small audience, never a large one. Finally arriving in Washington, for the first time, Guiteau peddled his pamphlets to government workers for twenty-five cents each. He went from there to New England, then to Newark, New Jersey and eventually to Wisconsin, lecturing always to small audiences and selling pamphlets. In August 1878 he opened a law office in Milwaukee.

But he could not resist the lure of the lecture hall, and he composed two new lectures which he tried out in other cities. He then had the lectures published in a book entitled *The Truth: A Companion to the Bible.* He was able to sell several hundred copies of the book, especially to Sunday School teachers.

The sale of the book eventually fell off, and he tried to sell insurance without success. Then his interest turned to politics.

General Grant was completing his second term in the White House, and was seeking the Republican nomination for a third term. The men who sought Grant's nomination were known as Stalwarts. Opposing Grant was a group contemptuously known as the Half Breeds, who wanted James G. Blaine of Maine to have the nomination. Guiteau favored the Stalwart selection and went to the Public Library in Boston, where he was living at the time, and wrote a speech urging the election of the General. After a long struggle between the factions at the national convention in Chicago, the Republicans turned to James A. Garfield as a compromise candidate. Guiteau quickly rewrote his speech to urge Garfield's election. Then he left Boston for New York to offer his services to Garfield and the Republican party. Afterwards, he said, "He had the distinct feeling that he was on his way to the White House in some way."

He wanted to be a speaker in the campaign, and tried to convince several high ranking Republicans, including Chester Arthur, the vice presidential candidate, of the value of his assistance. None of them accepted his offer.

Undeterred, he went to Poughkeepsie and Saratoga Springs to deliver his speech, but no one came in to hear him at either place. So characteristically, he returned to New York and had the lecture printed. Distributing it to Republican leaders in person, he asked them how they liked it. They said they did, probably because it was the polite thing to do, and he was overjoyed. He spent the rest of the campaign hanging around various campaign headquarters, shaking hands with Republican leaders, discussing Garfield's prospects—and sometimes the prospects of his getting a job should Garfield win.

One night he started to make a speech on a street corner in New York, but gave it up when the crowd and the noise from the street were too much for him. Although he spoke only for a few minutes, he presented reporters copies of the talk he had intended to give before leaving the corner. In the speech he claimed that a victory for Garfield was a victory for the North and insured the future growth of the nation. On the other hand, if victory went to the Democratic candidate, Hancock, who had distinguished himself as a general in the Northern army during the Civil War, the debts of the Southern Confederacy would be assumed and paid by the Federal government, the nation would become bankrupt and there would be another Civil War.

One day he met General Grant in the lobby of the hotel where the Republican headquarters were located, and asked him to sign a letter in which Garfield was urged to appoint him, Charles Guiteau as Ambassador to Austria. Grant refused. But Guiteau did not give up his dreams of a diplomatic post—eventually it became an obsession and led to the assassination of a President.

He sent a copy of his speech to Garfield, in the hope of impressing him favorably, and followed it with a letter in which he said he would like the Austrian Ambassadorship as a reward for his services during the campaign. Garfield did not acknowledge receipt of either the speech or the letter. Among the campaign workers Guiteau was considered pretty much of a joke.

After Garfield's election Guiteau went to Washington, and managed to get in to see the new President. At his trial he described the meeting. "As soon as General Garfield was at leisure I stepped up to him and gave him my speech. Of course he recognized me at once. I marked my name and 'Paris consulship' at the end of it—connecting it with my name—and I gave it to him and I told him that I was an applicant for the Paris consulship, and he looked at it, and I left him reading the speech . . . that was the only interview I ever had with General Garfield on the subject."

He remained in the capitol, seeing different people about his appointment, but getting nowhere. Once he talked with Blaine, who had become Secretary of State. He sent Blaine a letter in which he said he claimed credit for the election of Garfield on the basis of his speech.

He sent a letter to the President in which he said, in part, "I understand from Col. Hooker of the nat. committee that I am to have a consulship. I hope it is the consulship at Paris as that is the only one I care to take. Now that Mr. Phelps has the Austrian Mission, I think I have the right to press for the consulship at Paris. I think Gen. Logan and Secretary Blaine are favorable to this and wish you would send in my name for the consulship at Paris . . . . . the men that did the business last fall are the ones to be remembered. Senator Logan has my papers and he said he would see you about this."

Meanwhile he was living in good hotels and boarding houses, giving as references the President and Secretary Blaine. He had to move whenever a bill was presented, however.

Every day he went to the White House to send in a note to the President—on White House stationery—asking, "Can I have the Paris consulship?" He would help himself to the stationery, and once told a White House clerk who protested, "Do you know who I am? I am one of the men who made Garfield President." Every day he visited the State Department and left a note for Blaine. And every day he tried to get a petition started among members of Congress which read, "We recommend Charles J. Guiteau for the Paris consulship."

All these efforts were futile. No one signed the petition, the notes to the President brought an invariable answer that he was too busy to see Guiteau that day. The notes for Blaine were ignored.

The consulship at Paris became an obsession with him. Gradually he grew shabby in appearance as he made his daily rounds. He no longer attempted to hold lectures or sell pamphlets. He concentrated on obtaining the consulship in Paris.

He tried to find means of moving Garfield and Blaine to take the action he sought—and which they obviously would not take. He hinted in a note to Blaine that four years hence he would return from Paris—if he were appointed consul there—to assist Blaine obtain the Republican nomination. (As it turned out, Blaine got the nomination.) He also sent a note to Garfield telling him that the President could obtain the nomination for a second time if he played his cards right, over his opponents. His leading opponents, said Guiteau, would be Grant and Blaine. He added a post-script saying, "I will see you about the Paris consulship tomorrow unless you happen to send in my name today."

It was four days later that Guiteau encountered Blaine walking along a corridor in the State House and button-holed him. He asked about the position.

Blaine, who had managed to escape Guiteau in the daily visits, was exasperated now. "Never speak to me again about the Paris consulship as long as you live," he said to Guiteau.

"I am going to see the President about this," said Guiteau, confidently. "I think I can get the President to remove Mr. Walker."

Blaine was quite willing to let someone else deal with this crackpot. "Well, if he will," he said.

But when Guiteau arrived at the White House he was not admitted. The staff had been instructed to keep him out.

The order had been issued by the President's private secretary, who sought to keep Garfield from being bothered.

The President was having even more trouble over patronage than that represented by Guiteau. The day Guiteau had been refused admission to the White House, a row between the President and the Stalwarts broke out over jobs. The two Senators from New York, Roscoe Conklin and Thomas C. Platt, resigned in protest over Garfield's nomination to fill the post of Collector of Customs in New York City. Both Senators were Stalwarts. Many newspapers saw in this conflict a threat to the Republican party. Guiteau read an editorial from the *Brooklyn Eagle*—he had the clipping in his pocket when he shot Garfield—which said, "It's outcome would seem to involve the disintegration and overthrow of that organization (the Republican party) in the State and probably in the Union."

The papers continued to carry news of the row, which involved the giving out of jobs by the administration. There was no Civil Service then and the final responsibility was in the hands of the President. Guiteau, who thought of himself as a Stalwart, was disturbed by all this. Later Guiteau said: "After I saw the President and General Grant and Conklin and the kind of men who were wrestling and at loggerheads, I saw that this nation was coming to grief."

It was on the night of May 18th—four days after the rebuff from Blaine and the refusal of the White House staff to admit him, that he went to bed, he testified later, much distressed and disturbed. But he could not sleep, the row between the President and the Stalwarts was in his mind— and probably his failure to get the consulship in Paris.

"It was about half-past eight (he had retired at eight)

161

before I had gone to sleep, when an impression came over my mind like a flash that if the President was out of the way, this whole thing would be solved and everything would go well. That is the first impression I had with reference to removing the President."

The "impression" lingered in his mind, even though he fought against it, he testified at his trial. In fact, he said that at that stage it was not divinely inspired but simply an "embryo inspiration." But the idea grew stronger day by day.

He continued to read editorials in the newspapers dealing with the dissent within the Republican party, and the more he thought about it the more he became convinced that the assassination of Garfield was the only solution. Nevertheless, he did not give up the idea of obtaining the consulship; he sent Garfield a letter in which he quoted a Mr. Farrell of Chicago as saying that Blaine was a "vindicative politician" and "an evil genius." Guiteau added his own opinion that the Secretary of State was "a wicked man and you ought to demand his immediate resignation; otherwise you and the Republican Party will come to grief. I will see you in the morning, if I can talk with you."

There was no answer from Garfield, and Guiteau kept thinking about killing the President without actually making up his mind. At his trial he said that he tried to shake off the idea, but that "It kept growing upon me, pressing me, goading me . . . At the end of two weeks my mind was thoroughly fixed as to the necessary for the President's removal and the divinity of the inspiration. I never had the slightest doubt as to the divinity of the inspiration from the first of June. That was the day my mind became thoroughly fixed as to the necessary for his removal."

Guiteau kept thinking about this "necessity." He also thought that the assassination would revive interest in the book he had written, entitled *The Truth: A Companion to the Bible*. The more books were sold, the more souls would be saved, he explained later. He added another chapter to the book, in anticipation of this renewed interest and increased sales.

It was two weeks after he had sent the letter to Garfield, and five after the "inspiration" had become fixed in his mind, that he bought the revolver.

* * * *

The trial lasted for ten and a half weeks, and was spectacular. At it Guiteau insulted witnesses, the district attorney and even his own attorney, calling them names. He sometimes gave speeches, made comments on the proceedings, and sometimes created such disorder that the judge and court officials had difficulty in maintaining order. The judge, only sixteen years previously, had been the attorney for Michael O'Laughlin and Samuel B. Arnold, members of the Booth gang, who had received life sentences. It has been suggested that the judge, who had disliked the rigidity of the military trial of the Booth conspirators, leaned backward in the case of Guiteau.

Throngs attended the trial to see Guiteau and to witness the proceedings, sometimes filling even the corridors outside the courtroom. It was not uncommon for the audience to cheer or hiss or even laugh during the proceedings.

Guiteau obviously enjoyed the trial. He thought of himself as a hero who had done a wonderful thing. He expected Chester A. Arthur, who had become President because of the bullet he had fired, to contribute to his defense. This was not forthcoming. In answer to a letter, President Arthur said that he had seen the defendant a number of times at the Republican campaign headquarters in New York and had discussed his appeal for assignment as a stump speaker. He said he had also seen him in Washington. He emphasized that he had never encouraged him in his quest for an appointment to a government position.

Guiteau cavorted at the trial, pleased with himself, although not always pleased with the proceedings. Once he said that there might be divine inercession.

Not only did throngs attend the trial, but they also visited Guiteau at the jail. Guiteau, encouraged by this, told the court, "public opinion don't want me hung."

This attention fed his ego. He received hundreds of letters, most of them favorable to him. Some of them suggested that he should be President—a suggestion very dear to his heart. "I shall get the nomination just as General Grant and President Lincoln did," he declared. He decided to play hard-to-get, and added shortly after, "I don't care a snap about being President of the United States, and I don't know as I should take it if I was elected."

There were many other people, however, who despised Guiteau. A guard attempted to kill him by shooting at him in the cell, but only grazed his head; another man shot at him as he was being transferred from court to jail, nipping his arm. Certainly, most Americans hated Guiteau and the deed that he had committed.

Guiteau's lawyers had entered a plea of innocent because of insanity. The defense produced a number of witnesses, including medical people, but Guiteau himself said he was not insane execept during the period between June 1st, when the idea became fixed in his mind, and the moment when he shot Garfield on July 2nd. During that period, he declared, he was in an "Abrahamic" state of insanity, explaining that he was in the same state of mind then as Abraham had been when he planned to kill his son, Isaac, at the command of Diety. He told the court that the United States would incur the wrath of God, should he be convicted and executed.

Although the trial had lasted two and a half months, it took the jury only an hour and five minutes to find Guiteau sane and guilty. He shouted. "God will avenge this outrage!"

The trial ended late in January and the date of the execution was set for June 30th—a year, lacking two days after he killed Garfield. The day before the sentence was to be carried out, Guiteau wrote a letter to a clergyman, which has since been called "Guiteau's will," in which he bequeathed his body to the minister and also his book, *The Truth: A Companion to the Bible,* and all rights to it, "to be used by him in writing a truthful history of my life and execution." He also said that the title of the book should be *The Life and Work of Charles Guiteau.*

He gave instructions that his body never be used "for any mercenary purpose whatsoever." Then he said that if a monument were ever erected to his memory it should have inscribed on it, "Here lies the body of Charles Guiteau, Patriot and Christian. His soul is in glory."

PLOTS AGAINST PRESIDENTS

Nearly four thousand persons witnessed the hanging. Guiteau had his shoes shined that morning as he had the day he assassinated Garfield, mounted the scaffold and delivered a prayer which he had prepared especially for the occasion, in which he once again said he had been the agent of God, and reviewed his reasons for shooting Garfield.

He then recited a poem in which he said, "I am going to the Lordy; I am so Glad." One stanza went:

> "I save my party and my land;
> Glory Hallelujah!
> But they have murdered me for it
> And that is the reason
> I am going to the Lordy.
> Glory Hallelujah! Glory Hallelujah!
> I am going to the Lordy.

His last words were, "Glory, glory, glory."

IX

Powder Burns On A Vest

Friday, September 6, 1901, was a special day in Buffalo, New York. It was the day that the President of the United States, William McKinley, was to appear at the Pan American Exposition then being held in the city, and shake hands with his fellow citizens. It had been announced in the city's newspapers, and thousands of men, women and children thronged the Expositions, to see the sights, and to clasp the hand of the President. He was to stand in a receiving line and exchange handshakes with anyone who wished to do so.

It was also a special day for Leon Czolgosz. It was the day he planned to kill the President.

It was a hot day and Czolgosz, after a fitful night in a room up over Novak's saloon, awakened early. Because it was a special day, he did special things. After dressing, he cleaned up the room he knew he would never return to, making a packet of papers and pamphlets, then went down the bare stairs of the "hotel" where he had signed the regis- ter as "John Doe," into the street.

Even though it was early, people were already stream- ing into the city to enjoy the fair. Czolgosz dropped the packet of papers into a drain, and then went to a nearby eating place and had breakfast. He was almost out of money, but he made a point of eating a substantial meal, for he did not want to become weak or faint, and be unable to kill President McKinley. In his right hip pocket was a loaded revolver.

Breakfast over, he went to a barber shop for a shave. He wanted to look his best on this special day.

When he left the barber shop, he looked like a mechanic, dressed in his best, come to the fair to see the President, and the sights.

He was five feet, seven and a half inches tall, and weighed a hundred and forty pounds. He wore a striped grey suit, a flannel shirt and a string tie. On his head he wore a cap. His shoulders were slightly stooped. His face was smooth and round and not bad looking. On his left cheek was a small scar received in an accident in a wire mill in Ohio. His eyes were blue, his eyelids heavy, his hair was light brown and wavy. His expression was slightly sullen.

He took a train to Niagara Falls, where the President was to appear that morning. He hoped to get another look at the man he intended to kill, but he did not plan to

169

shoot him there. The day before he had been in the throng of an estimated fifty thousand persons who had heard McKinley deliver a speech on the Exposition grounds. Perhaps he simply had a curiosity to see his intended victim at close hand, perhaps he wished to be sure he would recognize him as the President before he shot him later in the day. Whatever the reason, he missed the President's appearance at the Falls.

He did not linger there when he learned he had missed McKinley. He took the train back to Buffalo and went to the Exposition. He was familiar with the Exposition grounds, for he had spent several days there.

The President was due to shake hands with the populace in the Hall of Music—where on other days Czolgosz had heard John Philip Sousa lead the Marine Band in a program of stirring marches. He arrived there a full hour before the President was due.

There were police in uniform, Secret Service men, detectives, and even some soldiers in and about the Hall of Music, when McKinley arrived. He had been urged not to hold the public reception by people close to him, but he felt there was no danger. Even his private secretary had advised against it. But McKinley had answered with a question, "Why should anyone want to harm me?"

It was a good question, for he has a popular President. He had been the head of the nation during the Spanish-American War which had been won so easily, and which had given the nation possessions in the Carribean and in the Pacific, as well as freeing Cuba.

It was an extremely warm day, and when McKinley arrived he was hot as well as tired. He accepted some refreshment gratefully before taking his place inside, between two men in front of a bower of potted plants, with a backdrop of flags.

Police stood nearby, as the doors opened at four o'clock, and the lines of people approached. Some of the men were mopping their foreheads with handkerchiefs. Czolgosz had a handkerchief in his right hand, wrapped about it as though it were a bandage. Secret Service men and detectives scanning the lines, saw nothing amiss.

It was seven minutes after four o'clock. McKinley was smiling as the people moved past, gripping his hand momentarily and then moving on. Only ten minutes had been planned for this public reception but the line was long and possibly the President thought that he would have to stay longer.

Czolgosz came up to the three men in front of the potted palm trees, his right hand with the handkerchief wrapped about it held close to his body. Inside the handkerchief his finger tightened on the trigger. McKinley, seeing the apparently bandaged hand, pulled back his own outstretched right hand and was about to extend his left for the handshake.

Before he could grasp Czolgosz's hand, the right hand moved. Czolgosz pulled the trigger.

There was a sharp explosion. He pulled it again, and there was another.

The President stumbled, then swayed. Czolgosz stood in front of him, mumbling something. For a moment, everyone appeared frozen.

McKinley fell backward, but was caught by the men about him. Soldiers and Secret Service men suddenly came to life. They flung themselves upon Czolgosz, hitting him with their fists and the butts of guns. He was knocked to the floor, where he was kicked, and hit again. A soldier lifted a rifle with a bayonet on it, but before he could run the fallen man through, the wounded President gasped, "Easy with him."

He was rushed past the throng of civilians, many of them trying to reach and attack him, to a small room. Blood covered his face. He was thrown bodily upon a table. A tall Negro waiter who was in the room pulled a knife and put the point of it against the throat of the prone and bleeding man.

Czolgosz, his eyes looking up at the Negro, but showing little emotion, said "It was my duty."

Outside a throng of people tried to get into the room. Police, aided by the soldiers and the Secret Service, kept them out, and later Czolgosz was taken to Buffalo Police Headquarters.

"Are you an anarchist?" the police wanted to know.

"Yes," was the answer. He added that he bore no grudge against McKinley but that he did not believe in government of any kind, nor in religion or marriage. That night he wrote out his confession.

"I killed President McKinley because I done my duty," he wrote. "I don't believe one man should have so much service and another man should have none."

* * *

The President was mortally wounded. He was taken in an ambulance to an emergency hospital on the Exposition grounds for an emergency operation, that lasted for an hour and thirty-one minutes. Several doctors, working in the extreme heat, searched for the two bullets in vain, and then closed the stomach wound. The bullets had been fired so close to the President that there were powder burns on his vest.

The President was then taken to the home of John Milburn, chairman of the Exposition, where Mrs. McKinley was resting. She had been ill earlier in the summer and her sickness had postponed the President's appearance at the fair by three months. The day before, exhausted by the heat, noise and excitement, she had fainted shortly after their arrival at Buffalo.

For six days the President fought to regain his health. He had suffered one bullet in the abdomen, the bullet going through both walls of the stomach and coming to rest, it was believed, in a back muscle. Actually, it had lodged in the rear of the pancreas—a wound very much like the one suffered by Garfield twenty years before. The other bullet had struck the breastbone, but had not penetrated.

Across the country prayers for his recovery were given. At the end of the six days he appeared to be better. Suddenly there was a change in his condition and he appeared to be losing ground rapidly. On September 13th, the President realized he was dying and said good-by to his family. He breathed his last at two o'clock the next morning, September 14, 1901.

Czolgosz was immediately charged with murder. Newspapers throughout the nation, carrying the news of the President's death, compared it with the assassinations of Lincoln and Garfield. Across the country, police arrested known

and suspected anarchists: it was widely believed that the
assassination had been part of a conspiracy.

* * * *

Leon F. Czolgosz was born in Detroit in 1873, where his
father, observing that most Americans had middle initials,
gave him one, the letter F, which stood for nothing. He was
one of eight children of a Polish immigrant who earned a
living cleaning out sewers. The mother took in washing until
her eighth child was born, when she died in childbirth.
Leon and his brothers and sisters were brought up in various
Polish communities in Michigan, until 1889 when they
moved to Natrona, a Polish community near Pittsburgh. All
told, he had about five and a half years of schooling, including public school, parochial high school and night school.
But these years gave him the reputation of being an educated
person within his own family and among the neighbors. It
also gave him a taste for reading, most of which was in the
Polish language.

He was sixteen when he went to work in a bottle factory,
receiving seventy-five cents a day to start and eventually
reaching a dollar a day. After two years the family moved
to Cleveland and he got a new job in a wire factory. He was
a good, quiet worker and he seldom missed a day. He was
frugal and saved from his earnings of about ten dollars a
week, and was able to contribute about four hundred dollars
when the family decided to buy a farm twelve miles outside
the city.

He was twenty years old when there was a strike at the
wire factory, an event that made a deep impression on his

mind. Even though he had had a reputation as a quiet, steady man who gave no one any trouble, he was outspoken during the strike, often addressing meetings of the strikers. When the strike was settled, Leon believed that the new head of the factory would retaliate against him, and so he signed his name on the factory rolls as Fred C. Nieman.

During the strike Leon, and his brother Waldek, who also worked in the mill, prayed fervently, but they felt that they had had poor results. They went to see the parish priest, but he told them to pray harder. They did, and they also read a Polish Bible they had bought. They drifted away from the Church. Leon continued to believe in God, but felt that the priests deceived people. They read many pamphlets regarding religion, for which they sent away. It was said that three years after the strike, the brothers had left the church in which they had been brought up.

In their search for guidance, they came across a publication entitled *The Free Thinker* which they read avidly.

Leon came in contact with a local anarchist named Anton Zwolinski, who repaired chairs, and who was a crusader. He told the young wire worker about anarchism. Zwolinski talked about the wrongs in the American system, he said governments, all governments, were wrong, and that rulers—all rulers whether presidents, kings, or czars—were evil because they were part of an evil system. He declared that police forces, all authority, existed to keep the poor man downtrodden and enslaved. According to Zwolinski, even marriage was wrong,—part of the system.

It was not long before the young man was embracing these beliefs, accepting them for his own.

He attended meetings of a Polish "educational circle"

regularly, at which many topics were discussed, usually from the viewpoint of socialists and anarchists. While the two groups had been opposed to each other in the past and were to be again, at the Cleveland meetings adherents of both mingled freely and apparently without friction.

At the meetings they talked about many things, but apparently the idea of killing a president never came up, for Czolgosz stated later that "the relations of the anarchists' principles they talked over sometimes, but at no time during these discussions that we had was the subject of killing the President brought up. It wasn't referred to in any way with anyone—with the President or anybody else." But the idea that all rulers, including presidents, were bad was sometimes discussed.

While he attended the meetings Czolgosz took little part in them. He listened intently, but rarely spoke of the topics under consideration with other members. He was thought of as being on the stupid side. Essentially he was a loner, preferring to keep to himself even when in the presence of others. In the saloon run by his father he sometimes drank a glass of beer, or an occasional whiskey, but only watched others play cards and other games. He never joined in but was always the spectator on the edge of the group. He held back so much from the activities about him that many people thought of him as timid. He did not swear and was very neat in appearance.

He didn't like to kill. He would catch flies with a swift movement of his hands, but he would not crush them; instead he would hold them cupped in his hands, go to the door and release them outside. He was careful not to step on worms when he was at his father's farm.

He was a hard working, industrious man, who sometimes boasted that he could do as much work as the next man and did. He worked steadily, quietly, and apparently had no difficulty in holding his job.

Then in 1898, when he was twenty-five years old, he suffered a change in his physical condition. He became sickly, and had what may have been a breakdown. Years later, Doctor Walter Channing, who undertook a study of Czolgosz, aided by Doctor L. Vernon Briggs, noted that this change from good health to bad probably was accompanied by a change from a normal to an abnormal mental state. Doctor Channing, then a professor of Mental Diseases at Tufts Medical College, later became chairman of the board of trustees of Boston State Hospital. Doctor Briggs became secretary of the Massachusetts State Board of Insanity and head of the National Committee for Mental Hygiene, paid special attention to this period of Czolgosz's life, and the effects of the physical upon the mental state. The two alienists made their study after the execution of the assassin, but nevertheless their investigation was intense. Doctor Briggs talked with many people in the different communities in which Czolgosz had lived.

The nature of the illness that changed Czolgosz is not known, but its effect upon his personality is fairly clear. He had been content, while in good health, to listen to anarchist debates, and was ready to accept their arguments, once he lost his health he began to feel the need to demonstrate that he was not inferior, that he was able and willing to do as much as others, if not in daily work, than in some other way.

He embraced two illusions. One was that he was an

anarchist. The other was that it was his duty to kill the President, whom he thought of as an enemy of the working people.

How soon after his illness he embraced the second idea is not known. Probably it was not until some time had passed after his breakdown.

He became pale and weak and was unable to continue work. He gave up his job in August, never to work regularly again. He went to live on the farm, outside the city, that his father owned, and except for some occasional chores, did nothing but read and sleep. He dozed and had frequent naps during the day, in addition to his sleep at night. He read a lot, mostly anarchist publications.

Sometimes he went into the city to see doctors or attend meetings, but he refused to go to a hospital, declaring that they were not for poor people. He drew benefits from a non-radical benevolent association whose members were supposed to believe in God and Christianity.

He did not get along well with his father, they had frequent quarrels, and eventually he stopped eating with the family, preparing and eating his own meals alone in his room.

According to Doctor Channing, this action indicated "the possibilty that he may have been drifting in the direction of dementia praecox."

Nearly two years after he gave up his job, Czolgosz read newspaper accounts of the assassination of King Umberto of Italy by Gaetano Bresci, an anarchist from Paterson, New Jersey, who had practiced his shooting along the banks of the Potomac—as Guiteau had two decades before him. Czolgosz read the newspaper accounts of the assassination with profound interest. No one knows if he had the idea of killing the President before reading about this. No one knows if the killing of the Italian King suggested a similar action to the sickly Czolgosz, or if it just strengthened and encouraged an idea he already had.

He, himself, said that he thought of killing McKinley only a few days before he fired the shots at Buffalo, but a study of other events and influences on Czolgosz suggests that he had the idea, subconsciously at least, for some time before that fatal afternoon. He had a clipping about the assassination of King Umberto which he carried about with him, reading it over and over, digesting every word and phrase.

The following spring he got the four hundred dollars back from his father which he had contributed toward the purchase of the farm, and went to Cleveland to hear a lecture by Emma Goldman, who was emerging as a leader of the American anarchists. Her talk, however, could not have stirred up Czolgosz for she said that the popular conception of an anarchist as a person favoring violence was wrong. She held that anarchy was the only true form of freedom and denounced both government and church organizations. A couple of weeks later Czolgosz decided to join an anarchist club in Cleveland and went to see its leader. He requested literature, which was supplied to him. Sometime later he returned to the leader and asked about secret clubs, saying he understood that the anarchists were "plotting something like Bresci."

The leader denied this. During the months that followed Czolgosz saw the leader and other anarchists a number of times, but could not gain admission and his application for admittance to the club was rejected. They felt he had no true understanding of anarchism and had a false impression about them and their intentions. Eventually they were to issue a warning about him to other anarchist groups, in which it was stated that he was a spy, who pretended "to be greatly interested in the cause, asking for names or soliciting aid for acts of violence."

While they thought of him as a police spy, he thought of himself as an anarchist.

In July with seventy dollars in his pocket—part of the four hundred he had received from his family—he left home, saying to one relative that he was going to Kansas, and to California for his health to another. Instead he went to Chicago. He looked up Emma Goldman, but she was about to leave for her home in Rochester, New York. He went to the railroad station with her and there, as she said good-by to friends, he told her that he was a Socialist, and that they had a mutual friend in the leader of the group in Cleveland. There was not much conversation, and she departed.

Then he moved to West Seneca, not far from Buffalo. No one knows why he went there; Czolgosz himself said that he went looking for work. But there were greater opportunities for employment elsewhere; in addition, he told people in West Seneca that he was not seeking a position, that he never worked during the summer months. He spent most of July and August reading, and taking frequent naps during the day. His meagre supply of money dwindled.

One day he read in a Buffalo newspaper that President McKinley had promised to attend the Pan American Exposition sometime early in September. The Exposition had opened in May, and had designated June 13th as President's

Day, when the head of the United States would visit the affair and receive the plaudits of the people. But Mrs. McKinley had been ill, and the date had had to be postponed. Now, even though she was still weak, she and her husband would come to the Exposition.

Czolgosz read this with deep interest. A few days later he told the boardinghouse keeper where he then lived, that he was leaving for Baltimore, Detroit, Cleveland or possibly Pittsburgh. He explained that he was nearly out of money, and gave the man a defective revolver in lieu of money. The bill was for only a dollar and seventy-five cents. He then paid a boy ten cents to carry his bag to the trolley for Buffalo.

In Buffalo he took a ship to Cleveland where he stayed only twenty-four hours before returning to Buffalo. Apparently the trip was part of the aimless wandering that he had been engaged in that summer. Back in Buffalo, he hired a room in a "hotel" over Novak's saloon. He paid two dollars for a week's rent, and signed the register "John Doe" for some unexplained reason. It was now August 31st.

He spent the days that followed walking about the grounds of the Exposition, sometimes listening to Sousa's concerts or watching the display of electric lights—illumination by electricity was a novelty in the United States in 1901.

He wandered among the throngs of happy laughing people, a silent, unsmiling figure. He became familiar with the grounds, with the Temple of Music and other buildings.

He read carefully newspaper accounts describing the coming visit of President McKinley. It was then, he later told police, that he decided to kill the President—four days before he did so.

On Main Street he entered a shop and bought a cheap revolver, paying four dollars and fifty cents for it. Back in his room he examined it carefully, and got used to handling it. It was there that he conceived the idea of holding it concealed by a handkerchief in his hand.

The President and his wife arrived in a special train from their home in Canton, Ohio, late in the afternoon, Wednesday, September 4th. They were greeted by a large and happy throng—and by a drunken lieutenant of artillery who had stationed his battery too near the train. When the battery fired a salute to the President it was so near the President and Mrs. McKinley, that it shattered the windows in the Presidential car and the tired First Lady fainted.

The next day an estimated one hundred thousand persons crowded the Exposition grounds, and about half of them heard the President deliver a speech, his last, in which he indicated that he had made a change in his attitude toward high tariffs. Among those listening to him and witnessing the military review and other events of the day was Czolgosz. He watched but he did not join in the applause and the cheering.

"I thought it wasn't right for any one man to get so much ceremony," he told authorities who questioned him later. "I saw a great many there saluting him, bowing to him, paying homage to him, and honoring the President."

Czolgosz spent the rest of the afternoon at the Exposition, and then went to a park, where he sat for a while. It is almost certain that he spent much of the time in the park thinking of what he intended to do the next day. It is significant that he gave much thought to the killing he expected to do, but none at all to escaping after he had committed the deed. It was about ten o'clock that night when he returned to his hot and dingy room.

The next day, at seven minutes after four o'clock in the afternoon, he fatally shot the President.

* * * *

Czolgosz was placed on trial in Buffalo, on September 23rd, four days after the slain President's funeral. He entered a plea of guilty but the court directed that the plea be changed to not guilty because in New York State a man could not plead guilty in a case where the penalty might be death. He had no lawyers, and two days before the trial began two elderly but respected Buffalo lawyers were assigned to his defense. They were further hampered by Czolgosz himself, who said he did not believe in courts, and appeared to have little interest in the outcome of the trial.

The defense was unable to shake the position taken by the prosecution that Czolgosz was sane. The alienist appeared to be in agreement that he was sane in the legal sense of the word.

The prosecution was unable to establish any formal, organizational link between Czolgosz and the various anarchist groups of leaders in the country. Czolgosz was a loner.

The trial lasted less than nine hours, and the jury spent thirty-four minutes of that time in coming to a decision. He was found guilty and sentenced to be put to death.

On October 29th, at twelve minutes after seven o'clock

in the morning, he was strapped to an electric chair in Auburn State Prison. He said, "I killed the President because he was the enemy of the good people—the good working people. I am not sorry for my crime." The switch was turned.

His body was placed in a coffin and a carboy of sulfuric acid was poured into the casket. He was buried just inside the entrance to Fort Hill Cemetery in Auburn.

It was estimated that the body disintegrated in twelve hours.

X

Saved By A Long Speech

The quiet, short man in the fedora hat and the batwing collar had been there, outside the hotel, since four o'clock that afternoon, and four hours later in the darkness of early evening, few persons noticed him. When Theodore Roosevelt, the former President now seeking a third term, emerged from the hotel a cheer went up from the thousand persons who had gathered there.

Roosevelt strode from the hotel, across the sidewalk and climbed into an open motor car. He turned and waved to the cheering throng. The man who had been waiting so long moved in closer—he had been near the car all those hours—pulled a revolver from his pocket, held it between the heads of two spectators, and pulled the trigger.

For a moment Roosevelt stood there, then he staggered a bit, but steadied himself with a hand against the rear seat. He felt a flash of heat in his chest, but no pain.

Pandemonium broke out. A stenographer of Roosevelt's, who had played football at the University of Detroit, hit the would be assassin with a flying tackle, knocking him to the ground, where the revolver was pulled from his grasp. The crowd, now aware of what had happened, surged about and there were cries of "lynch him, lynch him."

The wounded ex-President interceded. "Don't hurt him," he said.

Roosevelt was unaware of how badly he was wounded. He coughed, with his hands at his mouth, but there was no blood. This convinced him that the wound was not fatal. He instructed the driver to take him to the Milwaukee Auditorium, where he was due to make a major address in his campaign.

His companions urged him to go to the hospital instead, to ascertain how seriously he was wounded but he refused.

"I shall deliver this speech or die. It is one thing or another," he said.

They drove reluctantly from the milling, excited crowd at the hotel to the auditorium. There was blood on his vest as he mounted the platform, and when he took out his speech of one hundred typewritten pages there were bullet holes in it. It had been in his vest pocket, folded twice, and the bullet, after going through a steel spectacle case, had passed through the speech, and on into his chest.

The audience had learned of the shooting and cheered

him even while shouting pleas that he go to the hospital. He refused.

"It takes more than that to kill a Bull Moose," he told the throng of some three thousand. He then delivered the speech, talking for fifty minutes. The speech finished and the cheers acknowledged, he was then rushed to the hospital, where he was found to be suffering from shock and loss of blood. Doctors found that the bullet had struck him below the right nipple, penetrated about four inches in an upward course and had fractured his fourth rib.

* * * *

The man in the fedora hat who had fired the shot was John Schrank, a mild-mannered man who made a good impression on strangers and who had never been in trouble before. He had sought to kill the former President because the ghost of William McKinley had instructed him to do so. Roosevelt had succeeded to the Presidency at the death of McKinley.

He had failed only because of the mischance that had sent the bullet through the spectacle case and also the text of a long speech. He had not aimed, but had simply fired in the direction of the Bull Moose leader. The same chance might have made him miss altogether, or it might have sent a bullet through Roosevelt's heart, or some other vital part of his body.

He had been stalking the former President for days, and once before he had stood close to Roosevelt, gun in his pocket, but he had preferred to wait until another opportunity because he had never seen his intended victim before and he simply wanted to look at him.

There was another time, in Chicago, when he was across the street from the fromer President but he did not attempt to shoot him then for fear of hitting a bystander.

The opportunity he had been seeking for weeks came that evening of Monday, October 14, 1912.

Roosevelt's recovery was rapid and in eight days he was able to take the train back to his home in Oyster Bay, New York. He was unable to continue his campaigning, except for two appearances at Madison Square Garden, where he received ovations. But he lost the election, Woodrow Wilson, the Democratic candidate, received four hundred and thirty-eight electoral votes to Roosevelt's eighty-eight. The third candidate was William Howard Taft, the regular Republican candidate, who received only eight votes.

The bullet was never removed from Roosevelt's chest and he carried it to his grave in 1919.

* * * *

On the morning of September 15, 1901, John Schrank had a dream that he was in a room in which there was a coffin, surrounded by flowers. Suddenly a figure sat up in the coffin and pointed toward a corner of the room. Schrank looked. A man in a monk's garb sat there, and he recognized the man as Theodore Roosevelt, who had just been sworn in as President, following the death of McKinley.

"There is my murderer," said the man in the coffin, "Avenge my death."

The figure in the coffin was William McKinley, the

assassinated President. Schrank said that his face was white as paper.

The dream remained fixed in Schrank's mind—a mind much concerned with politics and history. It was a mind that was twisted, that distorted things and was often confused. Ultimately it was to be fixed on a single idea—the assassination of Theodore Roosevelt.

John Schrank was a quiet man, thoughtful, silent most of the time, a man who lived alone most of the time, who never married and despite his ability to make friends of strangers, had none who were close. In many ways he resembled Czolgosz, the assassin of President McKinley, who too had been a loner and had thought his intended victim was greedy for power.

In appearance Schrank was a dreamy looking person who in fact had many dreams—especially day dreams. He had wide set blue-grey eyes, a broad and pudgy face and heavy eyelids. His light brown hair was close cut and receding from his forehead. His nose was prominent. He was five feet four and a half inches in height and weighed one hundred forty-five pounds. He was hardly the sort of man who would attract attention; it is easy to understand why he was not noticed as he waited outside the hotel in Chicago for the opportunity to shoot Roosevelt.

The highway to that place and to that moment of attempted murder goes back through most of Schrank's adult life. No one knows when his mind first became twisted, when thoughts and misgivings and fears produced the dream of the dead McKinley accusing his successor of assassination.

Schrank was born in Bavaria, outside Munich on March

5, 1876, the son of a brewer and a charwoman. The father died when the boy was still young, the mother remarried and instead of keeping her son, left him with an uncle and aunt, Dominick and Anna Flammang. He had five years of schooling, from age eight to thirteen, while working during his spare time as a gardener. The Flammangs moved to New York City in 1889, taking him with them. They bought and operated a saloon and lived over it.

The boy helped around the saloon, while attending night school. He learned to speak English. When he was fifteen his uncle gave him a job as bartender. It was a respectable saloon, popular with the largely German population of the neighborhood. It paid tribute to Tammany, giving the money to police officers for the privilege of staying open on Sunday, which was against the law.

Young Schrank had an interest in history and politics, although he never sought office or participated in any of the campaigning for candidates. A naturalized citizen, he always voted for the Republican candidate in national elections, and for Democratic candidates in local elections because, in the latter case, he wished to retain the friendship of Tammany for the saloon.

But things did not go well for the saloon, due to a change of municipal administration. In 1895 the city got a new president of the Board of Police Commissioners who tried to stamp out corruption in the police department. In the process some of the saloons which had been paying bribes were hurt. For two months the Flammang's saloon was closed with a policeman stationed at the door. The Flammangs saloon was one of many closed for violating municipal regulations. The president of the Board of Police Commissioners was Theodore Roosevelt.

While later Schrank said that this had nothing to do with his decision to kill Roosevelt, there were many indications in his life of his dislike for Roosevelt dating back to that period.

He had been brought up as a Roman Catholic and about the time he was twenty-one he stopped attending Mass, but his interest in religion continued and among the books he read later was the Bible.

At one time, when he was nearly twenty-eight years old, he became interested in a girl who lived nearby. She went on a church excursion on June 15, 1904, but Schrank, who had planned to accompany her, could not. He had to tend the bar in the saloon. The girl was among the one thousand and twenty-one persons who died when the excursion steamer, General Slocum, caught fire and burned in the East River at Hell Gate. It was Schrank who went to the morgue and identified her body.

There is no indication that he ever again had an interest in a woman. And except for his aunt and uncle, he never had a friend in his entire life, he said later.

The autumn after the death of the girl, Theodore Roosevelt, then President, ran for re-election but this time Schrank voted for the Democratic candidate, who was unsuccessful.

It was about this time that his uncle decided to retire from the saloon and turned it over to the nephew. The uncle purchased a tenement house uptown and lived there. Schrank—he was known in the neighborhood as John Flammang until he acquired the saloon—ran the saloon for a couple of years and then sold it, going to live with his uncle and aunt and serving as a handyman there.

As time went on he read more and more. He read newspapers, and books, writing many notes of comment and observation. Some of these were incoherent to authorities who read them after his attempted slaying of Roosevelt.

He read the Constitution, the Bill of Rights and the Bible, time and time again, and some of the books which he perused were outstanding histories. He read a little Socialist literature but not much because he did not accept Socialist philosophy.

He greatly admired George Washington, Thaddeus Kosciusko, the Polish born hero of the American Revolution; Carl Schurz, the German-born politician of the post Civil War period; and Louis Kossuth, Hungarian patriot. Many Americans admired these same men and obviously there was no indication in his admiration for them that his mind was anything but normal.

During the presidential campaign of 1912, the *New York Herald* and the *New York World* were both opposed to Theodore Roosevelt's efforts to obtain a third term in the White House. Roosevelt had been unable to secure the regular Republican nomination for a third term, it went instead to Taft, who had succeeded Roosevelt four years before. Thereupon Roosevelt organized his following into the Progressive party and ran as its nominee for the Presidency. The party was sometimes referred to as the Bull Moose Party. The traditionally Republican *Herald* would not mention Roosevelt by name during the campaign, but referred to him as a "third termer," the "third-term candidate," or simply as "the Bull Moose candidate." This made a deep impression on Schrank, who was against Roosevelt, and he said, against the third term as a matter of principle. No President had served a third term up to then and in fact only seven of the twenty Presidents up to that time had had even second terms.

By this time Schrank had inherited the tenement from his uncle and aunt, but did not stay there. After spending some time in an apartment in the tenement, he moved out because he did not like the tenants, and went to a small hotel in Brooklyn, called the Homestead. The income from the tenement was only eight hundred dollars a year, and he sometimes worked as a bartender for additional income. He liked to walk about the city, and a favorite was to walk across the Brooklyn Bridge. He composed a little poetry, not very much and not very good, but interesting to the alienist who later examined him.

He was a lonely man, without friends, and apparently without enemies. He joined a Republican Club located near the tenement and he sometimes attended political meetings, but always as a silent spectator, rather than as a participant. He was moody, and at times he thought of his dream about McKinley accusing Roosevelt of being responsible for his assassination.

Meanwhile he continued a habit of making notes in which he stated opinions, not only about things he read, but about matters in general. Once he wrote what he called "The Four Pillars of the Republic," which were, in substance, the two term principle for President; the Monroe Doctrine, renouncing of wars of conquest and limiting the Presidency to Protestants. Although Schrank had been brought up a

Catholic he believed that the men who organized the government had had that precept in mind.

He was especially concerned with the two-term question which was being discussed from coast to coast as Roosevelt waged his campaign.

He thought a lot about Roosevelt, about his campaign to win the election, and he thought, too, of the dream that he had had in 1901—eleven years before. As time went on, the idea of Roosevelt being the instigator of the killing that made him President seemed more and more likely to him.

Then early on the morning of September 14, 1912—he placed the time at half past one—while he was writing a poem in which a phrase, "Be a Man," appeared repeatedly, he had' another supernatural visitation.

The ghost of McKinley came up to him, said Schrank, touched him on the shoulder and said in a low voice, "Let not a murderer take the Presidential chair. Avenge my death." Schrank looked up and saw, he said, the face of McKinley, chalk white.

This occurred while he was alone, in his room in a small hotel; ironically it called itself the White House.

It did not take Schrank long to decide that Roosevelt had in fact been responsible for McKinley's death, that he was a menace to the nation and that he, Schrank, had been called upon to kill Roosevelt. Over the years this had grown out of the bitterness that Schrank had felt ever since the closing of his uncle's saloon.

Just as Guiteau had written messages to the American people, so now did Schrank. It is not known if he knew about Guiteau's messages of this sort.

The day after he had seen the vision of McKinley at his

shoulder, Schrank sat down and wrote out an explanation of what he intended to do.

TO THE PEOPLE OF THE UNITED STATES

Sept. 15, 1901—1:30 A.M. in a dream I saw President McKinley sit up in his coffin pointing at a man in a monk's attire, in whom I recognized Theo. Roosevelt.

The dead President said This is my murderer, avenge my death.

Sept. 14, 1912, 1:30 A.M.: While writing a poem, some one tapped me on the shoulder and said Let not a murderer take the presidential chair, avenge my death. I could clearly see Mr. McKinley's features.

Before the Allmighty god I swear that the above written is nothing but the truth.

So long as Japan could rise to be one of the greatest powers of the world despite her surving a tradition more than 2,000 years old, as General Nogi so nobly demonstrated, it is the duty of the U. S. A. to uphold the third term tradition. Let every third termer be regarded as a traitor to the American cause let it be the right and duty of evey citizen to forcibly remove a third termer. To prevent is better than to defend. Never let a third term emblem appear on an official ballot.

I am willing to die for my country. God has called me to be his instrument, so help me God.

Eine feste Berg ist unser Gott (A mighty fortress is our God.)

INNOCENT GUILTY

Having written what he considered his justification, Schrank now proceeded to plan the murder of Theodore Roosevelt, a man he had never seen.

First he purchased a revolver at a gunshop near where

he lived, on September 21st, just before sailing on a steamer for Charleston and Jacksonville. Before boarding the ship he had packed a new suitcase with his belongings. Included in the various items he took with him were many of the notes he had made and his naturalization papers. Also a receipted water and light bill on the back of which he had written one of his frequent diatribes against the man he now intended to kill.

> Theodore Roosevelt is in conspiracy with European monarchs to overthrow our Republic. Theodore Roosevelt's unscrupulous ambition has been the murder of President McKinley to satiate his thirst for power. Down with Theodore Roosevelt. We want no King. We want no murderer. The United States is no Carthage. We will not yield to Rome.

Schrank boarded the ship at noon, but as he sailed down the coast he began to have some doubts that he could reach New Orleans by September, when Roosevelt was due there. Certainly Jacksonville would be far distant from the Louisiana city.

Anxious to intercept Roosevelt, he left the ship at Charleston on the 23rd and hired a room for a week, registering under his own name. He decided he could not get to New Orleans in time so he took a train two days later for Augusta, leaving his suitcase behind. He carried on his person the loaded revolver and six extra shells. He had cut a hole in a pocket on the right hand side of his vest, and this became an improvised holster. The barrel hung down into his trousers; the handle of the gun could not be seen when his coat was closed.

He had expected to intercept Roosevelt at Augusta, having read a newspaper story to the effect that the Bull Moose candidate would stop there while swinging through the South. The newspaper account was in error and Roosevelt did not stop there but proceeded to New Orleans. He moved about in the South with Schrank trying to catch up with him. The would-be assassin finally succeeded on September 29th, at Chattanooga. Roosevelt arrived there at ten o'clock that night and Schrank was waiting in the crowd. Schrank pushed through the throng until he was only a few feet from the automobile in which Roosevelt acknowledged the cheers. Schrank made no attempt to kill his intended victim then explaining later, "because it was a new thing to me. I didn't just exactly have courage enough and he started off so fast in his automobile."

Roosevelt, unmindful of the fact that he was being stalked, went back to Oyster Bay, New York, to rest for a few days. Schrank, knowing that Roosevelt was going to campaign in the Mid-West, gradually moved northward, arriving in Chicago on October 12th—the same day that his intended victim did. Schrank had copied Roosevelt's itinerary from a newspaper and knew that the candidate would be in the Windy City on that date. Both arrived in the morning.

Later in the day there was a reception for Roosevelt at a hotel, and Schrank got his second look at him. He stood across the street, but decided again not to shoot then. This time, he said, because it would look bad for the city of Chicago, "if at the reception he got shot down."

Schrank continued to wait for his opportunity. That night he went to the Chicago Coliseum but when Roosevelt came along there were so many people jammed about him that

Schrank could not get near enough to him. He waited for Roosevelt to come out after delivering his speech, but was disappointed again. Roosevelt had left by a different entrance.

The next day both the hunter and his intended victim went by train to Milwaukee. Roosevelt was scheduled to speak Monday evening. Schrank spent the afternoon strolling about the city seeing the sights and in the early part of the evening he visited a saloon near the Hotel Gilpatrick, where, he said later, he had ten or twelve beers, and enjoyed the music. He asked the musicians to play "The Stars and Stripes Forever," "The Watch on the Rhine," and "Where the River Shannon Flows." He enjoyed the music and tipped the musicians.

It was a pleasant affair for him, quite in contrast to the sinister thoughts that he had had for many weeks. He sang with the crowd at times, and came as near coming out of his shell as he had for years.

He did not stay long in the saloon, but left early as he customarily went to bed early. He got room number one in the Argyle, a small hotel, and paid one dollar in advance, signing the register as Walter Ross.

Shortly after noon the next day, October 14th, Roosevelt, who had intended to remain in his private Pullman car until it was time for him to go to the Milwaukee Auditorium, left for the Hotel Gilpatrick. The proprietor of the hotel, an ardent Progressive, had planned to give a small dinner for Roosevelt, and the candidate agreed to attend.

The news spread, and somewhere Schrank heard it. He made his way to the Gilpatrick and waited there patiently near the open car that was to take Roosevelt to the Auditorium. When the candidate emerged from the hotel and a cheer went up, Schrank put his right hand into his vest and pulled out the revolver.

* * * *

Schrank was arrested by the police and was taken to the police station where he was charged with armed assult with intent to kill. It was punishable then in Wisconsin by imprisonment from one to fifteen years. The Municipal Court named five alienists to examine him, and they kept him under observation for nine days and then told the court that Schrank was "suffering from insane delusions," that he was insane "at the present moment." The alienists' report said in part;

> He gives the impression that he feels himself to be an instrument in the hands of God and that he is one of a band of historic heroes paralleled by such characters as Joan d'Arc and other saviors of nations. He undoubtedly considers himself a man of heroic mold. At no time did he express remorse for his act.

On the testimony of the alienists—one mentioned homicidal tendencies in Schrank's mind—the Judge committed Schrank to the State Hospital for the Insane. Later he was transferred to another state-run mental institution. He was confined for thirty-two years, a quiet, well-behaved patient. When Theodore Roosevelt died Schrank said, "I am sorry to learn of his death. He was a great American. His loss will be a great one for the country."

When another Roosevelt became a candidate for a third

term, in 1940, Schrank became very much upset. He told his doctors that he would do something about it if he were free. After all, he had saved the nation once from a third termer, he declared. It was his duty he believed, to save it again.

He died on September 15, 1943, without ever having a visitor or receiving a letter during his imprisonment. Had he been found sane, and guilty of the charges against him, he would have spent less than half of those thirty-one years in jail.

His death came on the forty-second anniversary of seeing McKinley point an accusing finger at Roosevelt, and one day after the thirty-first anniversary of seeing McKinley at his elbow.

By the time of his death, another President had escaped assassination.

XI

Any President Would Do

The plan was a simple one. He would simply go to the amphitheatre, sit in the front row, and shoot the President-elect. But things did not go right for Giuseppe Zangara, mainly because he could not get a front row seat, even though he tried. If he had succeeded he might have changed the course of history.

It was February 15, 1933, a balmy night in Miami, Florida, and the man who had been elected President the previous fall was to address the public in Bayfront Park. In a little more than two weeks he was scheduled to be inaugurated. He had been on a vacation, fishing off the Florida coast.

Zangara, thirty-two years old, was barely five feet tall and weighed one hundred and six pounds. His face was narrow and swarthy, with a square jaw. He had bushy black hair and his eyes were dark brown. He was a dangerous, sullen man, with a overwhelming urge to kill a president.

He had that idea on his mind that winter's night in Miami—to kill Franklin D. Roosevelt, not because he disliked him, but because Roosevelt was going to be President. Zangara wanted to kill a president, and Roosevelt qualified in his mind, even though he had not yet assumed the office to which he had been elected.

In his pocket he had a loaded revolver. In his head he had a diseased mind. It was a bad combination.

Zangara went to the park an hour and a half before Roosevelt was due to speak, only to find that there were thousands of men and women already there, and the front row seats were all filled. In fact almost all the seats in the auditorium were taken, and the aisles were beginning to fill up. The auditorium had a capacity of eight thousand persons, but before the evening was over there would be another two thousand persons sitting in the aisles or standing in the rear.

Zangara wore white striped trousers and a white shirt open at the neck, as did many of the men in the audience. He was not noticed particularly by the others in the throng, except for his short stature.

Dismayed at what he saw, he pushed his way down the left side aisle and squirmed his way through until he was within a few rows of the front rows. There a visitor from Iowa stopped him.

"Where do you think you are going," said the Iowa man as Zangara tried to push past him.

"I'm going right down front," answered Zangara.

"Well, I'm sorry but you cannot go down there. It is full."

"It don't look like to me it is full," Zangara protested.

"There are many people sitting on the ground—ladies and children sitting on the ground," the Iowa man stated. "It isn't proper for you to go and stand out and push yourself in front of someone else."

Zangara stopped trying to reach the front—where he would be close to Roosevelt when the latter arrived, and remained where he was.

Before him was a gaudy bandstand, originally constructed for a Shriners' convention, with onion topped roof, and with some of the original oriental decorations still showing, despite the erosion of time and weather.

Roosevelt was due to arrive in an open car, drive to the area in front of the stage, and deliver his address from his car. On the stage itself, which was to serve as a backdrop, would be a number of dignitaries, including the Mayor of Chicago, Anton Cermak.

Zangara waited, the pistol in his pocket. It was around nine-thirty when the crowd began to shout as the President-elect drove up in front of the bandstand, waving and acknowledging the cheers of the throng. He drove by the aisle in which Zangara waited, and for a moment was only about twenty feet away from him, but Zangara, because of his short stature, had difficulty in seeing Roosevelt—certainly he could not see him well enough to aim his revolver and attempt a shot. He had to get a better vantage point.

Roosevelt was about thirty feet away when the car stopped, but there was a curve in the driveway, and when Roosevelt addressed the crowd his back was to the waiting gunman.

Sitting on the top of the rear seat, small microphone in hand, Roosevelt gave a short and informal talk lasting only about three minutes. The talk over, he slid down into the seat.

Zangara had been unable to gain the position he needed. Many people stood—some even stood on their seats, during Roosevelt's short address. He again waited for the opportunity he needed.

Roosevelt saw Mayor Cermak sitting in the front row on the stage, and called out for him to come down to the car. They shook hands and talked for a minute or so, and then the Mayor turned to start back to the stage. Roosevelt leaned over to look at a telegram that another man had given to him. The crowd started to break up.

It was at this moment—at about twenty-five minutes before ten o'clock—that Zangara acted. The opportunity to kill had arrived.

Zangara leaped upon a seat that had just been vacated, and saw that he could shoot the President-elect from that spot. He had a clear range. He drew the revolver from his pocket, aimed it at Roosevelt's head and fired. It was a five shot revolver and he kept pulling the trigger until all the bullets had been fired.

One bullet hit the Chicago mayor in the right armpit and penetrated the left lung. Another bullet hit a woman spectator in the abdomen, seriously wounding her. A New York city detective on vacation, a woman visitor from Newark, New Jersey, and a man from Cocoanut Grove, Florida, also suffered minor wounds, Roosevelt was not hit.

There were many theories regarding his failure to hit the man he hoped to kill. A woman said that she grabbed his arm and deflected his aim. A man made a similar claim. Zangara himself said that the seat on which he stood teetered as he opened fire.

He was seized almost at once, disarmed and thrown onto the trunk rack of one of the cars with Roosevelt. Three detectives sat on him and he was rushed out of the amphitheatre and to jail. Behind was pandemonium.

Secret Service men started to rush Roosevelt from the scene, but he ordered them to stop. They objected but he insisted. He had seen that Mayor Cermak was wounded and ordered him placed in the seat beside him. He held the mayor in his arms as the car sped to the hospital. The mayor gasped to Roosevelt: "Better me than you." He died on March 6th, two days after Roosevelt had taken the presidential oath.

Zangara, on his arrival at the jail, learned that he had missed shooting Roosevelt. He said that he was sorry that he had and hoped that he would have another chance. He did not.

* * *

Giuseppe Zangara was obsessed with two things—a desire to kill a President, and with a stomach ache. In his own twisted mind they were related. In court, after the attempted assassination he said, "The capitalists get to be boss to my father, keep the money from my father, and my father send me to work and I have no school, and I have trouble with my stomach and that way I make my idea to kill the President—kill any President, any King."

He had hoped to kill a king, and eleven years before,

while he was still in his native Italy, he bought a pistol with the intention of killing King Victor Emmanuel, but he was unable to get past the Royal guards, and at public occasions he was unable to get close enough because of the crowds. When he migrated to the United States he brought the idea along with him. He also brought his stomach ache.

After his arrival he considered assassinating Calvin Coolidge, who was then President, but never made an attempt to do so. But the idea of killing a President—like the pain in his stomach—would not go away.

He was born in a town near the toe of the Italian boot, on September 7, 1900. It was a poor family, superstitious and ignorant. At the age of six the boy went to school, but two months later his father took him out of school and got him a job. This was deeply resented by the boy who blamed the capitalists for it. He believed that they did not pay his father enough—that they withheld money rightfully his father's—so that he could not go to school as did the sons and daughters of "capitalists."

At six years of age he was shovelling dirt on highways, and doing other heavy manual work. In time he learned the mason's trade, which he was to follow from then on.

During the first World War he served in the Italian Army, and in 1923 he migrated to the United States. He went to live with his uncle in Paterson, New Jersey. His uncle, also a bricklayer, aided him in obtaining work. The next year Zangara filed his first papers for citizenship and in 1924 he became a naturalized citizen. He secured this citizenship, not because he wished to be a citizen, but because the union—which he disliked—made it a condition of membership.

For eight years he worked as a bricklayer, and for a time, as a small contractor in and around Paterson. He got good pay and saved quite bit of it, even though he sent money regularly to his father in Italy. But he was still being bothered by the pain in his stomach. He was a quiet, hardworking man who usually kept to himself. He was a bachelor and appeared to have no interest in girls.

As time went on he became more and more addicted to solitude, and once, when he was living in another New Jersey city, he hired two rooms. He lived in one, the other room, empty, insured him of not having any neighbors.

He did not talk much, and when he played chess occasionally—which was the nearest activity he had to a recreation—he played silently. He appeared to have little interest in anything but his stomach and the pain which he said he had there. He did not smoke; he said smoking would kill him. He did not drink because he said alcoholic beverages set his stomach on fire. Once his uncle suggested that he return to his native Italy and find himself a wife; he answered that he was too sick to think about marriage. He hated the cold weather and said, "When it is cold my stomach hurts."

The only other interest he appeared to have was his concern for the plight of the poor working man. Sometimes at lunch time he would expound on the evils of the capitalists. These discussions were about economics and social conditions and not politics.

After his arrest authorities were surprised to find that he was not an anarchist, socialist, or any kind of radical but that he was a registered Republican.

He continued to suffer from stomach pains, or at least he

thought he did. Certainly he thought of himself as in poor health but after his death doctors, who performed an autopsy, said he was healthy and well nourished. But he, himself attributed the pain he said he had to the hard work he had done as a small boy. It was swinging a pick, especially, he said, that first brought on the pain. "It spoils all my machinery—my stomach, all my insides. Everything inside, no good." A doctor at that time said it was probably due to strain and gave him some medicine, which Zangara said was no good. The doctor was quoted by Zangara as saying that he would never be any good again. Despite this, Zangara was able to work along with others, do as much as they did, work steadily and industriously. But in his mind he thought of himself as an invalid. He remembered what the doctor had said, and he would not face reality.

"What's the use of living half-dead from the capitalists?" he asked.

Two years after his arrival in this country he went to a hospital, complaining of an ache in his right side. The doctors examined him, and while they found nothing wrong, they took no chances of an infected appendix and operated. When they removed it they found it was in good condition. After his discharge from the hospital he resumed his complaints about the pain in his stomach.

Just as quiet, hardworking, lonely Czolgosz suddenly experienced a change in his condition, so did Zangara, when he was around thirty-one years old. He appeared to lose interest in his work and stopped seeking employment as a bricklayer, and lived on his savings, except for a few dollars he earned showing tourists around Miami, until his arrest. Jobs were harder to get in his field, but his stomach still pained, and he stopped working. He expressed some interest in travel, especially south to escape the northern winters, and his doctor encouraged him in this.

During the next three years he went to Miami, returned briefly to New Jersey, made a visit to Los Angeles, went back to New Jersey again, and then again went to Florida in 1932. In Miami he loafed about, hanging around the waterfront, sometimes trying to pick up some money by betting on the horses and dogs and losing. He had to eat in the cheapest restaurants and at the time of his arrest he was living in a two dollar a week attic room.

It was while he was living in Miami that the idea of killing a President—which had long been dormant in his mind—reasserted itself. This time it was stronger than ever. Perhaps it was a newspaper story about the assassination of Lincoln, perhaps it was just that he had more time now to think about it. He wanted to kill a President,—any President. At that time the President of the United States was Herbert Hoover, who headed the nation when it was experiencing its deep economic depression. But it was not the economic state of the country, or politics, that motivated Zangara but his stomach ache which he attributed to the "capitalists" and men who ruled, whether they were kings, presidents or others, somehow to him they represented capitalists.

Zangara considered going to Washington and killing President Hoover but it was cold in the North, even Washington, and it was warm in Miami, so he kept delaying his trip to the nation's capital. Then one day, probably February 13th, he read in a Miami newspaper that Franklin D. Roosevelt, the President-elect, then cruising and vacationing off the

Florida coast, would come to Miami on the night of February 15th and give a short address at Bayfront Park.

Zangara decided that he would kill Roosevelt instead of Hoover because he could do it right there in Miami where it was nice and warm. Although Hoover still had some time to serve and Roosevelt was not yet a President, Zangara equated the President-elect with President.

Zangara, having decided on Roosevelt, went to a pawnshop in downtown Miami and paid eight dollars for a revolver and ten bullets. He loaded the revolver and put the other five bullets in his pocket.

* * * *

He was tried two times. The first time he was charged on four charges of assault, five days after the shooting. His court-appointed lawyers, all prominent attorneys, agreed to his pleading guilty and he was sentenced to eighty years in jail. The charge involving the shooting of Mayor Cermak was deferred, but after the mayor died, Zangara was charged with murder. In both cases he pleaded guilty.

Alienists examined him and reported that he had "a perverse character wilfully wrong, remorseless and expressing contempt for the opinion of others . . . intelligence not necessarily inferior . . . distorted judgment . . . incapable of adjusting to the average social standards . . . inherently suspicious and anti-social. Such ill-balanced erratic types are classified as psychopathic personalities."

Zangara himself insisted he was sane, and the judge agreed with him. Zangara was found guilty and sentenced to death. On March 20th he was escorted to the electric chair in the State prison in Raiford, Florida. He strode past the electric chair to where the superintendent of the prison was standing and gave him three notebooks in which he had written his autobiography during the thirty-three days he had waited for the sentence to be carried out. The autobiography ended with the following: "I go contented because I go for my idea. I salute all the poor of the world."

He refused the services of the chaplain, and when the guards stepped up to escort him to the chair, he refused them, too, saying that he had no fear of it. He walked over, sat down and looked at them smiling.

Suddenly he noticed that there were no photographers present, and became angry. Ever since his arrest photographers from newspapers, magazines and news reels had taken pictures of him over and over, and this had pleased him. Now, at his great moment, there were none there to record it on film, none to carry his picture to the front pages of the newspapers.

"Lousy capitalists," he snarled, still blaming everything wrong on them. "No pictures. No one here to take picture. All capitalists lousy bunch of crooks!"

A black hood was placed over his head as he said, "Goodby. Adios to all the world." He continued to talk as the guards made the final preparations.

"Go ahead. Push the button," he said.

There was no button; the switch was pulled.

XII

All Dressed Up To Kill

The assassination of a President is a momentuous event and the two short, swarthy men were dressed for the occasion—in a literal sense they were dressed to kill. Both wore new suits and new snap brim hats.

They donned their new garments the day that they attempted to kill President Harry S. Truman who had succeeded Franklin Delano Roosevelt.

As it turned out, it was indeed a special day for them because before it was over, one of them would be dead and the other wounded and in jail, charged with attempted murder. Their intended victim would not even be shot at.

The two men were both short in stature and slender, as

are so many Puerto Ricans. Oscar Collazo, who was to be wounded, stood five feet, six inches, weighed about one hundred forty pounds, and was thirty-six years old. Griselio Torresola was an inch shorter, eighteen pounds lighter, and eleven years younger. The older man wore steel rim glasses. Both were devoted, even fanatical, members of the Nationalist party that sought to win independence for Puerto Rico, their native island.

The two men, both armed with revolvers and carrying extra ammunition, arrived in a taxicab at Fifteenth Street and Pennsylvania Avenue in Washington, at the Treasury building and only a short distance from the White House. Their intended victim, however, was not there. The Executive Mansion was undergoing repairs so President Truman was living at Blair House, diagonally across the street from the White House. All the two men had to do to reach Blair House was to walk down the street, past the White House on their left, and Lafayette Park on their right. This they did, strolling slowly so as to get a good look at Blair House, its entrance, and the position of the two guard stations on the sidewalk. After passing it, they turned around and walked back to Fifteenth and Pennsylvania, taking a second look as they passed Blair House.

It was the first day in November, 1950, and the weather was unseasonably hot. The temperature was up in the mid-eighties and most of the people on the street were more concerned with the heat than with the sight of two olive-skinned men who looked like foreigners, and who had obviously dressed up for their visit to the nation's capital.

The two men decided to separate. Collazo started to walk slowly along the sidewalk on the north side of the avenue, moving in the direction of Blair House. Torresola crossed the avenue, to the south side and walked a bit faster toward the temporary White House. The idea was that as Collazo approached Blair from one side, Torresola having passed Blair House, would turn back, so they would converge from opposite directions.

Inside Blair House, the President, unaware that two men would try to force their way into the mansion and shoot him, was having an after-lunch nap in a second floor bedroom. His wife and mother-in-law were in the house but not near him. His daughter was out of town.

In front of Blair House at that moment were three White House policemen and a Secret Service agent. One of the policemen, Leslie Coffelt, a private, was seated in the west guard booth, which Torresola would approach first when he made the turn back. On the other or east side, Joseph O. Davidson, private, sat in the other guard booth, chatting with Floyd M. Boring, Secret Service agent then standing at the entrance to Blair House. The latter was in charge of the detail assigned that day to accompany the President when he left his quarters. Standing nearby, on the steps leading to the door was Donald T. Birdzell of the White House police.

At twenty minutes after two o'clock Collazo, moving along in the steady stream of pedestrians, suddenly stopped, pulled out his revolver and aimed it at Birdzell, who was facing away from him, and pulled the trigger. There was a click, sounding loudly in the quiet of the afternoon, but the weapon did not discharge. Birdzell looked over his shoulder and saw Collazo holding the revolver against his chest and hitting it with his other hand. The gun went off and Birdzell was hit by a bullet in his right leg.

The wounded officer ran out into the middle of Pennsylvania Avenue, drawing his revolver and turning around, fired. He saw Collazo starting up the stairs as Boring and Davidson went into action. They fired from the east booth. Collazo stopped and crouched on the steps and returned their fire, using up the remaining bullets in his clip. He quickly inserted a second clip, as the two officers tried to line up their sights on him. Their target was partially hidden by the iron picket fence that stood in front of Blair House. Nevertheless they continued firing although some of their bullets hit the iron bars of the fence and were deflected from their target.

For a moment Collazo appeared to have a charmed life. One bullet took off his hat without hitting him, he was cut on his nostril and on one of his ears, but he was not really hit by either of the two men firing at him, even though both were expert marksmen.

Vincent P. Mroz, a Secret Service agent, emerging from Blair House, fired a single shot at Collazo. Davidson thought he saw Collazo reel, and shouted to the others to hold their fire. But the Puerto Rican turned and fired at the officer who leaped for cover into a doorway leading to the basement of Blair House, and from which he fired again at the Puerto Rican.

While this was going on, Torresola was walking back to Blair House. He drew his revolver, looked into the windows of the west guard booth as he reached it, and seeing Coffelt inside, dashed to the doorway of the booth and opened fire on Coffelt. He held the revolver close to his chest with both hands, but nevertheless, he managed to hit Coffelt twice out of three tries, once in the abdomen and once in the left side. Coffelt went down.

Another White House policeman appeared on the scene, Joseph H. Downs, who had been about to enter Blair House through a basement door on the west end of the building, was seen by Torresola who quickly aimed his pistol at Downs, firing three times and hitting him each time. The third bullet struck Downs as he was falling and penetrated his left shoulder, going up through his neck and out through his cap.

Torresola jumped over the hedge to help Collazo, who was still on the steps. Birdzell was shooting at Collazo from the middle of Pennsylvania Avenue. Torresola, aware of this, turned and fired at the officer, hitting him on the left knee. Birdzell, wounded now in both legs, collapsed.

Coffelt, despite his wounds—from which he was to die— came rushing out of the guard booth, drew his revolver, aimed quickly and sent a bullet through Torresola's brain, as he was reloading his pistol. The Puerto Rican seemed to stop and shake his head before toppling to the ground behind the hedge, dead.

Collazo had also fallen, he had been hit by a bullet in his chest. He sprawled out on the sidewalk, face downward, his right arm outstretched, his left under his body.

The gun battle had taken only about three minutes, and no one knew for sure who had wounded Collazo. The two Puerto Ricans had fired seventeen times and the officers had fired ten.

The President, awakened by the shooting, came to a second story window, and saw Collazo laying on the sidewalk. But one of the guards fearful that there might be more shooting—there might be others in the throng quickly gathering who were accomplices—shouted, "Get back! Get back!" The President obeyed.

The shooting was over, however. One man was dead, another was dying, and three others were wounded but would recover. The badly wounded Coffelt was rushed to the hospital but died during an emergency operation three hours and forty minutes after the shooting. Collazo appeared to be dying, but the bullet in his chest had been deflected by his breastbone, and had gone out through his right arm pit, and lodged in his arm. Downs, despite his three wounds, survived, as did the twice wounded Birdzell.

During the fighting the front door of Blair House had been open, because of the heat of the day, but the screen door was locked. Had either of the Puerto Ricans reached the screen door he undoubtedly would have been cut down, for when the shooting started a Secret Service man inside quickly grabbed a sub machine gun and posted himself where he could shoot anyone coming through the doorway.

At the hospital Collazo told a nurse that he had come to Washington with Torresola to kill the President. Neither of the two Puerto Ricans had thought out just how they were going to accomplish this, and even the attack that they made was poorly coordinated. They had planned this final step only a few minutes before they started firing. Nor had they even thought about getting away after the assassination. Their thinking went just to that moment when they hoped to gun down the Chief Executive of the United States.

* * * *

They had come to Washington to kill the President because they hoped in doing this they would advance the cause of Puerto Rican independence which they ardently embraced. Unlike all the other men who have tried to kill our Presidents, they had no history of mental imbalance, nor did they appear to be anti-social or in need of psychiatric assistance. And unlike the other attempts, this one was purely for political reasons.

Collazo told authorities that they thought the killing of President Truman would start a revolution in the United States, and during the ensuing confusion and disorder Puerto Rico would be able to gain its independence. They had made the attempt, however, without consulting the leadership of the Independence movement in their native island.

They misjudged their ability to reach and kill the President, and obviously knew little about the political system and tradition of this country—for while four Presidents have been assassinated there has never been a political upheaval as a result. And they apparently also miscalculated the strength of the Nationalist movement in Puerto Rico, which collapsed shortly after their attempt. There remained a small group of men and women who continued to seek independence, but with little public interest or support.

* * * *

Griselio Torresola had wanted to take part in the fight for the liberation of Puerto Rico. Collazo and he had talked about the small uprising then going on in their native land. They both lived in New York City and considered for a while returning to Puerto Rico and joining the forces actively engaged in the uprising. However they finally decided that they could do more for their cause by striking down the leader of the forces trying to surpress the rebellion. So they went to Washington instead.

Torresola's family in Puerto Rico, was strongly committed to the fight. His sister, Doris, was secretary to Pedro Albizu Campos, the President of the Nationalist party in Puerto Rico and she had been wounded during a four-day seige of Campos's house by forces of the established Puerto Rican government.

His brother, Elio, an ardent Nationalist, was one of a gang who allegedly set fire to a post office; later he was sentenced to life imprisonment for killing a policeman during the abortive uprising.

Grieselio Torresola knew how to handle firearms and had a liking for side arms. Before he died in front of Blair House, he demonstrated his skill as a a marksman for despite the fact that he was moving about as were the police and Secret Service men, he fired eight times and only missed once.

He was born in Jayuya, Puerto Rico, and had two years of high school. He became a member of the Nationalist party in Jayuya eventually becoming the local treasurer.

The migration of thousands of Puerto Ricans to the mainland of the United States included him, despite his Nationalist beliefs which he brought with him. He arrived in New York City in 1948. He got a job at a stationery and smoke shop, but lost it in 1950 for being inefficient. In the years that followed he sometimes lived on relief, but it is unclear what work, if any he did. He continued to be interested in the Nationalist movement, but this was not too apparent, for some of his friends said later he did not appear to have much interest in politics.

He was married several times, to women in New York and Puerto Rico, although it is not known if he was married to all the women he lived with. He had two daughters. His friends thought of him as a lighthearted somewhat irresponsible young man. In the months preceding his death, he lived with his current wife and one of his daughters in New York City; the other daughter was in Puerto Rico. In September, a few weeks before the assault on Blair House, he went to Puerto Rico and during the visit he met Campos, who revived some of his former devotion to the cause of Puerto Rican Nationalism.

Campos authorized Torresola to take over the leadership of the Nationalist party in the United States if it should be necessary, and also to collect funds for the party.

It is believed by many people in the government in Washington that Campos selected Torresola for the assasination of President Truman. This, the American government has never been able to prove.

Torresola had met Collazo some years before in his native town of Jayuya, and they met again in New York City. In October Torresola visited Collazo in the latter's apartment and showed him a copy of a Spanish-language newspaper printed in New York City which contained an account of the uprising in Puerto Rico. They went outside and walked along the streets discussing this news for a couple of hours. Torresola said they should return to Puerto Rico and join in the fighting, and Collazo agreed. He then gave Torresola fifty dollars with which to purchase a revolver.

The next day Collazo heard on the radio that government forces in Puerto Rico had strafed Jayuya, where he had lived as a boy. That night he and Torresola met again, and the latter had the revolver he had bought also fifteen dollars change. Both men were upset by the day's news, and they talked again about aiding the uprising.

It was Collazo, the quiet, friendly man, who suggested that they assassinate President Truman instead of joining the handful of compatriots fighting the government in Puerto Rico.

"I told him that a better idea would be to come to Washington. As long as the American people didn't know what Puerto Rico was or where Puerto Rico was or which was the real government of Puerto Rico they would never care what was happening in Puerto Rico; that by coming to Washington and making some kind of demonstration in the capital of the nation we would be in a better situation to make the American people understand the real situation in Puerto Rico."

The demonstration, they agreed, would be assassination.

They agreed to take the train for Washington the next afternoon, before they parted.

*   *   *   *

Oscar Collazo was born in Florida, a small town in central Puerto Rico, one of fourteen children. His father owned a good sized farm and at one time employed as many as twenty persons. His father died when Oscar was only seven, and according to Oscar he died of frustration and disappointment that stemmed from an American embargo on Puerto Rican sugar, although the United States purchased large amounts of Cuban sugar. However, his sister said that the father's death was due to failing health.

The oldest son in the family took seven year old Oscar to live with him in another town, Manati, and later Jayuya. He did odd jobs for his brother, while going to school. In 1931 conditions got very bad in Puerto Rico, as they did on the mainland, so Collazo went to New York City seeking employment. His new landlord helped him to get a job in the kitchen of a club.

The job lasted for a year but he was unable to find another in depression-stricken New York City, so in 1932 he returned to Puerto Rico.

One day in April, in San Juan, he attended an out-door meeting of the Nationalists which was addressed by Campos, the leader of the movement. That night he went to the party headquarters and joined. While he was undoubtedly influenced by Campos's speech, there can be no question that an incident that had occurred some time before helped prepare him for this step.

A doctor from the mainland, working in a hospital in San Juan, wrote a letter with certain sarcastic passages in which he said he was transplanting cancer to some of his native Puerto Rican patients, and that several of them had died. In addition he described the native population as dirty, lazy, thieving and degenerate and said that what was needed was a tidal wave to exterminate the entire population. The letter was not sent and fell into Nationalist hands and was published in newspapers. Campos even sought to have the

League of Nations take some action about it. The doctor said he was simply parodying anti-American attitudes of some of the Puerto Ricans.

The matter was investigated by both the medical and health agencies in Puerto Rico, the Rockefeller Institute and the Puerto Rican Attorney General. The doctor was exonerated. However, thousands of Puerto Ricans thought the letter was a statement of fact—not sarcastic as it had been intended—and were influenced by it in their attitudes toward the United States. In fact it is doubtful that the influence of the letter is ended yet.

Collazo joined actively in the work of the party, and one of the assignments he undertook was to go from village to village seeking signatures for a petition to put Campos's name on the ballot as a candidate for the Puerto Rican Senate.

He did not remain in Puerto Rico; he made frequent trips back and forth to New York City, staying for a while in one place, then another, working at menial, low-paying jobs.

In 1934 he was in Puerto Rico, working at two jobs to support himself. During the day he worked in a sugar refinery and at night in a drug store. It was during this time he met and married a Puerto Rican woman. They had a daughter the next year.

Even with two jobs he found it hard to support his family, and so he returned to New York City, taking his two-year old daughter with him, but leaving his wife in Puerto Rico. He worked in a variety of jobs—working hard and long. He sent the child back to Puerto Rico with relatives. Later he returned to Puerto Rico to divorce his wife on the grounds of infidelity. He then worked for a while in a grocery store but again decided to return to New York City. When he did he left his daughter behind with his relatives.

He met a divorcee, Rosa Mercado, who had two daughters. She was a Puerto Rican and a member of the Nationalist party. She lived in Moosup, Connecticut, and worked as a metal polisher in a factory there. Collazo had no job at this time so she got him one in the factory where she worked. He had a room in a neighboring town.

At the plant he was quiet and a good workman, but he mingled very little with the other workers. He did not join in the social activities of the employees and remained pretty much by himself. He would not express opinions about anything until he was asked.

A month after he started work, Collazo married Rosa. Later they moved to New York City, where he continued to work as a metal worker.

For several years Collazo and his wife had a settled, quiet existence, happy with their three daughters, living in a Puerto Rican neighborhood.

In 1943 an event occurred that changed the quiet, apparently contented Collazo, that ultimately was to cause him to take a revolver and seek the death of the President of the United States.

Albizu, a fiery leader in the Nationalist party in Puerto Rico, came to live in the same building as the Collazo family. He had just been released from the Federal penitentiary in Atlanta, after serving six years for attempting to overthrow the government of the United States. During his imprisonment the Nationalist cause had languished, now it was about to be revived.

Collazo and he became friends, they visited each other in their apartments, and it was not long before the younger man was visiting the Nationalist headquarters in New York City, and becoming active in the party. He spoke at party gatherings and became a leader in the party's neighborhood clubs. He obtained a mimeograph machine, set it up in his apartment and rolled out political notices. His activities extended to include social clubs, and he opened doors for Nationalist programs within them. He served as secretary of one such club.

It was not long before he was named one of four editors of a slickpaper monthly publication of the party in New York City. In 1945, when the United Nations organized, he prepared literature for distribution among the delegates, calling for an end of United States colonialism in Puerto Rico.

He went back to Puerto Rico for a year, working on a Spanish-language newspaper while studying shorthand and typing on the side. On his return he got another job as a metal polisher. Later his employer said that he was one of the best workers in the shop. The plant was in New Rochelle, and everyone there liked the quiet, hard working and dependable Puerto Rican. He still had solitary ways, usually eating his lunch alone, and he would not join in discussions about politics or social conditions. When it came time for the union to seek a new contract with the company, he was chosen to be one of the negotiators for the workers and he did a creditable job. When the new contract was approved, he typed up copies and distributed them to his fellow employees.

His existence was placid, comfortable and routine during this period—the period just before he went to Washington. He liked to take their daughters out, especially to museums and galleries, and he was deeply interested in their education. He did a great deal of reading. But whenever he thought about his native island and what he considered the oppressive policies of the United States toward it, he showed considerable emotion and sometimes became quite excited.

The serenity of this existence came to an end on Sunday, October 29, 1950, when his old friend, Torresola visited him at his apartment and showed him a copy of a Spanish-language newspaper, printed in New York City, which told of an uprising in Puerto Rico. Torresola suggested they go to Puerto Rico to aid their fellow compatriots but the next day Collazo convinced his friend that they could help their cause more by shooting President Truman. They agreed to leave for Washington the next day at three o'clock in the afternoon.

The next morning Collazo took his dog for a walk, returned to his apartment and told his wife to notify the plant he would not be in to work that day, and then went out and bought a new suit, three new shirts, three new undershirts and a new blue canvas bag. He drew a hundred dollars from the family bank account.

When he left the apartment, dressed in the new suit and carrying the bag, his wife went with him as he looked for a cab. A few minutes later he spotted one. He turned to her and said, "Good-by. Pray for me," and drove off to meet Torresola at Pennsylvania Station.

On the train the two men read newspaper accounts of the fighting in Puerto Rico, and in Philadelphia they obtained a copy of the Inquirer and read about an unsuccessful attempt to kill Governor Louis Munoz Marin.

Neither man had been in Washington before and after their arrival they walked to the nearest hotel, the Harris, and pretending they were not together, registered under aliases. They then went out, had a meal, roamed about for a while, bought some more newspapers and then returned to Collazo's room. There they discussed what they intended to do, and charted their movements for the next day on a map found in a hotel directory in the room. It was late when they retired for the night.

They had an early breakfast the next morning, walked about the Capitol grounds, and then took a cab for Blair House. They looked the place over from the cab and the driver told them that the President was living there while the White House was undergoing renovation. After the cab left them, they looked at the guards and the white guard booths in front of the ancient building. They noted that pedestrians passed freely by the building, which was separated from the sidewalk by only a small area, spanned by a short flight of stairs leading to the front door.

They decided that they needed to be more familiar with the neighborhood so walked about for a while, lunched and returned to their hotel.

Collazo knew nothing about firearms, and Torresola now gave him some instruction. For two hours Torresola showed him how to fire a revolver, how to eject clips and insert others.

It was just a few minutes before two o'clock that afternoon

that the two men, both armed, set off on their mission at Blair House.

* * * *

Collazo was found guilty of killing the guard, Coffelt, of assaulting Downs and Birdzell with intent to kill, and with attempting to enter Blair House with the intention of killing the President of the United States.

At the trial he said that there was no intention of killing Truman, simply to make a demonstration that would bring the "plight" of Puerto Rico to the attention of the public.

"I never had any feeling of hatred or dislike for Mr. Truman, or any other American or anybody else, for that matter," he told the court.

Collazo insisted he was sane, and two alienists who examined him agreed, even though they termed him fanatical in his attitudes.

It took the jury an hour and forty-five minutes to arrive at a verdict of guilty and the judge sentenced him to be executed on two counts—the killing of the guard and the attempt to enter Blair House and shoot the President. Also he was to serve from five to fifteen years in jail for the assaults on the other two guards.

Collazo showed no emotion when he heard the sentences. He refused to ask the President—whose death he had sought —for clemency lest it reflect in some way on his cause, but he received it anyway. On July 4, 1951, while Collazo was living in the death row in prison, President Truman commuted his sentence to life imprisonment. He took this action without explanation, eight days before Collazo was scheduled to die.

XIII

Double Death In Dallas

It was early in the morning, between six-thirty and seven, when the night watchman at the hotel in Mexico City helped the slender young man get a taxicab that took him to the bus depot of the Transportes del Norte. There the young man claimed seat number twelve which had been reserved the day before in the name of O. H. Lee.

At thirty minutes after eight the bus rolled out of the terminal and started on its long journey to the United States border some five hundred miles to the north.

He was almost twenty-four years old, of medium height and slender built. His face was narrow and dominated by a large nose. His thin lips were twisted slightly to one side, giving him a slightly sardonic look. His name was not O. H. Lee; it was Lee Harvey Oswald.

As the bus loaded with Mexican and North American passengers pushed on north from the mountains toward the lowlands around Laredo the face of Oswald must have reflected some of the frustration that he felt. He talked very little with the other passengers. He was a "loner," a man who kept by himself, who did not share his thoughts with others, and on this day, Wednesday, October 2, 1963, the thoughts he had were not happy ones.

The trip north to the border was an unhappy one for him, in contrast to the journey southward from Texas a week before.

Then he had had high hopes of achieving something that would mark him as a person of special importance. He had hoped, then, to become a prominent Communist and the confidant of Communist leaders. He had planned to go to Cuba by way of Mexico, even have a discussion with Fidel Castro, and then go on to the Soviet Union. After all, he had been to Russia once before, he had a Russian wife, he was a self-styled Marxist, and on his own initiative he had espoused the cause of Castro in New Orleans where he had used an alias and posed as the leader of the Fair Play for Cuba Committee. There was no such committee; its only member was himself. He had been interviewed on a New Orleans television program and had voiced the ideas of the "committee." He had even been arrested—the only time in his life—because of a scuffle while carrying a placard supporting Castro.

These things would ensure him an open-arms reception in Cuba and in Russia, he had reasoned. On the way down

233

from Texas to Mexico City he had told a couple of fellow passengers that he was on his way to Cuba and the Soviet Union, giving up momentarily his usual trait of keeping his own counsel. The whole thing had been certain in his mind.

A few days before he left for Mexico City the newspapers in Dallas had carried the news that President Kennedy was planning a visit to several Texas cities, including Dallas. The day that he left the papers had carried a confirmation of the first report but whether he read it is not known. Certain it was that he had thought about assassination before he stepped aboard the bus; five months before he had attempted to kill General Edwin A. Walker and had sent a bullet into a room occupied by the nationally known rightist.

On another occasion he had planned to take a pistol with him when he went to a meeting where former Vice President Richard Nixon was to be the speaker, but his wife had pleaded with him not to, and they had struggled for possession of the weapon.

He had arrived in Mexico City late at night. The next day he had wasted no time; he had gone immediately to the Cuban and Soviet embassies. Americans were banned by their government from travelling to Castro's Cuba, but at the Cuban embassy they were friendly and agreed to issue him a permit for him to enter their country if the Russians were willing to let him visit their homeland.

But the Russians would not agree. No one knows why not, but it is easy to imagine what their reasons were. During his stay in the Soviet Union he had worked in a factory, had married a Russian woman, and he had displayed some of the resentment against Soviet authority that he had shown toward his own country. Perhaps the Russians did not want him because he had made a false statement on his application. He had said he was a Communist; as a matter of fact he belonged to no Communist organization. He had thought of himself as a Communist but even in this his traits as a loner had continued.

So now, instead of being on his way to Cuba, a hero to be welcomed by Castro, he was on his way back to his native United States. The knowledge that he had spent quite a bit of money—for him—on the fruitless journey could not have been pleasant to him. He was a careful, even reluctant spender.

The bus roared steadily along the highway, gradually losing altitude as the day went by. He spent some of the time looking out the window at the passing Mexican countryside; other times he read. He may have talked to an elderly woman; later it was recalled that a slender young American had conversed with such a passenger and it might have been the unhappy Oswald.

After it became dark he switched on the light over him and read until he remembered that the American authorities at the border probably would not let him bring in any fruit. He had several bananas, of which he was especially fond, and he hurriedly ate them before the bus pulled to a stop at Nuevo Laredo on the Mexican side of the Rio Grande. It was then after midnight.

The Mexican authorities made him get off, claiming there were irregularities in his papers. A few minutes later he returned to his seat, mumbling complaints against the Mexican officials. The bus crossed the river and arrived at Loredo,

Texas at thirty-five minutes after one in the morning. At three he boarded another bus headed for San Antonio and Dallas.

No one knowns when Oswald first thought of killing President John F. Kennedy, as the Warren Report points out. It is possible, even likely, that the idea came to him during the long ride back to the United States seven weeks and a day before the assassination. We know that he thought of assassinating others even before this time, and that he knew the President was planning to visit Dallas. He had failed in his plan to go to the Communist lands as one of their heroes; he had failed in his efforts to impress others with the small things he had done in New Orleans—to him they were not small things. He had gone to Mexico City a hero in his own eyes, a person of importance, a person to be reckoned with. He returned a failure, disappointed and bitter.

If he killed Kennedy, if he destroyed the man who had defied both Russia and Cuba in the missile crisis the previous year, he would be important, too important to ignore, he must have told himself during that homeward journey. No one would deny him permission to enter Cuba and Russia, if he killed the President of the United States—he must have reasoned. All his life he had wanted to be important, now he would be important by committing murder.

Not many things in the life of Lee Harvey Oswald had gone right and most of the responsibility for this was due to himself, to flaws—psychological flaws—in his character. He had been unable to fit into the regimen of the Marine Corps; he had been unable to acquire Soviet citizenship after he had defected; he had been unable to keep a job that he apparently liked; his marriage was in real trouble; he had been unable to enlist a single follower when he set up his Fair Play for Cuba "committee," and now both Cuba and the Soviet Union had denied him admission. But he could wipe out this long list of failures and frustrations if he could do something big, such as killing the President.

It was twenty minutes after two in the afternoon when the bus pulled into Dallas. Oswald did not go to his expectant wife and their daughter then living in Irving a few miles away. They were living with a friend, Mrs. Ruth Paine. Instead he got a room at the Y.M.C.A., registering as a serviceman so that he would not have to pay for his lodging. Then he went to a local office of the Employment Commission and filled a claim for unemployment compensation. He said he was looking for work.

The next day he called his wife, Marina, and asked her to see if Mrs. Paine would drive into Dallas and pick him up, but she refused and so he hitch-hiked to Irving where he spent part or all of the weekend. Marina found him much more agreeable than he had been and she was encouraged by this, even though she still refused to live with him. Marina was carrying their second child and she was near the end of her term.

He told her what had happened in Mexico but said nothing about planning to kill the President—he never did. Sometimes in the past he had told her of his plans, such as one to hijack a plane in Mexico and take it to Cuba, but not always. He had not told her of his attempt to kill General Walker until after he had failed.

Once, during that weekend, Marina found her husband in a room by himself, crying.

He went back to Dallas and resumed his job hunting, calling his wife every night. He took a room for a week, but the landlady did not like him and refused to let him stay longer. He returned to Irving for another weekend with Marina. He was discouraged by his failure to obtain work and by the fact that his unemployment compensation was running out. He seemed to be especially concerned about Marina and the impending birth, and sometimes he called her twice in a day, even though he needed to conserve the little money he had.

He returned to Dallas and his quest for employment, obtaining a new room. Mrs. Paine learned of an opening at the Texas School Book Depository and when he called Marina that night, she told him about it. The next day, October fourteenth, he obtained the job, starting work Wednesday, October fifteenth. It was a temporary job and he received a dollar and twenty-five cents an hour. He worked from eight in the morning until four forty-five, in the afternoon, filling orders for books.

Both Oswald and his wife were happy about the job but he hoped to find a better one which would pay more. During the first week he became acquainted with a fellow employee, B. Wesley Frazier, who lived in Irving near the Paines. He arranged to go back and forth with him on weekends. In general he did not become acquainted with the others at the Depository and continued to stay pretty much by himself. Even when he went back and forth to Irving with nineteen-year-old Frazier he was silent most of the time.

Oswald's birthday was Friday, October eighteenth, and when he arrived at the Paine's he found a small family party had been arranged for him. It was a happy time. Two days later Mrs. Paine drove Marina to the Parkland Hospital in Dallas where she gave birth to their second child, another daughter. In less than five weeks President Kennedy would die in the same hospital, and so would Oswald.

Monday, October twenty-first, Oswald went to see Marina at the end of the day. He was happy about the birth, saying that two daughters were good for each other. He wept a little. After two hours at the hospital he went out to Irving with Mrs. Paine.

The birth of a second daughter which had elated him, the improvement in his relation with his wife, and the job he had were all positive things that should have encouraged him and eased some of the sense of frustration that he apparently felt, but they did not. He still dreamed of going back to Russia, presumably with a different status than he had had before. It is probable that he continued to think of killing Kennedy, because in his poor, distorted mind, it would be another positive thing to be eagerly sought.

Meanwhile leaders in Dallas had indicated concern over the possibility of unpleasant incidents occuring during the visit of the President the next month. They were especially concerned over possible acts by ultra right wing groups which appeared to be both strong and numerous in the city. Two nights after his visit to Marina in the hospital he attended a meeting of such a group headed by General Walker. Later he reported this to a member of the Communist party.

The day after the meeting of the Walker group there occured an incident in Dallas that showed how well grounded were the fears of the authorities. Adlai Stevenson, the United States ambassador to the United Nations, delivered an address in the city. Pickets had tried to disrupt the meeting and some of them shouted: "Kennedy will get his reward in hell." As he left the auditorium Stevenson was nearly mobbed, was spat upon and was struck on the head with a placard.

After the incident President Kennedy asked White House aide Arthur Schlesinger to telephone Stevenson and tell him he had conducted himself well. Stevenson, in reply, told Schlesinger to urge Kennedy to stay out of Dallas. Schlesinger did not pass on the message and a few days later Stevenson changed his mind.

On October twenty-fifth—four weeks before the Kennedy assassination—the Dallas Chief of Police announced that he would have a hundred extra men on duty to protect the President during his visit. That night Oswald went to a meeting of a local Civil Liberties group and joined in the discussion. When someone said that the John Birch Society was not anti-semetic he declared that he had been at a Birch Society meeting earlier that week and had heard statements that were both anti-semetic and anti-Catholic. He became involved in further discussion.

He expressed Marxist sentiments and described himself as a Marxist but not a Communist. He conceded that the United States was ahead of the Soviet Union in the field of civil rights. He praised the man many persons considered responsible for the recent betterment of the civil rights situation—President Kennedy. Undoubtedly he was planning even then to kill the President.

After the meeting he went to Irving to spend the weekend with his wife and two daughters. Marina and the new baby were back from the hospital.

The following Friday, November first, he obtained a post office box at a postal substation near the Book Depository which was to be used, he told a postal worker, to receive mail for the Fair Play for Cuba Committee and the American Civil Liberties Union. That night he went to Irving, as usual, for the weekend.

There he heard disturbing news. An FBI agent had visited the Paine home, inquiring about him. The agent had spoken briefly to Mrs. Paine and the latter had written down the agent's name, which she gave to Oswald. Marina, in compliance with instructions Oswald had given her some time before, had taken down the license number on the agent's automobile.

Oswald returned to work Monday, and Tuesday the agent returned to the Paine house, accompanied by another agent. Oswald was upset when he learned of this second visit and declared the FBI was trying to "inhibit" his activities. He wrote to the Soviet embassy in Washington and said that the FBI agent had warned him against further activity in the Fair Play for Cuba Committee and had tried to persuade Marina to "defect" and place herself under the protection of the FBI. This simply was not so, according to Mrs. Paine and Marina, in testimony they gave later.

Oswald still hoped to return to Russia and kept sending letters to Soviet and Communist officials in this country. Meanwhile at work he was making no friends. He did his work quietly and well but stayed pretty much by himself He did not discuss politics with his fellow workers who appeared to have no special feelings of like or dislike toward him. But he had earned the dislike of Michael Paine who had been with him at the Civil Liberties meeting, and so, on the weekend of November sixteen and seventeen—the weekend prior to the assassination—he did not go to Irving. Marina, knowing that Mr. Paine was going to be home, asked her husband not to come. She wished to avoid any unpleasantries.

Sunday morning Marina wanted to talk too him and because she knew little English she asked Mrs. Paine to get him on the telephone, giving the address where Oswald has said he was living. But the landlady said that no one named Oswald lived there. Marina became confused—and angry.

Actually Oswald was living there under an assumed name —O.H. Lee, the same name he had used in securing bus reservations for his return from Mexico City.

If she had not attempted to reach her husband it is quite possible that the President would not have been shot five days later. For she was angry with her husband and she was to remain angry with him throughout the next few days.

The next day was Monday, November eighteenth. Dallas newspapers carried stories about the coming visit of the President and gave the route that his motorcade would follow from the airport to the Trade Mart where he was scheduled to make an address. Oswald must have been elated when he read that the motorcade would pass the Texas School Book Depository where he worked.

That night he phoned Marina. She told him about the attempt to reach him the previous day and he became angry. He said he lived there but was using a fictitious name and she should not have called. She became angry and there were bitter words. The next night, Wesnesday, he did not call her.

The newspapers had been carrying stories about the Kennedy visit. The Chamber of Commerce and local Republican leaders joined others in urging citizens to be friendly and courteous. Dallas had become notorious as a center of right wing groups and there was a real fear they might disrupt the reception to the nation's Chief Executive.

There appeared to be ample justification for those fears. On Thursday morning—the day before the President's scheduled arrival—there appeared in the streets handbills with front and profile photographs of the President under the heading "Wanted for Treason" and a list of charges of alleged Communist collaboration.

It was that morning that Oswald asked young Frazier if he could ride out to Irving with him that night and come back with him Friday morning. He explained he wished to pick up some curtain rods.

Oswald's arrival at the Paine house that evening was a surprise for he usually telephoned ahead to make sure everything was all right. He appeared as the penitent husband seeking to make peace with his wife. He said he had been lonely the previous weekend but Marina was still angry and refused to talk with him.

He went out on the lawn and played with his older daughter until dinner time. Again he attempted to talk to Marina, asking her to come live with him in Dallas where, he said, they would get an appartment.

She refused. Had she agreed, it is quite possible that Oswald would have returned to Dallas, his head filled with plans for the resumption of family life, and that he would not have gone on with his plans to assassinate the President the following day. But had she agreed, it is not likely that he would have given up the idea permanently. He had been thinking too long about assassination, and the compulsion to be important, to show himself if not others how important a person he was was too strong. Had Marina said "yes," on that fateful evening, it probably would have delayed the assassination, but there is still some question whether it would have made him forget the idea of murder. Perhaps he would never again have the opportunity such as presented itself on Friday.

But she refused—by not answering him. He went into the Paine's living room and watched television while the women washed the dinner dishes and prepared the children for bed. And sometime he went out of the house to the family garage, for later Mrs. Paine found the light still burning there. Some of the belongings of the Oswald's were stored in the garage. Among them was an Italian army carbine, rolled up in a blanket.

Around nine o'clock he went to bed. He had a big day ahead of him.

* * * *

President Kennedy was already in Texas. With him was his wife, Jacqueline.

> The presence of his wife by his side had saved him once from possible assassination. On Sunday morning, December eleven, 1960, a few weeks after his election to the Presidency, Kennedy emerged from the Kennedy home in Palm Beach, on his way to ten o'clock mass. Parked nearby was

a former mental patient from Belmont, New Hampshire. The man had come south with the intention of blowing up the President-elect. He had not liked Kennedy's victory over the Republican candidate, Richard Nixon, saying that it had been achieved in an "underhanded way." In the car with the ex-mental patient were seven sticks of dynamite, ready to be detonated. All the man had to do was to pull a switch. He hoped to drive his car into Kennedy's and set off the charge and kill himself and his intended victim.

By the time that Kennedy reached the gate leading to the street the man could see that the President-elect was not alone. With him were his wife and some of the Kennedy children. The man could not go through with his plan that morning because, he later told the authorities, he had no wish to harm her or the children. He drove away, planning to make the attempt at some other time. He never did. The authorities, tipped off by a postal worker in Belmont that the man had made threats against Kennedy, picked up the deranged would-be assassin.

Thursday morning President and Mrs. Kennedy kissed their children goodby in Washington and left aboard the Presidential plane. This trip was something special for them, for she had been unable to accompany him on trips since the death of their son Patrick, following his birth in August.

They flew to San Antonio where he spoke at the Aerospace Medical Center at Brooks Air Force Base. They were greeted by such enthusiastic crowds that the concern of their friends seemed meaningless. Boarding the plane again they flew on to Houston. Again they were greeted by a large and friendly throng indicative of the warmth of feeling held by so many Texans toward the youthful President and his beautiful First Lady. He addressed a dinner that evening and then flew on to Fort Worth where they spent the night.

* * * *

Friday, November twenty-two, 1963 dawned gloomy and overcast in Fort Worth, and, in nearby Dallas.

In Irving Lee Harvey Oswald got up early and prepared to go to work in Dallas, twelve miles away. He dressed himself in brown trousers, white T-shirt and blue jacket. He went into the kitchen and made himself a cup of coffee. The others in the house were not up. Before he left the house he put his wedding ring on a cup on his wife's dresser—a thing that he had never done before. He also left his wallet containing $170 in a drawer of the dresser. In his own pocket he had $13.87.

Before he left the room his wife, who had awakened, spoke to him. She told to be sure and take a jacket. It was the only time that she spoke to him during that last visit. Apparently he did not see this as an indication that she was getting over her anger.

He left the house at seven o'clock, went to the garage, took the Italian army rifle, wrapped up in brown paper, and walked to Frazier's home nearby. The rifle had telescopic lens. He had purchased it through a mail order house the previous March, paying $19.95. Before he left the garage he carefully arranged the blanket where it had been, so as to appear undisturbed.

Frazier's car was outside his house when Oswald arrived, and he placed the package in the back seat. He walked to the house and met Frazier as he came out the kitchen door. Frazier noticed the package when they got into the car and asked: "What's the package, Lee?"

"Curtain rods," answered Oswald, and then Frazier remembered Oswald had said he wanted to pick up some curtain rods at the Paine's.

Frazier parked his car in the company lot at the School Book Depository. Oswald took the package from the rear seat and walked to the Depository, not waiting for Frazier as he usually did.

Oswald's actions after entering the building were later reconstructed. He went to the sixth floor, to a window on the southeast corner. There he set up boxes—if he had not done so before—to screen himself from fellow employees while he was at the window. Later three boxes were found by the window which could serve as a rifle rest, and another, as a seat. Behind this were other boxes stacked high.

Normally, Oswald did most of his work as an order filler on this floor and on the first.

His fellow workers were excited. The Presidential motorcade was due to pass the building at lunch time and they would have an opportunity to see Kennedy at close hand.

A great many persons in Dallas were looking forward to the President's visit. The morning paper devoted considerable space to it. It also carried a full page advertisement critical of the President, his administration and his brother, Robert, then the Attorney General. It had been placed by an ad hoc right wing committee. The advertisement was bordered in heavy black.

*　　*　　*　　*

In nearby Fort Worth the President rose early and dressed in a gray suit, blue tie and striped shirt. He tucked a white handkerchief in the breast pocket of his coat. During the night a light rain had fallen but now it had stopped even though the skies were gloomy and overcast. But the President was far from gloomy. The reception he had experienced in Texas the day before had exhilerated him.

A throng had gathered in a parking lot outside, hoping for a glimpse of the President and his wife. He went outside—it was quarter of nine—and talked with the crowd for a few minutes. His wife was not with him and he explained; "Mrs. Kennedy is busy organizing herself. It takes a little longer, but then she looks better than we do when she does." The crowd applauded.

He returned to the hotel and went to a breakfast sponsored by the Fort Worth Chamber of Commerce, joining the then Vice President, Lyndon Johnson, and Governor John B. Connolly. The latter had been Secretary of the Navy when Oswald had been issued his dishonorable discharge from the Marines in 1960, and had received a letter of protest from him.

Again Mrs. Kennedy was not there and the breakfasters were disappointed. She came in shortly, dressed in a plum-pink tailored suit. On her head was a pill box hat of the same color. She was obviously happy and looked radiant. There was applause. When the President began his speech he brought a laugh by commenting "No one is interested in what Lyndon and I wear."

He made a statement later in his speech that was more somber and which was to be recalled by those present. "This is a very dangerous and uncertain world."

They went back to the hotel and there the President and the First Lady discussed the risks inherent in Presidential public appearances with Kenneth O'Donnell, the aide who had planned the details of the trip. The President was aware of those risks, and according to O'Donnell, said "if anyone really wanted to shoot the President of the United States it is not a very difficult job—all one had to do was get on a high building someday with a telescopic rifle and there was nothing anybody could do to defend against such an attempt."

In the middle of the forenoon they went to the airport and made the short flight to Dallas. The Vice President and Mrs. Johnson flew in the Air Force Two plane and arrived three minutes before other plane, Air Force One, carrying the President and his wife.

There was an official delegation on hand to welcome them. Nearby waited a White House limousine which had been flown from Washington for this occasion. It was a convertible, equipped with a glass dome to protect its passengers from bad weather. It was not intended as protection against bullets, although the glass windows on the sides were bullet proof. The day had turned clear and very warm and O'Donnell ordered the dome removed and the windows rolled down.

Mrs. Kennedy was presented a bouquet of dark red roses, and she walked with her husband to the car. There was a chain fence that held back a throng of people, waving and shouting their greetings which were acknowledged by the smiling couple. In the car the President and his wife sat in the rear seat, he on the right and she on the left and the bouquet of roses between them. The Governor and his wife sat in the jump seats, and the front seat was occupied by Secret Service men.

The motorcade started for downtown Dallas at ten minutes of twelve. Six Dallas Police motorcycles led the procession; their function was to keep the crowd back and prevent it from moving onto the roadway. The first car in the procession was a "rolling command car" driven by the Dallas Chief of Police carrying two Secret Service men and a deputy sheriff whose job it was to scan the crowds and buildings along the route, looking for trouble.

There were narrow running boards on the White House limousine so that Secret Service Men could ride there, holding onto handles. The President did not like Secret Service men riding there and so on this fateful day they were in a car behind. There were eight of them, all armed with pistols. Also in the car were a shot gun and an automatic rifle.

Four motorcycles had been assigned to guard the President's car, but instead of being beside it, they were in the rear, in deference to the President's wishes.

The third car in the procession carried the Vice President and Mrs. Johnson, a Secret Service agent, a Texas Highway patrolman who was the driver, and Senator Yarborough. Other cars included telephone and telegraph vehicles. White House communications car, three cars for press photographers, a bus for White House staff personnel, and two busses filled with reporters.

As the motorcade moved toward downtown Dallas it reached speeds of between twenty-five and thirty miles per hour at times in thinly populated suburban areas. Along the route were people gathered to watch their President and to wave and shout greetings to him. Once the President ordered the procession stopped so he could get out and shake the hands of a person who carried a placard urging him to do so. Secret Service men scrambled out of their car and moved close to the President to protect him should he need their assistance. There was another stop so Kennedy could talk for moment with a nun and a group of children with her. Again the Secret Service men assumed protective positions but few persons noticed this. The eyes of nearly everyone were on the President.

The two stops put the motorcade a bit behind schedule. The President was in a happy, jovial mood and his wife was radiant as she waved and smiled at the throngs lining the route.

In the downtown area of Dallas the crowds were dense and repeatedly Secret Service men had to leap from their cars and help keep people from the President's car. Once a teen-age boy broke from the sidewalk and ran toward the car, apparently intent on getting a handshake and a word or so from the nation's Chief Executive. Dallas' motorcycle police roamed up and down beside the motorcade trying to keep the people back.

The motorcade approached the Texas School Book Depository, made a hairpin turn and started for an overpass. The time was 12:30.

* * * *

During the forenoon a crew of men worked laying a new floor on the southwest corner of the sixth floor. Cartons of books and other materials had been moved from the area to the southeast section. No one paid any heed to the fact that there was a row of boxes over by the window on the southeast corner.

Oswald, who had taken the package of "curtain rods" to the window before starting work, carried on his duties as usual. There was some talk among the employees about the President passing the building around noon but no one remembers Oswald joining in this discussion or making any comment.

At about fifteen minutes before noon the floor laying crew quit work for their lunch, using both elevators to go down to the street floor where many of them joined others lining the street outside. The foreman, going down, saw Oswald on the fifth floor near the elevator shaft; reaching the street the foreman discovered he had left his cigarettes in his jacket on the sixth floor and went back up. When he arrived at the sixth floor he saw Oswald again.

Oswald, clipboard in hand, was walking toward the elevator from the area of the window at the southeast corner.

The foreman asked: "Boy, are you going downstairs? It's near lunch time."

"No, sir. When you get downstairs, close the gate to the elevator." This was the west elevator which operated by push button and would not run if the gate was open.

"Okay," said the foreman, who was using the east elevator. Downstairs the foreman found that the push button elevator was not there. The time was about five minutes before noon.

There are no witnesses to what Oswald did during the next thirty-five minutes but his actions may be reconstructed nevertheless. He went back to the window, took down the package of "curtain rods" from its hiding place, removed the brown wrapping paper, and put the two parts of the carbine together, checking carefully to see if everything was in order. The empty paper bag he tossed on the floor. He loaded the carbine with four cartridges.

He placed the rifle on the boxes by the window and which served as a rest. He approached the window and looked out at the scene below. People had gathered along the sidewalks, but there no great mass of people. He stepped back from the window, but returned several times to check on the situation below.

It was exactly 12:30 when the motorcade arrived, driving toward the building, passing it and continuing toward the overpass. Oswald rested his rifle carefully, squinted through the telescopic lens got the back of the President's head in his sights. He squeezed the trigger. He fired three times in quick succession.

*　*　*　*

Jacqueline Kennedy was smiling and waving to the people on the left of the highway and her husband was doing the same to those on the right, as the car completed the turn and started down the incline toward the overpass. Mrs. Connolly, riding in front of Mrs. Kennedy, had just turned and said: "Mr. President, they can't make you believe now there are not some in Dallas who love you and appreciate you, can they?"

"No, we sure can't," he replied.

Mrs. Connolly turned back in her seat, there was a bit more conversation.

Suddenly there was a sharp report; it sounded like a backfire from one of the motorcycles. The Secret Service man in the front seat heard the President exclaim: "My God! I am hit!"

Turning, the agent saw the President clutching his throat. The first bullet had struck him in the back near his neck.

Governor Connolly, realizing that it had not been a backfire, but a rifle shot, started to turn. He did not hear the second shot. A blow struck him in the back. The bullet passed through him, smashed a wrist watch, went through his wrist and penetrated his thigh. He cried out.

Mrs. Kennedy turned and saw her husband with his hands at his throat, a quizzical look on his face. A third shot rang out. The bullet struck him in the back of the head, blowing some of his forehead away as it emerged in front.

She cried out: "Oh, my God, they have shot my husband. I love you, Jack!"

Mrs. Connolly, unaware that her husband had been hit, turned and saw the President slump down, his hands still at his throat, a blank expression on his face.

The Secret Service man in the front seat, hearing the three shots in rapid succession, turned and saw the President.

"Let's get out of here; we are hit," he said to the driver. He grabbed the microphone and radioed the car ahead. "We are hit, Get us to the hospital immediately!"

The driver of the Presidential car accelerated. In the jump seats Mrs. Connolly cradled the body of her wounded husband. The Governor thought he was dying, and exclaimed: "Oh; no, no, no. They are trying to kill us all!"

"It's all right, be still," Mrs. Connolly told her husband.

Mrs. Kennedy left her seat and crawled out onto the rear of the car—later she had no memory of this. A Secret Service man riding on the running board of the following car jumped off at the first shot and raced forward and got hold of a handle, climbed aboard and then extending his arm, took hold of Mrs. Kennedy's hand and got her back into the rear seat as the car leaped forward. He threw himself flat on top of the rear seat where his body could serve as a barrier to any more shots. There were none.

Spectators along the side of the highway were throwing themselves down on the ground, in an effort to escape being hit. Further back in the motorcade the Secret Service man in the front seat of the Vice Presidential car saw this and saw the Presidential car suddenly roar forward. Realizing that something was wrong but not knowing that, he turned, hit Vice President Johnson on the shoulder, and yelled: "Get down!"

The agent looked forward again, then turned and threw himself on top of the Vice President, forcing the latter to the floor, and protecting him with his own body.

A spectator across the street from the Book Depository had noted a thin young man at the window at the sixth floor and had seen the young man come to the window several times and look out prior to the arrival of the motorcade. When the firing started the spectator looked up and could see the young man with a rifle pointed at the President's car. It looked to the spectator as though the man in the window was standing up as he fired.

The motorcade raced for the Parkland Hospital, which had been alerted. The Presidential car reached speeds of eighty miles an hour in its race to the hopsital. Twelve doctors were waiting to treat the wounded President.

When the Presidential car braked to an abrupt stop, two Secret Service men ran into the Emergency Room, one of the agents brandishing a submachine gun. The hospital people dived for cover. Another man came running into the room and a Secret Service man struck him hard. The man slammed against a wall. Dazed, he produced his F.B.I. credentials.

At the Emergency entrance staff members rushed out stretchers to the Presidential car. A Secret Service man had taken off his coat and placed it over the unconscious President so that press photographers could not take pictures of him. The photographers, however, had not arrived.

Governor Connolly, unconscious during most of the four mile dash, came to and attempted to get out of the way so that the President could be taken into the hospital first, but collapsed. Up to now he had felt no pain, but suddenly it came and was excruciating. He was lifted onto a stretcher and rushed inside.

Jacqueline Kennedy held her husband's head in her lap and for a moment refused to release him. The President's eyes were open and blank. His face was ashen and he had spasmodic respiration. A doctor walking beside the unconscious President, could hear chest sounds which he interpreted as heart beats.

The President was admitted to the hospital at 12:35—only five minutes after the first shot had been fired.

The doctors tried desperately to save the President's life while his wife alternated between watching them and waiting outside. The Secret Service were guarding the area, and additional men who had been posted along the route to the Trade Mart were hurriedly brought to the hospital to keep out unauthorized persons.

The Vice President and Mrs. Johnson, who arrived as the President was being wheeled into the hospital waited in a nearby room, which had been cleared of a patient and nurse. The shades were pulled down, and Secret Service men stood guard outside.

The President died at approximately one o'clock—thirty minutes after being hit by the first bullet. It had been the second wound—the third bullet—which caused his death.

A group of doctors spent the afternoon operating on the Governor who was seriously but not fatally wounded. He had been wounded three times by the same bullet as he turned to see what had happened to the President.

* * * *

In Irving Mrs. Paine and Oswald's wife, Marina, watched the television coverage of the visit by the President—it had not included the shooting. Mrs. Paine, who was learning Russian, translated for Marina who knew very little English.

When the word came that the President had been shot they cried. They did not connect the shooting with Oswald even though they knew that the motorcade passed the place where he worked. A few minutes after the shooting Mrs. Paine told Marina that the shots had come from the Texas School Book Depository.

"My heart stood still," Marina later said. "I then went to the garage to see whether the rifle was still there and I saw the blanket was still there and I said: 'Thank God.' " She did not unroll the blanket; it appeared to be undisturbed and she thought the rifle was still there. She went back to the house, her mind relieved.

* * * *

After firing the three quick shots Oswald placed the carbine on top of a pile of boxes, not bothering to pick up the three empty shells on the floor, and quickly left. He probably ran down the stairs rather than using the elevator.

The shots had frightened some pigeons resting near the window from which he fired and a Dallas motorcycle police officer just back from a hunting vacation looked up and saw them fluttering about. The officer, Marion L. Baker, who had passed the building, turned his vehicle and raced back. Dismounting, he pushed through the crowd.

He encountered Roy Truly, the building superintendent, and together they entered the Depository.

Meanwhile, outside, several persons told police they had seen a gun or rifle pointing out the window on the sixth floor and one man provided a description of the man. The description was sent out over the police radio. The description, issued four minutes after the shooting, was of a slender man, about five feet ten inches tall, and in his early thirties. The description came from a spectator who said he had seen the man take aim and fire at the President.

Baker and Truly raced to the two elevators on the street floor but both carriages were on upper floors. They ran up the stairs. Less than two minutes had elapsed.

On the second floor landing the officer thought he saw someone through a small glass window in the door separating the stairs from the hall area. Gun in hand, Baker ran to the door and threw it open. Twenty feet away was a man walking in a lunchroom leading off the vestibule. The man was empty handed. Baker ordered him to turn and come back.

Truly, who had started up the stairs toward the third floor, came back to see what was delaying the officer. He told Baker that the man worked in the Depository, and the two of them continued up the stairs. The man who had been identified by the superintendent was Oswald.

About a minute later Oswald passed through the second floor offices, a full Coke bottle in his hand. He had purchased it from a vending machine in the lunchroom. One of the clerical workers said: "Oh, the President has been shot but maybe they didn't hit him."

Oswald mumbled something and continued walking toward a doorway leading to the building's front entrance. He was clad in his T-Shirt and trousers; he had left his blue jacket behind.

He left the building and walked seven blocks east, then boarded a bus that normally would take him back past the Depository to a point in the area of his rooming house. There was a highway jam, however, caused by the motorcade and the shooting and the bus got stuck. Oswald got out, walked several blocks, and hired a taxicab to take him to the general area of the rooming house. He walked the final distance and arrived at his room at about one o'clock —the time that the President was declared dead.

His strange behavior in walking east from the building when his destination was west, and taking the taxicab to a point several blocks from his rooming house rather than directly to it, probably was to confuse anyone who might be following him.

He did not know it but the police had been broadcasting his description. Neither did he know that he had barely left the Depository when the police sealed it off, and that at that moment police were checking to see if any employees were missing.

Oswald picked up a revolver he had, took a short grey jacket to replace the blue one he had left in the Depository, and then left the Building, zipping up the jacket as he went.

* * * *

At 12:44 the police radio dispatcher ordered all available cars to the area of the shooting but before he could carry out this order Patrolman J.D. Tippit was told to go to the Oak Ridge neighborhood—this was where Oswald's rooming house was located. The officer, a veteran of eleven years of police work, was told to stand by for orders when he arrived at his destination. He had just heard a description of the man wanted for questioning in connection with the shooting of the President. In the next half hour he heard the description three more times over the police radio.

At 1:15 he was cruising along a street at about twelve miles an hour when he saw a man walking on the sidewalk to his right who answered to the description. The officer pulled up beside the pedestrian and said something to him. The man went to the car, now stopped, rested his elbows on the front right window sill and there was a short conversation.

The officer opened the door on his side and slowly got out of the car. He started around the front but when he reached the left wheel the man suddenly produced a revolver and fired several times. The officer dropped with four bullets in him; he was dead.

The man turned and ran across a corner lot, shaking the spent cartridges from his revolver and quickly reloading. He mumbled "poor damn cop" or "poor dumb cop" as he went by a taxi driver who had witnessed the shooting and who was now hiding in bushes on the lot.

The driver of a pickup truck who had witnessed the shooting as he drove along, quickly halted his vehicle and ran over to the patrol car. Using the car's radio he notified the police dispatcher of the shooting, and then picked up two empty shells that the gunman had shaken from his revolver. Later two other shells were found near the bushes on the corner lot.

The gunman was Oswald; several witnesses later identified him as the killer.

Oswald ran down a street, carrying the reloaded pistol in his right hand, and cut across a parking lot, halting long enough to shed his jacket and toss it under a car. He then walked rapidly away, his hands in his pockets, his right hand still clutching the loaded revolver. He continued to walk away from the spot where he had shot the policeman and he was about eight blocks away when he heard sirens, as police cars started to comb the area.

A shoe store proprietor saw Oswald—he did not know who it was at the time—suddenly step into the outside lobby area of his shop as a police car came roaring down the street. The car gone, Oswald stepped out onto the sidewalk and continued walking. The proprietor's suspicions were aroused by Oswald's strange behavior and he continued to watch him. Oswald, the proprietor said later, "looked funny to me . . . his hair was sort of messed up and he looked like he had been running and he looked scared."

Oswald had obviously lost his head and his actions attracted the attention of persons who had no idea that he committed two murders within the space of two hours. The shoe store proprietor went to the Texas Theatre a short distance away and asked the ticket seller if the man who had just entered the theatre had bought a ticket.

She had noticed him but had not seen him enter; she had been too interested in the police sirens and had left her booth and gone out onto the sidewalk to see what was going on. He told her about the man's strange behavior in ducking out of sight at the sound of the sirens. She asked the shoe store proprietor to go inside and see if he could locate the man and to keep an eye on the exits while she called the police. She knew about the assassination of the President and said: "I don't know if this is the man they want . . . but he is running from them for some reason."

About fifteen policemen converged on the theatre at 1:45. Entering, they asked the manager to turn on the house lights, and the shoe store proprietor pointed out Oswald seated in the rear of the orchestra floor. There were only a few other patrons.

A patrolman searched two puzzled patrons near the front and then walked to where Oswald was seated and told him to stand up. Oswald complied, bringing up both hands. As the officer started to search Oswald for a gun he heard Oswald mutter: "Well, it's all over now." Oswald struck the officer between the eyes with his left fist as he pulled a revolver from his waist. The officer struck back with his right hand and grabbed the gun with his left. They fell, struggling, into the seats.

Three other officers joined in the melee. The first officer clung desperately to the gun while the other two grabbed Oswald. The first officer heard the hammer of the gun fall but the gun did not fire.

The first officer was scratched on the cheek by the pistol as he wrenched it from Oswald's hand. Oswald was quickly handcuffed and led from the theatre, cursing and muttering about "police brutality."

The film showing in the theatre was "War is Hell."

He was taken to the police station where he was questioned. He gave his name and address and the information that he was employed at the Texas School Book Depository. He had been there less than a half hour when a police captain who had been in charge of the investigation at the Depository came in and issued orders for a search warrant for Oswald's rooming house and to pick him up for questioning.

"Captain, we will save you a trip, there he sits," said one of the officers.

At first Oswald was charged simply with the murder of Tippit; later he was also charged with the assassination of the President. He denied both charges, and said his only crime was that of carrying a pistol.

Around three that afternoon police officers went to Irving and questioned Marina Oswald about her husband. They asked her if he owned a rifle and she said he did. She led them to the garage and pointed to the rolled up blanket which she thought contained it. It looked as if it did. But a police officer lifted the blanket. It was limp; there was no rifle inside.

Oswald was questioned for about twelve hours, intermittently between 2:30 Friday afternoon and one o'clock Sunday morning. Agents of the F.B.I. and the Secret Service were present during much of the interrogation. Oswald lied repeatedly, and when he did not lie he refused to talk.

Meanwhile other police and Federal agents were obtaining additional information about him, his ownership of the carbine, his pistol, and his movements, as well as the alias he had used and so on. The evidence became overwhelming while his answers to questioning showed that he had no alibi or defense.

The situation at police headquarters was chaotic at times. More than a hundred representatives of newspapers, wire services, radio, television and other media had gathered at police headquarters and crowded the corridors through which Oswald was taken from his cell to the captain's office and returned. They sought to ask him questions as he passed— he went through the corridor at least fifteen times on Friday afternoon and Saturday.

Several officers released information to the reporters, some of it premature, some of it in error. The police arranged for Oswald to appear in a room where news photographers could take pictures of him. Among those in the room was at least one person who was neither a member of the press nor the police—Jack Ruby, operator of a strip tease joint in Dallas who frequented police headquarters at times.

The press was notified that Oswald would be moved Sunday morning from the city jail to the county jail about a mile away.

Sunday morning the basement of headquarters was filled with news people, radio and television people, and police. Cameras were set up to photograph Oswald as he entered the basement from an office and walked to a waiting car.

At about 11:20 Oswald emerged from the basement office, flanked by police officers. Cameras began to roll. For a moment Oswald was blinded by the bright television lights, but moved ahead.

Suddenly a man dashed past a battery of cameramen, ran up to Oswald and fired point blank. Oswald groaned with pain and fell to the floor, losing consciousness almost at once. He was rushed to the Parkland Hospital where he was pronounced dead at 1:07. He had been shot in the abdomen while millions of television viewers watched.

The man who shot Oswald was Jack Ruby.

* * * *

Some ten years before he shot the President, Oswald was described by a psychiatrist who examined him as "potentially dangerous," a boy with a schizoid personality, full of hate, confused in his thinking. A group of doctors at that time wanted him to receive treatment but his mother refused.

During the decade that followed he followed a pattern of loneliness, resentment toward authority, a desire for recognition and importance. His life with his mother was uncertain and unstable providing him with no opportunity for roots, or for lasting friendships. His marriage was marked by frustration, differences with his wife, disappointment,

even sexual impotence at times. All this contributed nega-
tively to the structure of his personality.

He was born on October eighteen, 1939, in New Orleans,
two months after the death of his father. His mother alter-
nately cared for him and her other children and had friends
and neighbors look after them while she worked in a variety
of jobs. Once Lee was placed in a Lutheran home for thirteen months. They moved about a great deal in New Orleans
and then went to Dallas where the same uncertain existence
for the boy continued.

During his first seventeen years, Lee and his mother moved
many times, going from Texas where they had resided in
several communities, to New York where they changed resi-
dences several times, back to New Orleans and the same
pattern of frequent change, and then returning to Texas.
During those seventeen years they lived in nineteen different
houses and apartments, and he was enrolled in thirteen
different schools.

Fatherless, he tried to transfer the feelings he ordinarily
would have for a male parent to a step father, whose marriage was stormy and short, and to his two brothers, both
older than he.

When he first attended school he did well in his studies,
getting A's and B's. He was a quiet boy who liked to be by
himself. As he grew older and was left alone following the
departure from the family of the two brothers, he became
a "loner," often morose and prone to violence. As he grew
older he did poorer work in school. While in New York,
where his mother moved several times, and caused him to
be transferred from one public school to another, he became

a truant—in contrast to his earlier years when he was faithful in his school attendance.

The authorities in New York gave him a thorough examination and found him in need of psychiatric treatment. He was sent to a Youth House for a while, where he was studied but before any treatment could be arranged the mother and son moved back to New Orleans. It was one of the examining psychiatrists in New York who described the unhappy thirteen year old boy as "potentially dangerous."

He grew up without roots, without friends, without the counsel or companionship of either a father or an adult male friend. He kept by himself as much as possible and was quiet in his manner. But beneath that quiet manner was a proneness to violence, an urge sometimes to strike out. He was resentful of the world, of others who had the things he lacked. Even though he held himself back, socially, nevertheless there was a need to be someone, a need for recognition.

For Lee Oswald, at sixteen years, the world was filled with strangers and enemies and almost everything was wrong—for him. His mother went back to New Orleans and he enrolled in a junior high school. It was about this time he began to read Communist literature. He found the social and political theories appealing even though he did not understand them—because they were opposite to those prevailing in the world in which he lived and which he hated.

One of his older brothers had joined the Marines at the age of sixteen and he hoped to do the same, but when he became sixteen he was rejected. During the next year he worked at a variety of small, low paying jobs, reading the

Marine manual which his brother had given him, reading Communist propaganda and moping about the house.

When he was seventeen the Marines accepted him, and at first he did well. He won a markmanship medal, received high ratings in training programs and was promoted to private first class. After a careful security check he was assigned to radar duty which involved some confidential work. After he completed his training he was sent overseas, to the Philippines and to Japan. Overseas, he was court martialled twice.

The first time was for unauthorized possession of a revolver; it was discovered when it fell out of his locker. The other was for pouring water on the head of a non-commissioned officer and swearing at him. He was found guilty both times, lost his rating of private, first class, and was confined for a period.

He read a great deal and appeared to be better informed on world affairs than the others, and he delighted in baiting officers and demonstrating his superiority. He read a lot of Communist literature and he studied the Russian language. At one time he sought a higher rating because of his knowledge of Russian but failed to obtain it.

By the time that he had completed his overseas duty he had made his interest in Russian things evident to the others, but few of them thought he was a Communist. He was sometimes called "Oswaldskovich" or "comrade." Both titles pleased him. He also had an interest in Latin America —he had studied the Spanish language while in school. He sometimes expressed an admiration for Castro.

He talked with another Marine about Castro and Cuba and the two of them discussed joining the Cuban government or army and leading expeditions to "free" some of the Carribean islands. He told the other Marine he was in touch with Cuban authorities in this country. The other Marine, later, said that he thought Oswald was simply telling another of his falsehoods.

Although he appeared to be less withdrawn during this period, he still had no real friends, and when he was on leave he did not remain with the other Marines. He was promoted to private first class again, and he carried out orders quietly and efficiently. But he would gripe about the officers and orders. He was sloppy in barracks and the others were constantly after him to smarten up.

While he was still in the service he applied for admission to Albert Schweitzer College in Switzerland, claiming to have completed his high school work by means of correspondence courses—which he had not; proficiency in the Russian language—an exaggeration; and that he had participated in school organizations for the control of juvenile delinquency—a falsehood. He said he belonged to the Y.M. C.A., which he had once, briefly, and the "A.Y.H. Association." He was accepted for the spring of 1960.

His mother was injured at work; he sent her money and he applied for a dependency discharge. He was released from active duty and assigned to the Marine Corps Reserve, in which he was expected to serve until September, 1962. He was released from active duty on September fourth and on the same day applied for a passport, saying that he planned to leave the country to attend Albert Schweitzer College, the University of Turku in Finland and to travel in England, France, Germany, Russia, the Dominican Republic and Cuba. Six days later he received the passport.

He gave a hundred dollars to his mother, and boarded a freighter at New Orleans.

He arrived at La Havre on October eighth; two days later he was in Helsinki where he obtained a visa from the Russian embassy to enter the Soviet Union. On October sixteenth—two days before his twentieth birthday—he arrived in Moscow. His permit was good for six days.

He immediately applied for Soviet citizenship and permission to remain permanently. But when the six days were up he was told he had to leave within two hours, and he cut his left wrist in an apparent attempt at suicide. He was committed to a psychiatric ward, and on his release sent a letter to the American embassy in which he renounced his American citizenship.

He was interviewed by American newspaper correspondents and denounced the "imperialism" of the United States. The Russians permitted him to remain indefinitely but did not give him the Soviet citizenship he had asked for. He offered to supply the Russians with information about American military radar operations which he had acquired while in the Marine Corps.

He was sent to Minsk to work in an electronic equipment factory, and while his pay was low, between seventy and eighty dollars a month, it was augmented by funds from an organization known as the "Red Cross," and which had no connection with either the American or International Red Cross organizations. He was also assigned a small apartment which ordinarily did not go to a worker until he had been employed for many years and was married.

At first he appeared to be happy. He had a social life for the first time and participated in many activities, and made some friends. There was some curiosity about him and about the United States and he had a certain undefined status among his fellow workers. He met and fell in love with a Russian girl, but she refused to marry him. Gradually the novelty wore off and he began to be disillusioned about Russian life. The work, while easy, was monotonous, the food in restaurants was poor and tiresome, he was required to attend innumerable meetings at the factory. He found that the peasants were extremely poor and much worse off than their counterparts in the United States. He was also disappointed that he had been unable to continue his education in a college.

In a diary which he kept he was critical of the Communist party officials, the political officers at the plant and the preferential treatment they received. He was also critical of the small army of examiners at the factory and enormous amount of paper work.

Gradually he came to a decision; he wanted to return to the United States. He wrote to the American embassy in Moscow asking help, saying that he was anxious to retract his renunciation of citizenship. There was some correspondence and he learned that officially he had never renounced his citizenship because, characteristically he had not followed prescribed procedure.

During this period he met a nineteen-year-old girl named Marina, a pharmacist, and after a short courtship, asked her to marry him. In his diary he said that when he was with her he kept seeing the face of the other girl who had rejected him. He told Marina that he could not return to America and that he wished to stay in Russia. He proposed several times before she accepted him. They were married in April,

1962. A month later he wrote in his diary that in spite of the other girl he now loved Marina. In May he notified the embassy in Moscow that he was now married and that his wife would accompany him when he returned to the United States. Apparently he had not told her this, however, and she was surprised when he told her some time later. She encouraged him in these plans.

At this time his marriage was a happy one and they continued to enjoy the friendship of other people. His knowledge of the Russian language increased although he never learned it well. He did most of his reading in English.

He visited the American embassy and asked for reassurances that he would not be prosecuted if he returned to the United States, saying that he had "learned a hard lesson the hard way," and that he had gained a new appreciation of the United States and the meaning of freedom.

The embassy returned his passport, which he had surrendered when he had tried to renounce his citizenship, and issued a visa for return to the United States. Meanwhile he had written his mother and brother, telling of his plans to return. He asked his mother to get some money for him —a gift, not a loan—which he needed. He also said not to send any of her money. He wrote to Governor Connolly, on the assumption that he was still Secretary of the Navy, protesting his undesirable discharge from the Marine Reserve and asking that it be changed to an honorable discharge. The letter was sent to the Navy Department and forwarded to the proper board, which refused his request.

The months dragged on. He could leave by himself if he wished but could not get a permit for his wife to leave the country. He attempted to bring pressure to bear, and wrote to Senator Tower of Texas, telling him of his plight and asking the U. S. government to intercede in his behalf.

On February tenth Marina gave birth to a daughter, and the other workers at the factory gave a number of presents for the infant and her parents.

Finally he obtained permission for Marina to leave Russia, and to enter the United States, borrowed $457 from the embassy; and Oswald, his wife and daughter left almost at once, arriving in the United States on June 13. The next day they enplaned for Fort Worth.

They lived for a while with his brother Robert and with his mother while he looked for work. Late in July he got a job as a sheet metal worker at $1.25 an hour. He was considered a good worker but he did not like the job, and as in the past, he remained pretty much by himself and did not mix with the other workers.

The Oswalds moved into a one bedroom, furnished apartment, and soon they were in contact with members of the Russian community in Fort Worth.

The group included native Russians as well as others with Russian interests or backgrounds. They tried to help the Oswalds get settled, and they welcomed them into the group. They were invited to the homes of members, to parties and to other events. There was at least one party given expressly for them. One member of the group was Mrs. Ruth Paine of suburban Irving, a young mother, who took a liking for Marina.

Gradually Lee became less popular with the group. He had expressed criticism toward the Soviet Union when he first arrived, but a few months later he was back to finding fault with the American system and praising the Soviet system. This attitude was not a popular one with members of the Russian community. Furthermore, he began to remain aloof from them, was moody and sullen. Marina noted the change in him and later said that he was not the man she had married in Russia. She was having difficulty with him, there were frequent fights and sometimes he struck her. He was opposed to her learning English—she knew only a few words in that language.

Abruptly he quit his job—he told Marina he had been fired but this was untrue—and went to Dallas where he found a job in a graphic arts plant. His salary was $1.35 an hour, and he was well liked at first, and apparently he liked the work. He soon earned a reputation as a good worker. He got a room in the YMCA, while Marina and their daughter went to live with a member of the Russian community, soon moved to the home of another member. In two weeks he rented a three room apartment and was rejoined by his family. His marital difficulties continued, he would not let her smoke, he argued with her a great deal, and apparently at this time he was sexually impotent, which added to his sense of frustration. Marina considered running away from him. When a friend tried to intercede in her behalf, Lee rebuffed him. Sometimes he beat Marina.

Matters steadily deterioted, and in a few weeks Marina and their daughter went to live with another woman, a member of the Russian community, with the intention of separating permanently from him. He resented this. She moved from one family to another, all of them eager to help her. Oswald made no attempt to find her for a while, then capitulated. He went to her, begged her forgiveness and asked her to return home. He wept and she agreed.

Their friends in the Russian community who had tried to help Marina were disappointed, and Lee and Marina saw them less frequently.

Even though they were reunited, they did not get along well; they continued to fight, and at one time Marina considered killing herself. He tried to join the Socialist Party but there was none in Texas; he kept in touch with the Russian embassy in Washington and asked that he be sent Russian literature. He subscribed to several Communist publications. As before he read a great deal, mostly books or other publications of a Communist nature, although Marina said later that included in the books her husband read was H. G. Wells' "Outline of History," and biographies of Khruschchev, Hitler—and President Kennedy.

He sent a Christmas card to the employees of the Soviet embassy, signing both his and Marina's name and wishing them "all the best." It was that Christmas that they met Mrs. Paine, who was learning to speak Russian. She became a close friend of the Oswald's, especially of Marina.

In January he enrolled for a typing course, hoping eventually to obtain office work but after a few weeks his interest lagged and he stopped going to class; he continued to use the textbook at home.

It was in January, too, that he ordered a pistol from a Los Angeles mail order firm, using the name "A. J. Hidell." It was the pistol with which he killed Officer Tippit.

In March he decided to kill Major General Edwin Walker, the militant right wing leader. On the weekend of March nine and ten Oswald photographed the alley which runs behind the General's residence, the rear of the house itself, and a nearby railroad yard. He sent away to a mail order firm in Chicago for an Italian army carbine, equipped with telescopic lens, which he had seen advertised in a magazine. It was the rifle used to kill the President.

He used the name "A. Hidell" in ordering the rifle, and it was about this time that he forged an identification card for himself, using the name Aleck James Hidell. It has been theorized that the Hidell was a variation of Fidel, the first name of the Cuban dictator. Aleck was the name that many of his friends in Russia used in referring to him; they had difficulty in pronouncing Lee.

He outlined his plan to kill the General in a notebook, which he went over time and again. He obtained a bus schedule and studied the timetables; he did not own a car and had to depend on public transportation.

The rifle arrived on March 20, 1963. He kept it in a small storeroom in their apartment and he spent quite a bit of time there. He told Marina she was not to enter the room. He told her that he had bought the rifle for hunting and that he was practicing handling it in the storeroom. He said nothing to her about his plan to kill the General.

One day he asked Marina to photograph him in their back yard. He posed with a revolver strapped to his waist and holding the rifle in his right arm. In his left hand he held copies of the Communist publications, *Worker* and *Militant*. Later he gave her one of the photographs and asked her to save it for their daughter, June.

Three and a half weeks after receiving the rifle he went to the home of General Walker, intending to shoot him but changed his mind at the last minute. He hid the rifle nearby and returned home.

A few nights later, on April eleven, Oswald left a note

for Marina, telling her what to do if he were apprehended, and went back to the Walker home. He retrieved the rifle and fired through a window at the General. The shot narrowly missed. Oswald again hid his rifle nearby and took the bus home. Later he went back and got the rifle.

The story of the attempted assassination was in the newspapers and Oswald told his wife that he had made the attempt. She became very angry and made him promise never to do anything like that again. He tried to explain that the shooting of General Walker was comparable to shooting Hitler. A few days later one of their friends saw the rifle in the Oswald home and jokingly intimated that Oswald had been unknown sniper who had tried to kill the General. Oswald thought that Marina had told their friend and he was visably shaken.

The attempt on the General's life had come right after he had lost his job. Despite a good beginning, he had gradually become an undesirable employee, hard to get along with. The management said that he could not do the job, but perhaps it was annoyed over his bringing a Russian language newspaper to work.

The loss of his job was a blow, because he liked it and wanted to continue at it. There was another blow: when he applied for unemployment benefits while he looked for new employment he was turned down because, he was told, he did not have enough credits to qualify. Later it turned out that he had, that there had been a mistake. Meanwhile the Oswalds were continuing to have trouble with their marriage. He urged her to return to Russia and once she even wrote to the Russian embassy asking for a visa. Later she said she was forced to write the letter by

Oswald, who fought with her a great deal and occasionally beat her.

Mrs. Paine visited them on April 20 and found him packed and about to leave for New Orleans where he hoped to find work, saying that he could not get a job in Dallas. Marina later said she thought his real reason for leaving Dallas was fear that the authorities would trace the attempted assassination of General Walker to him.

Mrs. Paine suggested that Marina and the child come live with her in Irving while he looked for employment in New Orleans, promising that she would bring them to him when he got settled there. Her offer was accepted.

In New Orleans he lived with an aunt while he looked for work, which he found in about two weeks. The job was in a peanut roasting plant, and he did not like it; he told Marina in a letter that he was employed as a commercial photographer. He rented an apartment and sent for her and the child.

Then began a period of special significance in his life, for it clearly showed how he was torn between a happy family life and that of an agent-provocateur and Communist. He took delight in showing her the city of his birth and early childhood. They had little money but they enjoyed themselves nevertheless, visiting the zoo, parks and beaches. Sometimes he hunted for crabs, a pastime he enjoyed. Sometimes they visited or were visited by his relatives in the city. True, it was not idyllic. He was not happy about his job, and the approaching birth of their second child posed an increased financial burden.

This happy period lasted only a few weeks and then slowly he changed. He lost his job after three months, being let go because of inefficiency. He looked for another job while the family lived on unemployment benefits. He read a great deal, but this did little to lift the mood of despair that settled upon him. He thought back to their life in Russia, of his happy life there with Marina, and of the friends he had made there. He thought less of the frustrations he had experienced there and of the criticisms he had expressed about the Communist state. He became increasingly interested, too, in affairs and events in Cuba where Fidel Castro had betrayed the revolution and delivered the country he had rescued from a right wing dictatorship of great harshness to a Communist dictatorship or even greater harshness and tyranny.

He continued to talk to Marina about returning to Russia, urging her to go with their daughter and the unborn child; he spoke, too, of going back with her. They fought again; their marriage was in trouble again.

Marina confided her troubles to Mrs. Paine but said nothing about Lee's plan to return to the Soviet Union, or of his political attitudes. She revealed how they had quarrelled and her own unhappiness. Mrs. Paine invited the expectant wife to come live with her in Irving if things got too bad. But for a few days relations between Marina and her husband improved and she decided to stay with Lee, promising, however, to go with Mrs. Paine if things became unbearable.

Lee set about organizing a New Orleans branch of the National Fair Play for Cuba Committee. At his own expense he had some handbills printed demanding "Hands Off Cuba," in large letters; application and membership forms. He used the alias "Lee Osborne."

On July 27 occured an event that appeared to be at variance to his attitude and his activities. At the invitation of a cousin who was studying for the priesthood he went to the Jesuit House of Studies at Mobile, Alabama, and talked before an audience of prospective priests about his experiences in the Soviet Union. He indicated that he was disillusioned by those experiences and expressed the thought that an ideal political system would embrace the best aspects of both capitalism and communism. He was articulate and apparently made a good impression upon his audience.

But nine days later he went to a store run by Carlos Bringuier, who had fled Castro's Cuba and now was the New Orleans delegate to the anti-Castro student directorate. He had a long talk with the Cuban, expressing a desire to join in the fight against Castro.

He offered to train exiled Cubans in guerilla warfare, saying that he was an ex-Marine trained in this kind of combat. He also offered to join in the fight himself. The following day he returned and gave Bringuier his copy of the Marine manual.

Three days later, however, the Cuban and some of his compatriots saw Oswald passing out his "Fair Play for Cuba" handbills. There was an angry argument between Oswald and the Cubans which the police had to break up. Oswald and three of the exiles were arrested and he spent that night in jail.

The next day he was interviewed by a captain of the New Orleans police and, at his request, by a member of the F.B.I. The F.B.I. had talked with him on his return from Russia and he asked that it take part in the questioning at police headquarters. He told them he was a member of the Fair Play for Cuba Committee's New Orleans branch and that he was in touch with its leader, A. J. Hidell. He claimed that the local group had thirty-five members. Actually he was Hidell and the only member of the local committee. He paid a fine of ten dollars for disturbing the peace. The charges against the three Cubans were dismissed.

The arrest and the night in jail upset Oswald and for a few days he was less active. But he could not remain so; he returned to pro-Castro activity like a moth to a flame. Soon he was passing out handbills again, assisted by at least one other person. A television station showed pictures of this that night and subsequently his search for employment became more difficult.

That evening a follower of Bringuier sent a man to Oswald's home, posing as a Castro sympathizer and asking about Oswald. However, Oswald apparently saw through this scheme and divulged nothing.

The next day a radio announcer visited Oswald and taped an interview which was aired that evening, and later the same announcer arranged for a radio debate on Castro between Oswald and Bringuier. Still later the announcer said that he thought Oswald conducted himself well, but that nevertheless, the debate finished the Fair Play for Cuba Committee in New Orleans.

Whatever the effect on the committee and the Castro cause in New Orleans, the interview and the debate did something to Oswald. He now felt more committed than ever before to Communism, and that his role was an important one.

He told Marina he hoped to go to Mexico and to Cuba. He told her he planned to hijack a plane in Mexico and have it flown to Cuba, as had been done by another pro-Castroite, but she persuaded him to give up the idea. But he was still determined to go to Mexico and on to Cuba, and on September seventeenth he obtained a tourist card from the Mexican consulate in New Orleans. The card was made out to "Lee, Harvey Oswald." The misplaced comma was to lead to some confusion later. He was listed as an employed person, even though he was not. This was characteristic of Oswald, for most of the applications he filled out during his adult life contained lies.

He was ready to leave, presumably with Cuba a destination, and possibly Russia as well. Marina felt he was more intent on the visit to Cuba and she was not sure he really intended to go to the Soviet Union.

Three days after he obtained the travel permit Mrs. Paine arrived for a visit and found relations between the two much improved. However, in view of his plans it was decided that Marina and their daughter would go to Irving and stay with Mrs. Paine at least until Marina had given birth to their second child. During the next three days he packed their household goods, and on September twenty-third, Sunday morning, Marina and her daughter went to Irving with Mrs. Paine. The latter did not know that Oswald planned to go to Mexico and assumed that he was going to stay in New Orleans and continue to seek employment. Lee had asked Marina not to tell anyone about his plans and she had complied.

Two days later he boarded a bus for Houston, arriving shortly before midnight. He had about two hundred dollars with him and two pieces of luggage. With him, among other things, were copies of his correspondence with the Soviet embassy in Washington, newspaper clippings about his arrest in New Orleans and other papers he thought would be useful.

He also carried some notepaper, and on it he wrote out a number of reasons why he thought he would be useful to the people he hoped to visit in Cuba, and possibly Russia. He listed his experience in the Marines, as a resident of the Soviet Union, his ability to speak Russian, and his experience as a "street agitator" and as radio speaker and lecturer, and a number of other things.

As the bus rolled southward to Loredo and on to Mexico City he was in a happy mood. Usually taciturn and secretive, he told two Australian girls and a British couple on the bus that he was on his way to Fidel Castro in Cuba.

* * * *

All his life he was a failure; he never had a good job and he invariably lost even the poor ones he managed to obtain. Sometimes the reason for his dismissal was incompetence or his inability to get along with people. He was a confirmed liar, putting falsehoods on papers even when there was no need to. He craved to be someone, to be a success. The world in which he lived was a hard one and he wanted to change it but he did not know how. Neither did he know what those changes should be.

His marriage, in general, was not a happy one. There had been at least one period when he was impotent. He fought with his wife and with their friends and was hostile much of the time—moody and withdrawn.

The only real success he achieved was in murdering John F. Kennedy—a man he had once said good things about. His desire to be important was fulfilled briefly when he managed to remove a President from office. He joined the small group of small men who had, for one reason or another, assassinated American presidents.

XIV

Poisoners In The White House?

The body of the dead President was badly swollen and the face and breast were "as black as though the blood had been drawn to the skin by bruises." A doctor present said only poison could have produced that result and urged that an investigation be made into the cause of the President's death. None was made.

So stated a hotelman from Philadelphia about the burial of President William Henry Harrison, ninth President of the United States who had died in the White House on April four, 1841—one month after his inauguration. The hotelman was Oliver H. P. Parker who had been proprietor of the Franklin House in Philadelphia. He made the statement in a long letter which he addressed to Abraham Lincoln one day in September, 1860, when it became obvious that Lincoln would win the Presidential election in November. Mr. Parker described what he considered Harrison's fate and warned him to be on guard against what he termed the Borgias of the White House.

Lincoln received a number of letters warning him of the possibility of his being poisoned but none of them went into such detail as did Parker's. The hotelman said that he had conducted a study over a period of time and was convinced that Lincoln because of his well-known stand against slavery, stood in mortal peril.

It was and is commonly believed that Harrison contacted a cold on his inauguration day—a cold, blustery day—and died of pneumonia a month later. There are other stories that he became ill at another outdoor event in March, and died. And many Americans then did not believe either; they were convinced that Harrison was the victim of foul play.

It was also widely believed that General Zachary Taylor of Mexican War fame was poisoned, dying some nine years after Harrison. Little credence has been given to the theory that either or both—the first to die in office—were victims of foul play and there is little to support the theory, except conjecture and incomplete circumstantial evidence. The fact that many Americans believed the two had died as a result of poisoning and at the hands of Southern or pro-slavery elements indicates the extent that suspicion and bitterness were to be found in the United States in the years leading up to the Civil War. Many persons in the North thought the worst of the people of the South, and many Southerners believed the worst about their fellow Americans north of the Mason and Dixon line.

The Philadelphia hotelman, Parker, stated the case well for the theory that Presidents Harrison and Taylor had been secretly murdered by political enemies. He pointed out that Harrison was nominated for the Presidency in 1840 by the Whigs and that, at the convention, not a single delegate from the South voted for Harrison. He said that John Tyler, a slave owner from Virginia, was nominated "to satisfy the slave interests."

"After Harrison's death his remains was placed in a sarcophagus to be conveyed to North Bend, the final resting place, and a committee of Congress was appointed to accompany the funeral cortege to North Bend," he wrote to Lincoln. "The Chairman of that committee was the Hon. Thos. Ewing, Senator from Ohio, and when they arrived at the place of destination the sarcophagus was opened and to the surprise of all, the head and chest of the corpse was very much swollen and the face and breast was a black as though the blood had been drawn to the skin by bruises;—The matter was talked over by the Committee and I am informed it was declared by a doctor who was present, that nothing but poison would produce that result, and suggested an investigation, when Mr. Ewing replied, close up the sarcophagus and deposit it in its final resting place, for said he, if in an investigation it should be found that poison was the cause of his death, it would involve the country in a civil war.;—Thus his body was consigned to the grave without investigation, and the people left in ignorance as to the real cause of Harrison's death, which was by poison beyond a possibility of doubt—"

Parker noted that Tyler succeed Harrison and followed a pro-slavery policy "and lived out his term of office." He reminded Lincoln that Polk and his vice president, George M. Dallas, followed a pro-slavery policy, too, and "they lived out their terms of office."

In 1848 General Zachary Taylor was elected President, wrote Parker, and followed a policy of opposition to the extension of slavery that won him the hostility and hatred of the South. "I am credibly informed that five days before his sudden death he had had high and angry words with some of his prominent Southern friends, on the subject of extending slavery into New Mexico . . . and he said to them . . . he would never with his consent agree to force or extend the damnable curse into any territory that is now free . . . and would use all his power against it; consequently he did not suit the Slave Oligarchy, and on the 9th of July, one year, four months and five days after his inauguration, he died suddenly, as did Harrison, and with the same apparent disease.

"His death was attributed to his eating a cherry pie the day before his death;—I have no doubt that the pie was the cause of his death, but in the pie was poison for I cannot believe that the old soldier who has been used to the hardships of camp life for thirty years could be killed by eating a simple cherry pie, if there had been no poison in it, but my opinion is that the Borgias were about;—"

Parker said that the vice president, Millard Fillmore, who had been anti-slavery in attitude, reversed his position after becoming President, lived out his term of office and retired to his native Buffalo after a triumphant tour through the Southern states.

PLOTS AGAINST PRESIDENTS

After the election of James Buchanan, wrote Parker, a group of Southerners headed by Governor Wise visited him. The President-elect's attitudes toward the extension of slavery was not what the delegation had hoped and it left, disappointed and discouraged. Parker said that "Old Buc" moved to Washington and took up quarters in the National Hotel. Some fifteen hundred persons registered there during the stay of the President-elect. Of these some five hundred were poisoned, said Parker, who intimated that the target had been "Old Buc." Had the poisoners succeeded, then John Breckenridge, a Southerner, would have stepped into the White House. But the plot did not succeed, according to Parker who said the five hundred who were poisoned—fifty died—were all from the North. According to Parker, he had investigated and found that ground glass had been mixed into some sugar which was served only to persons drinking tea. At that time tea was the universal drink of Northerners and coffee that of Southerners. Coffee drinkers were served sugar free of ground glass, he said.

Parker's letter was one of many that Lincoln received. It stands out because here was a man of some prominence who had organized his material and had attempted to present a strong case in support of his belief that two Presidents had died of poisoning, to say nothing of the large number of persons who had died from ground glass in their sugar. Yet he based his arguments on conjecture and hearsay, and he simply was unable to bring before Lincoln a single hard fact that would have held up in court.

The letter is interesting because it reveals some of the suspicion and hatred that was so common in pre-Civil War America. Many Northerners believed all Southerners to be bad, capable of any evil, of plotting the deaths of those who differed from them. There is no question that a similar attitude existed among Southerners toward the people of the North.

It is precisely because of this attitude of hostility and suspicion that we can safely reject the belief held by many Northerners that Southerners had engaged in assassination in order to remove opponents in the White House. When the two Presidents died in office a suspicion of foul play came into being almost instantly. There were many Americans eager to prove—or simply to believe—the worst of their fellow Americans. If there had been anything more than conjecture and hearsay, if there had been a shred of proof, there were men who would have been quick to proclaim it.

The hatred and suspicion that existed between the North and the South were strong contributing factors leading to the Civil War; they also practically guaranteed that the death of a President while in office would be carefully scrutinized, that every possibility of foul play would be fully explored by men eager to find out murder.

The leaders of the South and of the North were incapable of murder, secretly or openly, but there were others, men of less prominence and less character, who were capable. Looking back after more than a century to a period when passions ran higher than at any other time in our history, one sees no public clamor, no public accusations. Apparently there was little or no concrete evidence of any wrongdoing in connection with the deaths of the two Presidents.

Seventy three years after the death of President Taylor another Chief Executive died in office and again the rumor of poisoning reappeared. Warren G. Harding, with a history of heart ailments, died after collapsing while on an arduous speech-making tour of the West. While it has never been proven, and despite the fact that a group of distinguished doctors stated that he died of what appeared to be a coronary attack, the belief that President Harding was poisoned persisted, and indeed, still persists in the minds of many Americans.

Harding died on August third, 1923, in San Francisco, five days after his collapse. The collapse came after he had spent forty-one days touring the West, with a short visit to Vancouver, Canada. During the forty-one days he had delivered eighty-five speeches—averaging more than two a day. He had travelled hundreds of miles by railroad car and automobile, had shaken hands with thousands of his fellow citizens and had held innumerable conferences with government and political leaders.

Harding had been elected President in 1920, succeeding Woodrow Wilson, who had led this nation during World War I and its immediate aftermath. Harding had been a newspaper publisher in Marion, Ohio, and was an influential figure in political circles in his state and had served in the United States Senate. He was selected as a compromise candidate by the Republicans and had run on a platform promising a return to "normalcy." That expression had a great deal of appeal to the voters who were tired of the recent venture into world politics.

His administration has gone down as one of the most corrupt in the nation's history, although most of the corruption was not revealed until after his death. Some writers have expressed the belief that he was personally honest but that unknowingly he had appointed dishonest men to his cabinet and other important government posts, in fulfilling deals made in a "smoke filled hotel room" during the 1920 Republican convention.

During his administration there were rumors that his private life was not above suspicion, but for another reason. A woman wrote a book in which she claimed to have borne Harding an illegitimate daughter. The book was widely read—and widely believed.

In general, however, Harding was a popular president. He had received a landslide vote and he appeared to many Americans as the symbol of the "normalcy" he had promised them. He was a fine looking and affable man.

He encountered opposition to some of his policies and in June of 1923 decided to go before the people and appeal for support. He was not the first, nor the last President to go over the heads of Congress and seek support, directly from the voters.

Harding decided to ignore the summer heat and embark on a tour during June, July and August, making his appeal to the voters in the western half of the country. It was before the age of commercial aviation and he travelled by special train from Marion across the Plain States and the Mountain States. There was no air conditioning and the Presidential train was hot. It was also before light weight summer clothing had been introduced and the President and other members of his party sweltered night and day.

In addition to the formal addresses and the handshaking at major cities there were countless occasions when he appeared on the rear platform of his car at smaller communities to wave at crowds, and, if the train stopped, to say a few words of greeting.

It was a strenuous journey and many of his friends urged him to ease up but he was determined to continue and do his utmost in publicly soliciting support for his policies, and privately seeking party unity.

It is difficult to evaluate the results of these efforts for he faltered and collapsed while making a speech in Vancouver, across the Canadian line. He had planned to go to San Francisco by way of Yosemite but the plans were changed and the train bearing the stricken President went directly to the California city. By his bedside in the Presidential car was his wife.

The physician accompanying him said he was suffering from a stomach upset due to eating seafood; he appeared to be recovering when he suddenly died, at the age of fifty-eight. Calvin Coolidge, the vice president, was sworn in, taking the oath of office by the light of a flickering lamp in a Vermont farmhouse.

There were rumors of something irregular about Harding's death almost as soon as he was buried and they became stronger and more widely believed as time went on. The great Teapot Dome scandal and other instances of misconduct in office when Harding was the nation's chief executive were revealed early in Coolidge's administration, and many persons saw a connection between the sudden death of the president and the scandals that characterized his administration.

In 1915, during World War I but before this country's entrance into it, President Wilson designated oil resources at Teapot Dome, Wyoming, as belonging to the Navy. They were not tapped during the war—most of our naval ships used coal for fuel during this period. Shortly after he succeeded Wilson in the White House, Harding transferred this and other oil reserves to the Department of the Interior. This appeared to be a logical act for his administration was concerned with naval disarmament. The following year Teapot Dome and another oil field at Elk Hill, California were leased to Albert Fall, the Secretary of the Interior, without competitive bidding. He thereupon subleased Teapot Dome to the Sinclair oil interests and Elk Hill to a man named Doheney.

Reacting to public clamor regarding the leases and subleases, the Senate appointed a committee headed by Senator T.J. Walsh to make a thorough investigation—which it proceeded to do, despite lack of cooperation sometimes displayed by persons highly placed in the government. The Committee uncovered the major outline of a plot to defraud the government. Fall was forced to resign as Secretary of the Interior.

Attorney General Daugherty, whose department had presumably made an investigation of its own, and which had refused to let the Committee look at its records and reports, was also forced to resign. Criminal proceedings were initiated against the two former cabinet members and against others involved in the deal. Fall was found guilty, fined $100,000 (the amount he received for the sublease of the Elk Hill fields) and was sent to jail for a year. Daugherty and Doheney were acquitted. Sinclair was sentenced to serve ninety days in jail for contempt.

The rumor that there was something suspicious regarding Harding's death flourished during the period when the nation's newspapers headlined the day-to-day progress of the investigation and the subsequent trial. There was some speculation that Harding might have committed suicide when he learned how Fall and others had betrayed his trust. There were other stories that he had been poisoned by persons close to him who were afraid they might be implicated in other scandals and that he was poisoned so he could escape the indignity of the scandals about to be revealed.

Seven years after Harding's death a former investigator of the Department of Justice, Gaston B. Means, wrote a book, in collaboration with Mary Dixon, which was entitled *The Strange Death of President Harding*. In it he intimated strongly that Mrs. Harding had poisoned her husband to spare him the ordeal of the scandals about to break.

Means pointed out there was something strange about the diagnosis of the White House physician. The latter had identified the illness as ptomaine poisoning dating back to some sea food which the President had eaten on the trip, despite the fact that no seafood had been served on the Presidential train nor at the banquets he had attended. Means argued that the first physician's report was wrong, and wrong deliberately. The doctor was a close friend of Mrs. Harding.

Other persons besides Means pointed out that the President appeared to be getting better and then suddenly died when he was alone with his wife. Mrs. Harding refused to allow an autopsy—and it might be said here that relatives of many dead persons are reluctant to let surgical procedures of this nature be performed.

Later a group of distinguished physicians who had been

in attendence at the time of Harding's death issued a report in which they stated that the cause of death was related to the coronary illness from which he had suffered for many years.

Some time later the doctor who had issued the first report about ptomaine poisoning suddenly died, soon after being alone with Mrs. Harding, and the ailment appeared to be similar to the one that had taken the President's life.

There were whisperings that Mrs. Harding had made sure the doctor would never reveal the truth.

There were also stories that she had murdered her husband because of escapades in his private life. Nan Britton, who wrote a book in which she claimed to have borne Harding a daughter, had sometimes been in the White House during the Harding administration, according to Means. This was denied by close associates of the President, and by members of the White House housekeeping staff. According to some persons who believed that she had been a visitor to the Executive Mansion, the presence of Harding's mistress—if she was that—had infuriated Mrs. Harding and had steeled her resolve to kill her husband.

The story that Nan Britton frequented the White House was widely believed just as it was widely disbelieved. The story persisted and still does.

Means, who had been involved in the Teapot Dome scandal, was attacked by Harding's friends as an outright liar, and Mary Dixon, who had helped him write his book, publicly disclaimed it. Historians have divided opinions ragarding Nan Britton and her child but appear to be unanimous in rejecting Mean's allegations, and in general agreement that he was a scoundrel who had written a book of lies designed to sell copies rather than to tell the truth.

There was no investigation into the death of Harding. The statement of the group of doctors that Harding was the victim of a heart ailment during an unusually strenuous journey has been accepted by most persons on face value. His prior history of coronary illness was a matter of record.

* * *

So there have been three Presidents who died in office under circumstances that led many Americans to think they were poisoned. Yet there has never been any actual, any real, evidence to support the stories of secret murder. While it is possible that anyone or all three were poisoned, it is highly unlikely that they were.

The possibility of a President being poisoned has always existed. The Warren Commission, investigating the assassination of President Kennedy and the precautions taken to safeguard the person of the nation's Chief Executive, learned there was no one whose responsibilities included the tasting of food before it is served in the White House. John J. McCloy, a member of the Commission, asked the head of the Protective Research Section of the Treasury Department, Robert Inman Buck: "You don't have a royal taster, do you?" He referred to the ancient custom of assigning one person to tasting all food before it was served to royalty.

Mr. Buck answered that such an employee is not considered necessary, adding that "we find out from the White House where they would like to buy, we check on the employees of these establishments every six months, we check on the procedures by which it is handled and we check on the source of their food, where they get the raw materials."

"Have you had any poisoned food?"

"We think not but this we are always watching for," answered Mr. Buck. He said they had found food that appeared to be bad from spoilage or which had been prepared under unsanitary conditions "but we know of no actual case of intended poison."

As a matter of fact, poisoning appears to an out-of-date method of assassination. In the Middle Ages it was sometimes employed to get rid of opponents or enemies, as was the dagger, lance, bow and arrow or strangulation. With the advent of gun powder, firearms were employed more and have come to be preferred by assassins as more efficient, quicker and effective from a distance.

Four of our Presidents have died from bullet wounds and four others have escaped would be assassins using firearms. None have been attacked with knives, swords or other cutting instruments, and none, as far as can be definitely established, have died from poison.

XV

Who Was Behind The Assassins?

Who was really responsible for the death of Abraham Lincoln? Was it John Wilkes Booth, the man who fired the shot from a 44 calibre derringer, or was it some one else who was responsible, someone who conspired with him?

Who really killed John F. Kennedy? Was it Oswald acting alone? Or did someone else fire the fatal shot? Did he have accomplices in his plot to kill the President? Was he simply the executioner in a conspiracy that involved others?

These are questions that many persons have asked, not only about the first and the most recent Presidential assassinations, but also about the other assassinations and attempted killings, and they deserve some discussion.

WHO WAS BEHIND THE ASSASSINS?

Whenever a President is shot or even whenever an attempt is made on the life of a President, many persons have raised the question—was the man with the pistol or rifle acting alone or was he the agent of others? Quick answers have usually been given which later have been found to have little substantiation. Conjecture has sometimes been confused with evidence and fact.

When Lawrence tried to kill Andrew Jackson the irate President exclaimed that he knew who was behind the attempt. He assumed, as did many other persons, that it was the work of political enemies. One of his opponents, a leading political figure of the time, felt it necessary to deny publicly any complicity. However, when Lawrence was brought to trial it took the jury a very short time to decide he was insane and that he had no accomplices.

After Lincoln was shot there was an immediate widespread belief that Booth was an agent of the Confederate government and some of the notices sent out asking the public to assist in apprehending the assassin described him as working with Confederate leaders. The belief that Jefferson Davis had been involved persisted for some time but the trial of the conspirators revealed no evidence that the Confederate government or its leaders was involved in any way.

In time suspicions arose that Booth had been working with others, not the Confederate leaders, when he fired the fatal shot in Ford's Theatre. The idea of Confederate complicity has been dead for a century now, but there has been a steady stream of books and articles which purport to show that Booth was not the real leader of the conspiracy to kill Lincoln, but simply its instrument.

PLOTS AGAINST PRESIDENTS

When Charles Guiteau shot Garfield there was an assumption at the time that enemies of the President, within his own party, had plotted the assassination. The trial, lasting a long time, failed to bring forth any evidence to support the assumption.

Czolgosz gunned down McKinley, and because he described himself as an anarchist, it was widely accepted that the murder was part of an anarchist plot. Anarchist groups and individuals were attacked by mobs across the nation, and police and other authorities took known anarchists into custody. The trial revealed that Czolgosz had acted alone and that in fact the anarchists had rejected him, thinking him a police agent.

When the news was flashed around the world on November 22, 1963 that President Kennedy had been killed in Dallas, many persons instantly came to the conclusion he had been shot by rightist agents. This belief has persisted, especially in the Communist countries.

When it was learned Oswald had a history of Communist defection, had lived in Russia and had been engaged in what were believed to be Communist activities there was widespread belief he was working for the Communists, following orders when he fired at the President. This idea persists.

The trials of Lawrence, Guiteau and the other assassins and would be assassins pretty much disproved the existence of conspiracy and showed to the satisfaction of the courts and most Americans then and since that they were acting alone and on their own initiative. The assassinations of Lincoln and Kennedy differed from the others. In both instances the man who pulled the trigger never came to trial. Booth was killed by a trooper named Boston Corbett who ignored orders that no one was to shoot the actor. Booth never had the opportunity to testify regarding his crime. He never had the chance to reveal if there was any one else, in addition to his gang, who were involved.

There have been many books written about the assassination of Lincoln and a number of them have attempted to show Booth as the tool of others. The man most mentioned has been Edwin Stanton, Lincoln's Secretary of War; the argument has been he sought control of the government. It would have been easy for him to have done so on that Saturday morning, April fifteen, 1865. Lincoln was dead, Seward, the Secretary of State, was fighting for his life after being struck down by Paine. Stanton controlled the army at that moment.

But he did not seize control of the nation. It seems unlikely that he would have conceived and organized such a conspiracy, carried it through, and then at the last moment held back. He was not addicted to hesitation or indecision. Actually, for a few hours he was in virtual command of the nation, but there was no delay, no visable reluctance, in his turning over the reigns of control to the new President, Andrew Johnson.

The books that have placed the guilt for Lincoln's death on his head have been full of conjecture, half truths and meaningless whole truths. None of them have produced tangible evidence. But the fact that he could have done it has remained fixed in the minds of some writers.

The same sort of conjecture, half truths and the like have been assembled by other writers to "prove" that other persons were behind Booth, including, of all persons, the victim's wife, Mary Lincoln. The argument against Mrs. Lincoln was that she wanted her husband out of the way so she could marry someone else. It has been pointed out that sometimes she fought with her husband and that some of the arguments were bitter. There are many couples, past and present, who have fought bitterly and sometimes frequently, but few of them have resorted to murder. In the case of Mary Lincoln she was free to remarry at about twenty minutes after seven on Saturday morning, April fifteen, but she never did. All evidence points to the fact that she mourned him deeply until the day of her own death.

There are many unanswered questions regarding the death of Lincoln and about the conspiracy as well as the acts of some of the persons in authority at the time and after, and probably most of them will never be answered. The big question—who was behind the assassin—has been pretty well established—no one.

Booth wrote before the assassination that he was a Confederate acting on his own initiative—without the knowledge of the Southern government or its leaders. After he had killed Lincoln and was hiding from Union forces seeking him he rested for a while at a Virginia farmhouse where his identity was not known. There was a discussion about the murder of Lincoln and the farmer's daughter said she thought Booth killed Lincoln for money. Booth replied, without revealing his identity, that he thought Booth did it for fame.

Fables, folklore and other stories have risen around the assassination of Lincoln. One is that Booth escaped, that the man shot in the burning barn was someone else, that the man was so badly burned that he could not be recognized. The fact was that he was shot in the burning barn and taken from it, dying but still conscious. He was not burned. Yet the story persisted for many years that he escaped. In the mid-thirties a book purportedly written by a woman who claimed to be his daughter, was published, in which it was stated he had escaped and lived out his life. There were many other men who had some facial or other physical resemblence to Booth who claimed to be him, even though some of them were several inches taller than the actor had been.

Booth was clearly identified even before his death. He was buried in an unmarked grave at an army fort in Washington—there was a story still believed by many that he was buried in mud flats in the Potomac in the dark of night so no one would ever find his body. Actually the body was removed from the fort and reburied in the Booth family lot in Baltimore a few years after the assassination.

The stories about Booth escaping not only ignore the facts they also fail to take into account the nature of the man himself. He was not a man to hide, to shun the spotlight. When he shot Lincoln he did not do it secretly; he made certain that he would be known. He expected to be lionized in the South after he had escaped Washington. He thought he was doing something praiseworthy and he expected to be praised. He was a man who had sought adulation, applause, the aprobation of others. Had he escaped could he have surpressed the strongest drive in his personality the rest of his life? Or would he have made his way to some safe place, possibly in another country, proclaimed his identity and basked in the light of publicity?

If Boston Corbett had not shot Booth it is likely there

would be fewer loose ends, fewer unanswered questions regarding the murder of Abraham Lincoln. But Corbett did shoot Booth and the questions have gone unanswered even though there has been no lack of conjecture about them. There were a couple of pages torn from a diary kept by Booth during the days he was hiding in Virginia— who tore them out and why? Why did Mrs. Lincoln urge the appointment of the guard to the White House force who a month later abandoned his post outside the Presidential box that night at Ford's Theatre, allowing Booth to slip into the box and shoot the President? There are many such questions.

Conjecture about unanswered questions do not prove anything. The answers to those questions might or they might not prove something, if they were known. It is possible to build what looks like a case against a number of persons, by considering some knowledge of the conspiracy and ignoring other known facts and adding conjecture.

The similarity of the assassinations of Lincoln and Kennedy, the chain of coincidences that apparently exists, is well known. Oswald, like Booth, was killed before he was brought to trial. In both cases, there was conflicting testimony from survivors of the President, from witnesses and the authorities. While this may arouse suspicions among many persons, it is not an unusual situation; indeed, it is common. Witnesses to traffic accidents and other events often contradict each other, or give testimony that is inconsistent with other testimony; it is natural that such contradictions and omissions be found in information regarding the killing of Presidents.

The Warren Report records these inconsistences in many

instances while trying to obtain a comprehensive picture of what actually happened, and the background of the event and the principal actors in the tragedies. The Report does not rule out the possibility of others besides Oswald being involved in the assassination of President Kennedy. Nor does it suggest that there were others besides Oswald who were involved. It lacked information which only Oswald could provide and which he took to the grave. Had he not been killed by Ruby it is quite possible that the whole truth would now be known.

It is possible to build a case in almost any direction regarding the complicity of others with Oswald. It can be argued—by accepting some facts and ignoring others—that Oswald was a Communist agent, or a rightist agent or even that he was working for some agency of our government. In each case it is necessary not only to ignore the testimony of persons who knew Oswald—members of his family, police officers, etc.—but also to ignore other testimony from similar sources. It is then necessary to engage in conjecture to come to a conclusion.

There are many unanswered questions, many loose ends, in the theory that Oswald was acting alone and on his initiative when he fired the fatal shots at Kennedy. Yet it is generally accepted by the authorities who have investigated the assassination. Why? Because not only is it the most likely, the most plausible, but any other theory has more conjecture, more consideration of what might have been, what may have been possible. Nevertheless it is likely that these other theories which would involve a confederate or several working closely with Oswald, will continue to exist. Books probably will be written proclaiming these theories as facts. Rumors, guesses, testimony of unreliable witnesses, all will be taken literally in building these other theories, as they were during the century following the death of Lincoln. It will be strange if this does not happen again, in connection with the death of Kennedy.

There is always the possibility, of course, that new testimony, new evidence, of a reliable nature, will be forthcoming in the years ahead that will provide us with some or all the answers to the questions now being asked about Oswald—answers that will reveal new aspects of the assassination, that will reveal more of his true motives, if he had any accomplices, and so on.

Lincoln has been dead more than a century, many books have been written attempting or purporting to answer some of the questions that have persisted regarding the circumstances of his death. But nothing tangible has been produced and it appears to be the verdict of history that Booth was the leader of the band of conspirators and that he was not the tool of some other man or men—only of his own distorted, tortured mind.

Will time give the same verict in the case of Lee Harvey Oswald, the murderer of John Fitzgerald Kennedy?

Bibliography

Cuthbert, Norma B. *Lincoln and the Baltimore Plot,* 1948
Dana, Charles *Recollections of the Civil War,* 1896
Donovan, Robert J. *The Assassins,* 1955
Fowler, Robert H. *Album of the Lincoln Murder,* 1965
Fox, Sylvan *The Unanswered Questions About President Kennedy's Assassination,* 1965
Gribble, Leonard *Hands of Terror,* 1960
Halstead, Murat *Illustrated Life of William McKinley,* 1901
Holland, J. C. *Life of Abraham Lincoln,* 1865
James, Marquis *Andrew Jackson, Portrait of a President,* 1937
Kimmel, Stanley *Mr. Lincoln's Washington,* 1957
Leech, Margaret *Reveille in Washington, 1860-1865,* 1941
Means, David C. *The Lincoln Papers,* 1948
Potter, John Mason *Thirteen Desperate Days,* 1964
Power, John Carroll *Attempt to Steal Lincoln's Body,* 1890
Raymond, Henry J. *Life and Public Service of Abraham Lincoln,* 1865
Seward, Frederick W. *Seward in Washington,* 1891
Stern, Philip van Doren *The Man Who Killed Lincoln,* 1955
The Warren Report, 1965
The Witnesses, 1965